PENGUIN BOOKS

INSIDE THE SERAGLIO

John Freely was born in New York in 1926. He joined the US Navy at the age of seventeen and served with a commando unit in Burma and China during the last months of the Second World War. He received a Ph.D. in physics from New York University in 1960, and since then he has lived in New York, Boston, London, Athens, Istanbul and Venice. His first book was *Strolling Through Istanbul* (1971, with Hilary Sumner-Boyd). Since then he has written over twenty books, including *Classical Turkey*, *Strolling Through Athens*, *Strolling Through Venice* and most recently *Istanbul: The Imperial City*.

D0976244

INSIDE THE
SERAGLIO

*

PRIVATE LIVES
OF THE SULTANS
IN ISTANBUL

*

JOHN FREELY

PENGUIN BOOKS

PENGUIN BOOKS

Published by the Penguin Group
Penguin Books Ltd, 27 Wrights Lane, London w8 5tz, England
Penguin Putnam Inc., 375 Hudson Street, New York, New York 10014, USA
Penguin Books Australia Ltd, Ringwood, Victoria, Australia
Penguin Books Canada Ltd, 10 Alcorn Avenue, Toronto, Ontario, Canada m4v 3b2
Penguin Books (NZ) Ltd, Private Bag 102902, NSMC Auckland, New Zealand

Penguin Books Ltd, Registered Offices: Harmondsworth, Middlesex, England

First published by Viking 1999
Published in Penguin Books 2000
1

Set in Monotype Sabon
Printed in England by Clays Ltd, St Ives plc

For Toots
More Istanbul Memories

Acknowledgements

The author would like to thank Anthony E. Baker for the photographs he has supplied for the book. He would also like to acknowledge the kind assistance of Dr Anthony Greenwood, Director of the American Research Center in Istanbul; Köksal Seyhan, curator of rare books at the Bosphorus University Library; and Tunç Üstünel, for help in Turkish translation. He would also like to thank Eleo Gordon and Sarah Day for their help in preparing the manuscript for publication.

Contents

Picture Acknowledgements

Pages 3, 16, 23, 43, 61, 67, 121, 172, 219 and 238 are engravings by W. H. Bartlett from Julia Pardoe, *Beauties of the Bosphorus*, 1839; pages 11, 27, 34, 54, 70, 81, 93, 96, 101, 107, 127, 131, 135, 137, 145, 166, 169, 180, 190, 197, 200, 203, 211, 216, 225, 228, 233 and 250 are from the Topkapı Sarayı Museum; pages 39, 74, 192 and 206 are from R. P. Koleksiyon in Türk Kültürüne Hizmet Vakfı; pages 142, 326 and 328 are photographs by Anthony E. Baker; page 2 is from the German Archaeological Institute; pages 243, 255, 259, 278, 280, 288, 294, 296, 308, 317 and 319 are from the Çelik Gülersoy Archive; page 149 is from Fazil Yildiz, *Zanan-name*, Istanbul University Library; pages 41, 115, 161, 196, 261 and 327 are from Thomas Allom and Robert Walsh, *Constantinople and the Scenery of Asia Minor*, 1838; pages 4, 147, 170, 177 and 263 are from A.-I. Melling, *Voyage pittoresque de Constantinople et des rives du Bosphore*, 1839; pages 77 and 120 are from *Les quatres premiers livres des navigations et pérégrinations orientales de Nicolas de Nicolay*, Lyon, 1567; page 104 is from Comte de Choiseul-Gouffier, *Voyage pittoresque de la Grèce*, Paris 1782–1809; pages 38 and 84 are from M. I. d'Ohsson, *Tableau général de l'empire Othoman*, Paris 1787–1824; page 30 is from S. H. Eldem and F. Akozan, *Topkapı Sarayı: Bir Mimari Araştırma*, Istanbul, 1972; pages 47 and 59 are from Lokman, *Hünername*, c. 1584–5, Topkapı Sarayı Museum; pages 65 and 68 are from Lokman, *Tarih-i Sultan Süleyman*, 1579, Chester Beatty

Library, Dublin; page 71 is from Lokman, *Shahanshahname*, 1581–2; page 110 is from C. Vecellio, *Costumiantichi*, 1859, Biblioteca Nazionale Marciana di Venezia; pages 8 and 157 are from *Foggie Diverse del Vestire de' Turchi*, Biblioteca Nazionale Marciana di Venezia.

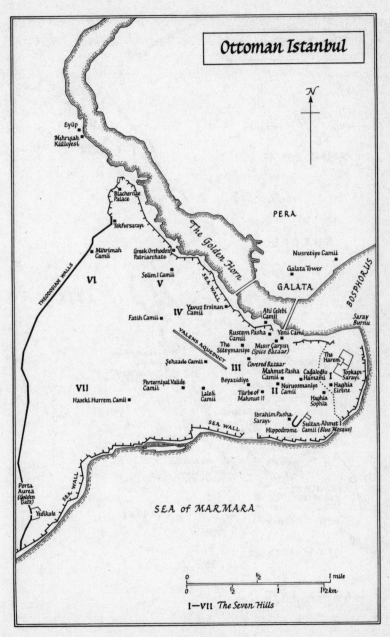

Ottoman Istanbul

N

Eyüp

Mihrişah Küllüyesi

Blachernae Palace

Tekfursarayi

The Golden Horn

PERA

Mihrimah Camii

VI

Greek Orthodox Patriarchate

Selim I Camii

V

THEODOSIAN WALLS

Nusretiye Camii

Galata Tower

GALATA

BOSPHORUS

Fatih Camii

IV

Yavuz Ersinan Camii

SEA WALL

Ahi Çelebi Camii

Yeni Cami

Saray Burnu

Rustem Pasha Camii

VALENS AQUEDUCT

Mısır Çarşısı *(Spice Bazaar)*

The Süleymaniye

Şehzade Camii

III

Covered Bazaar

Mahmut Pasha Camii

The Harem

Topkapı Sarayı

Perterniyal Valide Camii

VII

Beyazidiye

Nuruosmanlıye Camii

Çağaloğlu Hamamı

I

Haghia Eirene

Türbe of Mahmut II

II

Haghia Sophia

Laleli Camii

Haseki Hurrem Camii

Ibrahim Pasha Sarayi

Hippodrome

Sultan Ahmet I Camii *(Blue Mosque)*

SEA WALL

Porta Aurea (Golden Gate)

Yedikule

SEA WALL

SEA of MARMARA

0   ½   1 mile

0   ½   1   1½ km

I—VII *The Seven Hills*

[xiii]

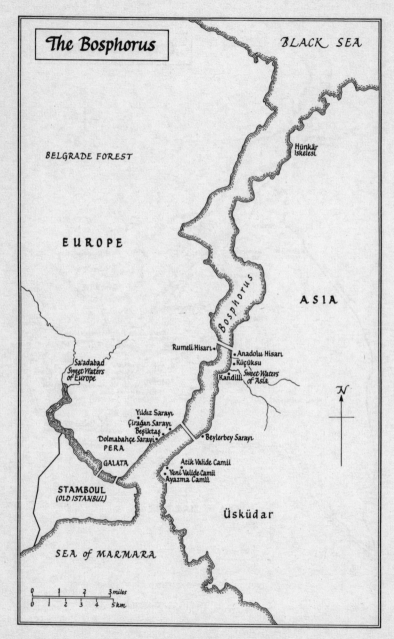

The Bosphorus

BLACK SEA

BELGRADE FOREST

EUROPE

ASIA

Bosphorus

Hünkâr
İskelesi

Rumeli Hisarı • • Anadolu Hisarı
• Küçüksu
Kandilli • Sweet Waters
of Asia

Sa'adabad
Sweet Waters
of Europe

Yıldız Sarayı
Çirağan Sarayı
Beşiktaş
Dolmabahçe Sarayi • • Beylerbey Sarayı
PERA
GALATA

Atik Valide Camii
Yeni Valide Camii
Ayazma Camii

STAMBOUL
(OLD ISTANBUL)

Üsküdar

N

SEA of MARMARA

0   1   2   3 miles
0 1 2 3 4 5 km

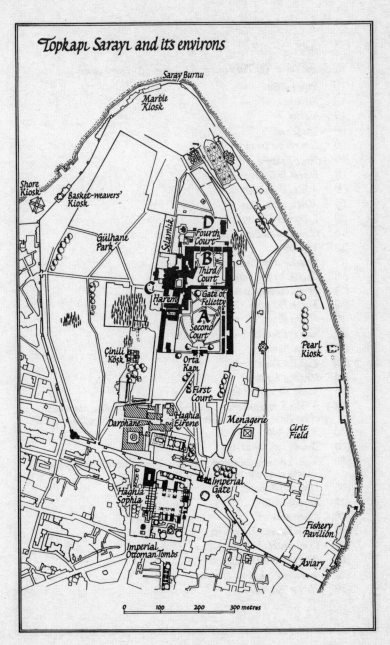

Topkapı Sarayı and its environs

Saray Burnu

Marble Kiosk

Shore Kiosk

Basket-weavers' Kiosk

Gülhane Park

Selamlık

D
Fourth Court

B
Third Court

Harem

Gate of Felicity

A
Second Court

Orta Kapı

First Court

Çinili Köşk

Pearl Kiosk

Darphane

Haghia Eirene

Menagerie

Cirit Field

Haghia Sophia

Imperial Gate

Imperial Ottoman Tombs

Fishery Pavilion

Aviary

0   100   200   300 metres

Key

(A) Second Court   (B) Third Court   (C) Harem   (D) Fourth Court

(1)   Imperial Gate
(2)   Kitchens
(3)   Stables
(4)   The Divan
(5)   Tower of the Divan
(6)   Inner Treasury
(7)   Gate of Felicity
(8)   Audience Chamber
(9)   Mosque of the Ağas
(10) Library of Ahmet III
(11) Chamber of the Expeditionary Force Pages
(12) Treasury
(13) Chamber of the Commissary Pages
(14) Chamber of the Treasury Pages
(15) Privy Chamber, Pavilion of the Holy Mantle
(16) Marble Pool
(17) Marble Terrace
(18) Sünnet Odası, Circumcision Chamber
(19) Revan Kiosk
(20) Baghdad Kiosk
(21) Mecidiye Kiosk
(22) Altın Yol, Golden Way
(23) Marble Terrace in front of Hall of the Favourites; the Gathering Place
      of the Jinns leads into its south-west corner past the Twin Pavilions (26)
(24) Marble Pool
(25) Chamber of Murat III
(26) Twin Pavilions, originally thought to be the Cage, which was probably in the
      unrestored complex of rooms to the south
(27) Library of Ahmet I
(28) Imperial Hall
(29) Imperial Baths
(30) Valide Sultan's Apartments
(31) Courtyard of the Valide Sultan
(32) Courtyard of the Concubines
(33) Quarters of the Black Eunuchs
(34) Harem Hospital

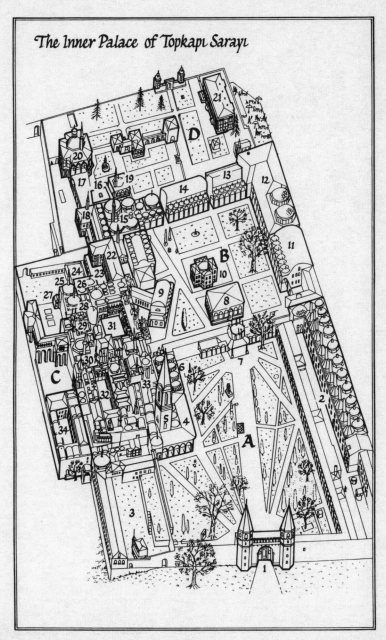

The Inner Palace of Topkapı Sarayı

Preface

This is the story of the House of Osman, the imperial dynasty that ruled the Ottoman Empire for more than seven centuries. Known to the Turks as the Osmanlı, they reigned over a Muslim empire that once stretched from central Europe to North Africa and from Persia to the Adriatic. The capital of this empire for the last four hundred and seventy years of its existence was Istanbul, the ancient Byzantium, known to the Greeks as Constantinople, the imperial city that stands astride Europe and Asia on the Bosphorus. During the first four centuries of Ottoman rule in Istanbul the sultans lived there in the great palace of Topkapı Sarayı, whose gardens and pavilions still grace the acropolis hill above the confluence of the Bosphorus and the Golden Horn, where their waters meet and flow together into the Sea of Marmara. This was the setting of the pleasure dome in which the sultans took their ease when they were not off on campaign, closed off from the outside world in the Inner Palace of Topkapı Sarayı, the imperial residence known as Dar-üs Saadet, the House of Felicity.

The chapters that follow are not a history of the Ottoman Empire. They are, rather, a family biography of the Osmanlı dynasty, the House of Osman, the thirty-six sultans who in turn ruled the Ottoman Empire through twenty-one generations. The book tells the story of this family, the sultans and their women and children and those who formed their court in Topkapı Sarayı and the other, later imperial palaces along the Bosphorus until the end of the empire in 1923. These palaces are now museums, but the rooms in which the sultans lived are still imbued with their presence, coming alive for those who know the story of their very private lives in the House of Felicity.

Turkish Spelling and Pronunciation

Throughout this book, modern Turkish spelling has been used for Turkish proper names and for things that are specifically Turkish, with a few exceptions for Turkish words that have made their way into English. Modern Turkish is rigorously logical and phonetic, and the few letters that are pronounced differently from in English are indicated below. Turkish is very slightly accented, most often on the last syllable, but all syllables should be clearly and almost evenly accented.

Vowels are accented as in French or German, i.e. *a* as in f*a*ther (the rarely used *â* sounds rather like *ay*), *e* as in m*e*t, *i* as in mach*i*ne, *o* as in *oh*, *u* as in m*u*te. In addition there are three other vowels that do not occur in English; these are *ı* (undotted), pronounced as the *u* in b*u*t, *ö* as in German or the *oy* as in ann*oy*, *ü* as in German or as the *ui* in s*ui*t.

Consonants are pronounced as in English, except the following:
c as *j* in *j*am, e.g. cami (mosque) = jahmy
ç as *ch* in *ch*at, e.g. çorba (soup) = chorba
g as in *g*et, never as in *g*em
ğ is almost silent and tends to lengthen the preceding vowel
ş as in *s*ugar; e.g. çeşme (fountain) = cheshme

Chapter 1

THE HOUSE OF OSMAN

Istanbul stands astride two continents, Asia and Europe, balanced precariously between two worlds, East and West. Oldest of the world's great cities, known to the ancients as Byzantium and the Greeks as Constantinople, it was the capital in turn of the Christian Byzantine Empire and the Muslim Ottoman Empire. The monuments of these empires still adorn its skyline above the Bosphorus, the Golden Horn and the Sea of Marmara, the waters that divide and surround the city.

The city is at the southern end of the Bosphorus, the historic strait that separates the continents as it flows for thirty kilometres from the Black Sea to the Marmara. Near its southern end the strait is joined by the Golden Horn, a scimitar-shaped stream whose waters merge with those of the Bosphorus as they flow together into the Marmara.

The oldest part of the city, ancient Byzantium, is on the European side of the Bosphorus, a huge triangular promontory bounded on its north by the Golden Horn, on the south by the Marmara, and on its western side by the late Roman walls of Byzantine Constantinople. It is a city of seven hills, six of them rising in succession from the ridge that parallels the Golden Horn, the seventh standing isolated above the Marmara shore just inside the land walls.

The first of the seven hills is at the seaward end of the promontory.

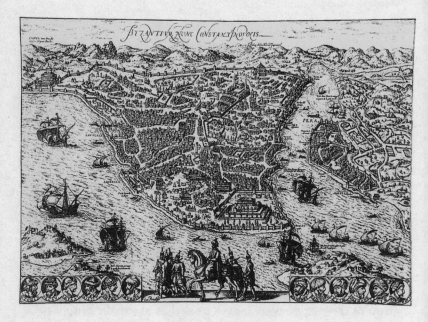

Map of Istanbul, late sixteenth century

The First Hill was the site of the Great Palace of the Byzantine emperors, of which only fragmentary ruins remain on the Marmara shore. Some of these ruins are built into the outer defence walls of Topkapı Sarayı, the imperial residence of the Ottoman sultans, whose cluster of domed pavilions crowns the summit of the First Hill, looking out over the Marmara, the Bosphorus and the Golden Horn.

The palace of Topkapı is now a museum, but it is still a place set apart from the rest of the city behind its encircling walls, its succession of arcaded courtyards opening off into a labyrinth of cloistered rooms and enclosed corridors, left empty and silent in the gathering darkness after all visitors and staff have departed.

The main entryway to Topkapı Sarayı is Bab-ı Hümayun, the Imperial Gate, where one passes into the first courtyard of the

*View of Topkapı Sarayı on the First Hill at the confluence
of the Bosphorus and the Golden Horn*

palace. Above the gateway there are two gilded inscriptions in
Arabic script, each of them bearing a *tuğra*, an imperial monogram
in interlaced calligraphy. The lower *tuğra* is that of Mahmut II, the
last sultan to live out his life in Topkapı Sarayı, which was abandoned
in the mid nineteenth century in favour of new palaces along the
Bosphorus. His inscription records repairs to the gate early in the
nineteenth century. The upper *tuğra* belongs to Mehmet II, known
to the Turks as Fatih, or the Conqueror, after his capture of Constantinople in 1453. Fatih's inscription records his completion of Topkapı
Sarayı in the quarter-century after his conquest of the city:

*This is a blessed castle that has been put up with the consent of
God and is secure and strong. May God the Most High make eternal
the sultanate of the sultan of the two seas, the shadow of God in
the two worlds, God's servant between the two horizons, the hero*

Bab-ı Hümayun,
the Imperial Gate of Topkapı Sarayı

of the water and the land, the conqueror of the stronghold of
Constantinople, Sultan Mehmet, son of Sultan Murat, son of Sultan
Mehmet Khan, and may He place his position above the north star.
Done in the month of Ramazan the Blessed in the year 883 [1478].

Fatih Mehmet was the seventh sultan in the House of Osman,
the Osmanlı dynasty, thirty-six of whom ruled the Ottoman Empire
in turn through twenty-one generations of the same family over the
course of more than six centuries. The dynasty was named for
Osman Gazi, the first of the line to take the title of sultan, ruling
from about 1282 until 1326. Gazi, or 'Warrior for the Faith', was
the name given to those who took up arms to conquer in the name of
Islam. Osman was known to early European historians as Othoman,

and thus the state that he founded came to be called the Ottoman Empire in the West, though in the Islamic world it was known as the realm of the Osmanlı. Osman's original realm was hardly an empire, comprising merely a tiny principality in Bithynia, the north-westernmost region in Asia Minor. The rest of Bithynia was part of the Byzantine Empire, which by then was in its last decline, and as Byzantium diminished the new Ottoman state expanded apace.

Osman's son and successor, Orhan Gazi, captured the Bithynian city of Prusa from the Byzantines in 1326. Known to the Turks as Bursa, this became the first Ottoman capital, and Orhan used it as a base to conquer the rest of Bithynia and cross the Dardanelles into Europe. Within half a century the Turks captured Adrianople, which they called Edirne, and in the third quarter of the fourteenth century they moved their capital there, giving them a base in the Balkans for their further expansion into Europe.

The Ottomans received their first setback when Orhan's grandson Beyazit I was defeated by Tamerlane at Ankara in 1402, dying soon afterwards in ignominious captivity. This halted Ottoman expansion until the accession of Beyazit's grandson, Murat II, who came to the throne in 1421 and soon afterwards resumed the Turkish march of conquest.

Early in Murat's reign he erected a mosque complex called the Muradiye in the old Ottoman capital of Bursa. Around the same time he also built a palace in the new capital called Edirne Sarayı, comprising a number of pavilions on an island in the Tunca, one of the two rivers that nearly encircle the city.

Murat's third son, the future Mehmet II, was born in Edirne Sarayı on 30 March 1432 to a slave-girl named Hüma Hatun (Lady). Little is known of Hüma's origins, for she was not one of Murat's four wives, but merely a concubine, probably a Greek of humble birth. Murat seems to have had little regard for her or Mehmet, preferring his second son, Alâeddin Ali, whose mother, the Türkmen princess Hadice Hatun, was his favourite wife. The mother of his eldest son, Ahmet, was probably also a concubine, though her name is not listed in the Ottoman genealogical records.

The first years of Mehmet's life were spent in the harem of Edirne Sarayı with his mother. When Mehmet was three years old he was sent off to Amasya in Anatolia, where his half-brother Ahmet was serving as provincial governor. Then in May 1437 Ahmet died suddenly, whereupon Mehmet was appointed to succeed him as governor, though he was only five years old. At the same time his half-brother Alâeddin Ali, who was then seven, was appointed as governor in Manisa. Both of the young princes were under the tutelage of advisors appointed by Murat from among his most trusted associates. Two years later the assignments were interchanged, with Mehmet transferred to Manisa and Alâeddin Ali to Amasya. Before they went off to their new governorates the two princes were recalled to Edirne, where Murat had them circumcised, marking the event with prolonged festivities at the palace. Sheikh Seyyid Natta of Baghdad provided leather tablecloths to be used in the sultan's dining-hall for the circumcision feast, a refinement hitherto unknown to the Ottomans.

Early in June 1443 Alâeddin Ali was murdered by his advisor Kara Hızır Pasha. This left Mehmet as heir to the throne, whereupon he was immediately recalled to Edirne by his father. Apparently Murat also wanted Mehmet to be at his side to help him face a serious threat to the empire, for Pope Eugenius IV had proclaimed a new crusade against the Turks. Mehmet's presence in his father's court at that time is mentioned by the Italian antiquarian Cyriacus of Ancona, who would later be Fatih's tutor in Greek and Latin. Cyriacus, who accompanied a Genoese trade mission to the Ottoman court at Edirne in 1443, reports that Murat received the visitors sitting on a carpet 'in regal splendour of a barbaric kind', while young Prince Mehmet stood behind in attendance with his father's vezirs.

Mehmet was by all accounts impetuous and headstrong, unwilling to obey his elders or to accept any criticism or advice, and being separated from his father during the first eleven years of his life there had been no one to control or discipline him. Murat had appointed several tutors for Mehmet, but he refused to heed any of them before the appearance of Molla Ahmet Gürani, a celebrated Kurdish cleric. Gürani was given a switch by Murat and told to use it if his pupil did not obey him. When Gürani told this to Mehmet the prince laughed at him, whereupon he gave the boy the first beating of his life. Mehmet stood in awe of Gürani after that and became a model student, or so say the Turkish sources. Eventually he studied philosophy and science as well as Islamic, Greek and Latin history and literature, which he read with Cyriacus of Ancona and other tutors from both Europe and Asia.

A rebellion by one of his Turkish vassals in Anatolia, the Karamanid emir Ibrahim, forced Murat to leave Edirne with a large part of his army on 12 June 1444. He appointed Mehmet to act as regent in his absence, with the grand vezir Halil Pasha Çandarlı serving as the prince's advisor. Almost immediately after Murat's departure, a Persian dervish of the Bektaşi sect began spreading heretical religious ideas among the troops of the garrison in Edirne. Mehmet found his ideas interesting and offered protection to the dervish and his followers. This scandalized the Mufti Fahrettin, chief cleric in the Ottoman court. Mehmet was alarmed at this and withdrew his protection of the dervish, whereupon Fahrettin incited a mob to burn him and his followers at the stake.

Later in June an insurrection broke out among the Janissaries, the élite corps of the Ottoman army, who demanded that Mehmet raise their pay. This corps was composed of Christian youths who had been conscripted in a periodic levy known as the *devşirme*, after which they converted to Islam and were trained to take their place in the Ottoman military hierarchy, a number of them rising to the post of grand vezir. Murat had used them with great effectiveness in his campaigns, but now that he was absent they had grown restive, feeling that they could take advantage of Mehmet's youth. After the Janissaries rioted and burned down the Edirne *bedesten*, or covered market, Mehmet gave in and increased their salary, setting a precedent that would be a constant source of trouble down to the last Ottoman century.

Meanwhile, the threatened crusade materialized, and a large

Janissary sergeant fully armed

Christian army under the Hungarian nobleman John Hunyadi began marching southward into the Balkans. When Halil Pasha learned of this he sent a message by courier to inform Murat, who immediately marched his forces back into Europe. Murat's army virtually annihilated the crusaders at the battle of Varna on 10 November 1444, with Hunyadi being one of the few Christians to escape with his life.

After his victory Murat returned to Edirne, where soon afterwards he astonished the court by announcing that he was abdicating in favour of his son, who on 1 December 1444 succeeded to the throne as Mehmet II. Murat, who was only forty at the time, then went off to his place of retirement in Manisa, leaving his son, who was not yet thirteen, to rule the empire on his own, with Halil Pasha as his grand vezir.

During the months that followed, Halil Pasha sent repeated

messages pleading with Murat to return, insisting that Mehmet was too young and immature to rule. Soon after he came to the throne Mehmet impetuously decided to attack Constantinople, but he was dissuaded by Halil Pasha, who reported the incident to Murat as another instance of his son's unfitness to rule. This led Murat to end his retirement, and in September 1446 he returned to Edirne. Halil Pasha persuaded Mehmet to abdicate in favour of his father, who was immediately reinstated as sultan, while his son withdrew to Manisa.

Meanwhile John Hunyadi had organized another crusade against the Turks, and in September 1448 he led his army across the Danube. Murat summoned Mehmet to join him in Edirne and mustered his army to confront the crusaders. The two armies met on 23 October of that year at Kosova, on the same field where Murat I had defeated the Serbs in 1389. The second battle of Kosova had the same outcome as the first, as the Turks routed the Christians in a three-day battle in which Mehmet had his baptism of fire, leading the Anatolian troops on the right wing of his father's army. Once again John Hunyadi escaped with his life, living to fight on against the Turks for another eight years.

Mehmet had become a father for the first time in January 1448, when his concubine Gülbahar gave birth to a son, the future Beyazit II. Little is known of Gülbahar's origins, but she was probably Greek, since the concubines in the imperial harem were almost always Christians, although high-born Muslim women were sometimes taken in as wives of the sultans in dynastic marriages. Murat arranged for such a marriage the following year, though without consulting his son until the plans were completed, which made Mehmet very resentful. The bride chosen by Murat was the princess Sitti Hatun, daughter of the emir Ibrahim, ruler of the Dulkadırlı Türkmen tribe in eastern Anatolia. The wedding took place in Edirne Sarayı in September 1449, followed by a celebration that lasted for two months, with music, dancing and competitions in poetry in which Anatolian bards sang verses in praise of the bride and groom. The bride was apparently quite beautiful, as evidenced by her portrait in a Greek codex preserved in Venice, as well as by the testimony of contemporary chronicles. But Mehmet seems to have had no love for Sitti, who never bore him a child, and he left her behind in Edirne when he moved to Istanbul after the Conquest. Sitti died in Edirne in 1467, alone and forlorn, buried in the garden of a mosque built in her memory by her niece Ayşe.

Mehmet's mother Hüma Hatun died in September 1449, after which she was buried in the garden of the Muradiye mosque in Bursa. The dedicatory inscription on her tomb records that it was built by her son Mehmet 'for his deceased mother, queen among women – may the earth of her grave be fragrant!'

The following year Mehmet's concubine Gülşah gave birth to his second son, Mustafa, who would always be his favourite. Later that year Murat fathered a son, Ahmet, nicknamed Küçük, or Little, to distinguish him from the late Prince Ahmet, the sultan's first son. Küçük Ahmet's mother was the princess Halima Hatun, daughter of the emir Ibrahim II, ruler of the Çandaroğlu Türkmen tribe in Anatolia. By this dynastic marriage, together with that of his son Mehmet, Murat cemented alliances with two powerful tribes against his most formidable enemy in Anatolia, the Karamanid Türkmen, who blocked the expansion of the Ottoman empire eastward in Asia Minor.

Early the following year Murat began work on building several new pavilions in Edirne Sarayı. But the project had barely begun when he died on 8 February 1451, stricken by apoplexy after a drinking bout. He was forty-seven years old and had ruled for three decades, most of which he had spent at war. Murat's death was kept secret by the grand vezir Halil Pasha so that Mehmet could be summoned from Manisa. He arrived fifteen days later and was immediately acclaimed by the army as sultan, one month before his nineteenth birthday.

When Mehmet came to the throne for the second time he was girded with the sword of his ancestor Osman Gazi, the Ottoman equivalent of coronation, in the presence of all the vezirs and nobles of the court. After the ceremony Mehmet reappointed Halil as grand

The House of Osman,
from Osman Gazi through to Abdül Mecit I

vezir, although he loathed his father's old advisor. Mehmet felt that Halil had sabotaged his first attempt to rule as sultan, and he suspected that the grand vezir had been taking bribes from the Byzantines and other enemies of the Ottomans. Nevertheless he allowed Halil to continue in office for the time being, while he waited for the right moment to eliminate him. Halil had just as deep a hatred for Mehmet, as the contemporary Greek historian Doukas reveals in writing of the grand vezir, whom he describes as 'a friend of the Byzantines and susceptible to bribes'. Doukas quotes Halil in calling Mehmet 'insolent, violent and savage', as compared to the deceased Murat, who had been 'a sincere friend and a man of upright conscience'.

Mehmet also retained another of his father's old vezirs, Ishak Pasha, whom he appointed as *beylerbey* (governor) of Anatolia, ordering him to conduct Murat's remains to Bursa for burial in the Muradiye. Directly after his accession Mehmet went to the harem of Edirne Sarayı. There he received the congratulations of Murat's women, who also offered him their condolences on the death of his father. The highest-ranking of Murat's wives at the time of his death was Halima Hatun, who fifteen months before had given birth to Murat's last son, Küçük Ahmet. The question of succession had been a matter of contention in the Ottoman dynasty, leading to two civil wars, and so Mehmet decided to settle the question at once by ordering the execution of Küçük Ahmet. While Mehmet was talking with Halima Hatun, one of his men was strangling her infant son in his bath. Mehmet justified the murder of his half-brother as being in accordance with the Ottoman code of fratricide, which had been practised on several occasions by his ancestors to prevent wars of succession. Appropriate verses from the Kuran were quoted, such as 'The execution of a prince is preferable to the loss of a province', and 'Death is better than disquiet.' Mehmet later had the code enacted into law, as stated in his imperial edict: 'Whichever of my sons inherits the sultan's throne, it behooves him to kill his brothers in the interest of the world order. Most of the jurists have approved this procedure. Let action be taken accordingly.'

Soon after Mehmet's accession he had to deal with another insurrection by the Janissaries, whom he once again appeased by raising their pay, though much against his will. Mehmet vented his rage on the commander of the corps, Kazancı Doğan, having him whipped and dismissing him from his post. He then reorganized the Janissaries in such a way as to take more direct control of the corps, which he was to use with great effectiveness in his subsequent campaigns.

The following year Mehmet set in motion his plan to besiege and conquer Constantinople, which was by now totally cut off from the outside world except by sea. During the summer of 1452 he constructed the great fortress of Rumeli Hisarı on the European shore of the Bosphorus, directly opposite Anadolu Hisarı, which Beyazit I had built in 1397. The Byzantine emperor, Constantine XI Dragases, was powerless to stop Mehmet from building the fortress, which completely isolated Constantinople from its grain supplies on the Black Sea, setting the stage for the coming siege.

The siege began on 6 April 1453, when Mehmet set up his tent outside the gate of St Romanus and ordered his artillery to commence the bombardment of the city. The bombardment continued at intervals for seven weeks, interspersed with attacks by the Janissaries and the Anatolian infantry, while Constantine led the entire civilian population in repairing the damage to the walls. Constantine rallied the Greeks and their Genoese allies in their desperate defence of the city, hoping for help from the Christian powers of Europe. But help never came, and after a last pitched battle the Turks broke into the city early on the morning of Tuesday 29 May 1453, the emperor Constantine dying in the final struggle before the defenders were forced to surrender.

Constantinople had been captured by the Turks and the world of Byzantium had ended, bringing to a close the history of an empire that had lasted for more than a thousand years. The House of Osman had replaced the Palaeologues, the last of the dynasties that had ruled Byzantium, whose ancient Christian realm was now part of a new and powerful Muslim empire.

Chapter 2

MEHMET THE CONQUEROR

Mehmet made his triumphal entry into the city early that May afternoon, and as he passed through the Adrianople Gate he was acclaimed by his troops as Fatih, the Conqueror, the name by which he would thenceforth be known to the Turks. The city that Fatih had conquered had been known to the Turks as Kostantiniye, but after the Conquest its name in common Turkish usage became Istanbul, a corruption of the Greek 'stin poli', meaning 'in the city' or 'to the city'.

The most detailed account of the Turkish conquest of Constantinople is the *History of Mehmed the Conqueror* by Kritovoulos of Imbros, a Greek who came to the city shortly after its fall. Kritovoulos describes the scene that greeted Fatih Mehmet when he entered the city, which he had allowed his soldiers to loot for three days, to his great regret:

After this the Sultan entered the City and looked about to see its great size, its situation, its grandeur and beauty, its teeming population, its loveliness, and the costliness of its churches and public buildings ... When he saw what a large number had been killed, and the wreckage of the buildings, and the wholesale ruin and desolation of the City, he was filled with compassion and repented not a little at the destruction and plundering. Tears fell from his eyes as he groaned deeply and passionately: 'What a city we have given over to plunder and destruction!'

Fatih rode into the city along the ancient thoroughfare known as the Mese, or Middle Way, which took him from the Sixth Hill to the First. This brought him to Haghia Sophia, the great church built in the years 532–7 by the Emperor Justinian. There he dismounted and fell to his knees, pouring a handful of earth over his turban in a gesture of humility, for the Great Church was as revered in Islam as it was in Christianity. After surveying the building, he ordered that it be immediately converted to Islamic worship under the name of Aya Sofya Camii Kabir, the Great Mosque of Haghia Sophia. This required the erection of a minaret for the *müezzin* to give the call to prayer, as well as some other internal constructions. This done, Fatih attended the noon prayer there on Friday 1 June 1453.

After Fatih's first visit to Haghia Sophia he also inspected the ruins of the Great Palace of Byzantium on the Marmara slope of the First Hill. This had been long abandoned by the Byzantine emperors in favour of the Blachernae Palace on the Sixth Hill, which was also in ruins, having been bombarded during the siege. When Fatih walked through the ruined halls of the palace on the Marmara he was deeply saddened, reciting a melancholy distich by the Persian poet Saadi:

The spider is the curtain-holder in the Palace of the Caesars.
The owl hoots its night-call on the Towers of Afrasiab.

Fatih could not use either of the Byzantine palaces as his residence, so after his first day in the city he returned to his tent outside the gate of St Romanus. Soon afterwards he decided to build a new imperial palace on the Third Hill, a site described by Kritovoulos as 'the most beautiful location in the centre of the City'. At the same time he ordered that the defence walls of the city be further repaired and a fortress constructed just inside the walls at the Golden Gate, the ancient triumphal entryway of the Byzantine city near the Marmara shore. This came to be known as Yedikule, the Castle of the Seven Towers, which Fatih and his successors used as a prison and also as a stronghold to store the State Treasury.

Istanbul was to be the new Ottoman capital, and Fatih gave

Interior of the mosque of Haghia Sophia

orders to have the city repaired as well as repopulated, bringing in subjects from both the European and Asian provinces of his empire, including Christians and Jews as well as Muslim Turks. The non-Muslims were grouped into '*millets*', or 'nations', according to their religion, each headed by its own religious leader. The post of Greek Orthodox Patriarch was vacant at the time of the Conquest, and so Fatih arranged for the election of the monk Gennadius, who was given the ancient church of the Holy Apostles as his patriarchate. Later, when Fatih decided to demolish the church to make way for his mosque, he allowed Gennadius to move into the monastery of the Pammakaristos, sending one of his own horses so that the patriarch could ride there in comfort. He also presented Gennadius with a *firman*, or imperial decree, which assured him 'that no one should vex or disturb him; that unmolested, untaxed, and unoppressed by any adversary, he should, with all the bishops under him, be exempted from all taxation for all time.'

Fatih freed a number of captive Greeks who had been high state or court officials. Among them was the grand duke Lucas Notaras, who had commanded the Greek forces during the siege. Notaras had been captured while trying to make his way back to protect his sick wife and their children, and he was kept under guard in his house until Fatih sent for him. Notaras confirmed the sultan's suspicions about his grand vezir, telling him that Halil Pasha had in fact been taking bribes from the Byzantines. Fatih immediately had Halil arrested and imprisoned, after which he had him tortured for more than a month before beheading him. Meanwhile Fatih treated Notaras with great consideration, for he thought that he might appoint him as commandant of the city. But the grand duke had many enemies among the high-ranking Greek captives, and they denounced Notaras to Fatih, who had him and his two sons beheaded.

Fatih appointed Karıştıran Süleyman Bey to oversee the work of restoring and resettling Istanbul, after which he returned to Edirne, arriving there at harvest-time, according to Kritovoulos. During the weeks that followed Fatih received a succession of foreign envoys at Edirne Sarayı, including representatives from the Venetians, Serbs, Albanians, Greeks, Egyptians, Persians and the Karamanid Türkmen, all of them seeking friendly relations with the young conqueror. One of the Venetian emissaries, Giacomo Languschi, describes him thus:

The sovereign, the Grand Turk Mehmet Bey, is a youth of twenty-six [actually twenty-two], well-built, of large rather than medium stature, expert at arms, of aspect more frightening than venerable, laughing seldom, full of circumspection, endowed with great generosity, obstinate in pursuing his plans, bold in all undertakings, as eager for fame as Alexander of Macedonia . . .

Turkish descriptions of Fatih are usually panegyrics couched in flowery language, although the sixteenth-century chronicler Mustafa Ali notes that on the sultan's return from campaign in 1454 'Mehmet spent many nights in debauchery with lovely-eyed, fairylike slave girls, and his days drinking with pages who looked like angels.' But then he goes on to say that 'Mehmet was only seemingly engaged in debauchery and wantonness; in reality he was working, guided by love of justice, to relieve the oppression of his subjects in the land.'

Fatih did not appoint a new grand vezir for a year after his execution of Halil Pasha, during which time Ishak Pasha acted as his first minister. Finally, in the summer of 1454, he named as his new grand vezir Mahmut Pasha, a Byzantine of noble Greek and Serbian lineage who had converted to Islam, and who served him faithfully and brilliantly for two decades.

Fatih returned to Istanbul for a short time early in 1454, before going off on campaign in Serbia. According to Kritovoulos, he stayed in the city 'just long enough to examine the buildings that had been constructed there, and gave orders about further work on them and on others, stipulating that it be done as quickly as possible'. He visited Istanbul again the following year, before another Serbian campaign, when, as Kritovoulos writes, he 'found the palace brilliantly completed, and the castle at the Golden Gate and all the walls of the city well built'. Kritovoulos goes on to note that Fatih 'commanded them to build a very large and very fine marketplace in the center of the city, somewhere near the palace'. The marketplace referred to by Kritovoulos is the Bedesten, the multi-domed building that now forms the core of the famous Covered Bazaar.

Fatih's Serbian campaign in 1456 brought him as far as the walls of Belgrade, where in mid July he was defeated by John Hunyadi and forced to withdraw. This was the first set-back in Fatih's meteoric career, with 24,000 of his troops killed and he himself wounded in the thigh by a javelin. The news that Belgrade had been saved gave rise to jubilation throughout Western Europe, with Pope Callistus III calling it 'the happiest event of his life', and there was talk of mounting another crusade against the Turks. But John Hunyadi died a month later in an epidemic of the plague, and thoughts of a crusade were soon abandoned.

After his withdrawal from Belgrade Fatih marched his army back to Edirne, where he remained for a year. The following spring he sent messengers throughout his empire and abroad to announce the coming circumcision of his two sons, Beyazit and Mustafa, the invited guests including the doge of Venice, Francesco Foscari, who sent his regrets.

The circumcision feast is described by the Turkish chronicler Aşıkpaşazade, who writes that for four days there were continuous festivities at Edirne Sarayı, on its island in the Tunca river. The island was covered with the tents of the notables who had come from all over the empire at the sultan's bidding. Fatih sat enthroned in his own imperial tent in the centre of the assemblage, flanked by four distinguished clerics. On the first day there were recitations from the Kuran which were commented upon by the scholars present, followed by recitations of poems composed for the occasion by the court poets. The scholars and poets were rewarded with gifts of money and robes of honour, after which everyone sat down to an abundant feast. The next day the poor of Edirne were lavishly entertained, and on the following day there was a feast for the nobles of the empire and honoured guests, with a display of martial exercises, horse races and an archery contest. Then, on the final day, the dignitaries presented gifts to the sultan, after which he cast handfuls of coins among the poor of the city who gathered around his throne. Throughout the festivities Mehmet remained in the highest humour, showing no sign that he had suffered the worst defeat of his life less than a year before.

Despite his humiliating defeat at Belgrade, Fatih's forces continued their march of conquest. After his army captured Athens Fatih went there in 1459 to see the ruined monuments of the ancient city, for his classical studies had imbued him with a deep reverence for classical Greek culture. Kritovoulos calls him a 'Philhellene' and writes:

He was greatly enamored of the city and the wonders in it, for he had heard many fine things about the wisdom and prudence of its ancient inhabitants, and also of their valor and virtues and of the many wonderful deeds they had done in their times when they fought against both Greeks and barbarians.

Three years later Fatih visited the site of ancient Troy, known to the Romans as Ilium, which he knew from his reading of Homer. Kritovoulos writes that Fatih's conquest of Byzantium made the sultan feel that he had evened the score with the Greeks for their victory over the 'Asiatics' at Troy, and that he only regretted that he did not have a poet like Homer to extol his deeds.

The palace on the Third Hill was not completed until 1458, but by then Fatih's wives and children were already living there along with the rest of his household. One of his concubines, a girl named Çiçek, or Flower, gave birth to his son Cem in the palace on 22 December 1459, the first of the Osmanlı line to be born in Istanbul. By that time Fatih's two older sons had been sent off to be provincial governors in Anatolia, with Beyazit in Amasya and Mustafa in Manisa, from where he would later be transferred to Konya.

Earlier in 1459 Fatih had ordered the construction of a vast *külliye*, or mosque complex, on the Fourth Hill, making way for it by demolishing what remained of the church of the Holy Apostles. This *külliye*, which came to be known as Fatih Camii, the Mosque of the Conqueror, took more than a decade to complete. Besides the great mosque itself, the largest erected up to that time in the Ottoman Empire, the complex included eight *medreses*, or colleges, along with a medical school, hospital, insane asylum, primary school, public kitchen, hospice, caravanserai, public bath and a cemetery with two domed *türbes*, or tombs, one for Fatih and the other for his wife Gülbahar, the mother of Prince Beyazit, the heir apparent. Mahmut Pasha followed Fatih's example and built a large mosque on the Second Hill, along with a public bath, a market and a *türbe*.

Fatih also began work in 1459 on a new imperial residence on the acropolis of the First Hill, the palace that would come to be known as Topkapı Sarayı. Although the palace on the Third Hill had been completed the previous year, Fatih seems to have felt the need for a more private dwelling place and administrative centre, which he created by constructing a high defence wall with towers around the promontory between the Golden Horn and the Marmara, the pavilions and courtyards of the palace to be laid out on the summit of the acropolis, with gardens and orchards around it on the lower ground. While Topkapı Sarayı was being built, Fatih and his household continued to dwell in their original residence on the Third Hill, which in time came to be called Eski Saray, or the Old Palace.

That same year Fatih commissioned a mosque complex outside the city at Eyüp, on the upper reaches of the Golden Horn. The site is named for Eba Eyüp Ensari, friend and standard-bearer of the Prophet Mohammed. Long after the Prophet's death Eyüp is said to have been among the leaders of the first Arab siege of Constantinople in the years 674–8, during which, according to Islamic tradition, he was killed and buried somewhere outside the walls of Constantinople. During the siege of the city in 1453 Mehmet launched a search for Eyüp's grave, which was miraculously discovered by the *şeyhülislam* Akşemsettin. Fatih thereupon reburied Eyüp in an ornate *türbe*, which he rebuilt in 1459 as part of his new mosque complex, Eyüp Camii. Eyüp's tomb became the most sacred Islamic shrine in Turkey, and in later times it was the custom for a new sultan to be girded there with the sword of Osman Gazi, as coronation.

Early in the spring of 1460 Fatih mounted a major campaign into the Peloponnesos, where Thomas and Demetrius Palaeologus, the two brothers of the late emperor Constantine, were still ruling as despots. Demetrius surrendered to Fatih at Mistra, his capital, on 29 May 1460, seven years to the day after the fall of Constantinople, while Thomas fled to Italy. Demetrius accompanied Fatih back to Edirne and was allowed to settle on an estate in the town of Didymoteichion, where he died in 1470. By that time the only other surviving fragment of Byzantium had come to an end with the fall of Trebizond to Fatih in August 1461. The last emperor of Trebizond, David Comnenus, was imprisoned in Edirne along with his family. Then on 1 November 1463 Fatih ordered the execution of David and his two elder sons. He spared the emperor's youngest son, George, and also his daughter Anna. George was given to a Turkish family and raised as a Muslim, disappearing from history, the last of the imperial dynasty of the Comneni. Anna was married off successively to two Turkish pashas, becoming a Muslim, and after the death of her second husband she ended her days in the sultan's harem in Istanbul.

All of the other high-born captives taken at Trebizond were executed, except the family of George Amirutzes, a relative of Mahmut Pasha, who were spared through the intercession of the grand vezir. Amirutzes was a distinguished philosopher and scientist, and he became Fatih's instructor in geography, astronomy and astrology.

The new palace of Topkapı was completed in 1465, according to Kritovoulos, although inscriptions indicate that work continued for another thirteen years. Apparently Fatih at first intended Topkapı Sarayı to be principally his administrative centre, keeping his harem in the Old Palace on the Third Hill. But from the description that Kritovoulos gives of the new palace it would seem that Fatih planned for his household to reside there at least part of the year:

In it he had towers built of unusual height and beauty and grandeur, and apartments for men and others for women, and bedrooms and lounging-rooms and sleeping quarters, and very many other fine rooms. There were also various out-buildings and vestibules and halls and porticoes and gateways and porches, and bakeshops and baths of notable design.

Giovanni Maria Angiolello, an Italian captive in the Ottoman service, says that the palace had three courts and was surrounded by a wall ten feet high; he notes that within the grounds there were both botanical and zoological gardens and a lake stocked with fowl where the sultan enjoyed shooting:

Third Court of Topkapı Sarayı

And here in the garden there were many kinds of fruit trees planted in order, and similarly pergolas with grapevines of many kinds, roses, lilacs, saffron, flowers of every sort, and everywhere there is an abundance of most gentle waters, that is, fountains and pools. Also in the garden are some separate places in which are kept many kinds of animals, such as deer, roes, roe deer, foxes, hare, sheep, goats and Indian cows, which are much larger than ours, and many other sorts of animals. The garden is inhabited by many sorts of birds, and when it is spring it is a pleasure to hear them sing, and likewise there is a marshy lake where a large number of wild geese and ducks dwell, and in that place the Grand Turk takes pleasure in hunting with a gun.

Fatih had always been interested in Christianity, perhaps because of his mother, who may have been Greek but had converted to Islam. Gülbahar, mother of the future Beyazit II, was probably also Greek, as were a number of Fatih's other women, all of whom became Muslims when they entered his harem. Fatih's interest in Christianity was particularly evident at the time when he had Gennadius appointed as the Greek Orthodox Patriarch. He called on Gennadius three times at the patriarchate, and in their conversations they ranged widely over Christian theology. Gennadius also wrote a summary of his work and had it translated into Turkish for Fatih's private study. Fatih's contacts with Gennadius and other Christian clerics and scholars gave rise to rumours that the sultan had inclinations towards Christianity. Teodoro Spandugino, an Italian who lived in Galata early in the sixteenth century, claims that Fatih took to worshipping Christian relics and always kept many candles burning in front of them. These rumours were strengthened by incidents such as the one reported by Brother George of Mühlenbach, who writes of a visit that Fatih made to the Franciscan monastery in Pera, the area in which most of the Europeans lived, on the heights above Galata:

The Franciscan brothers living in Pera have assured me that he came to their church and sat down in their choir to attend the ceremonies and the sacrifice of the Mass. To satisfy his curiosity, they ordered him an unconsecrated wafer at the elevation of the host, for pearls must not be cast before swine.

But Fatih's interest in Christianity appears to have been superficial, for he seems to have been basically irreligious, and in his observance of Islam he merely observed the forms of the Muslim faith, as was necessary for him as head of state. Angiolello writes that Prince Beyazit was heard to say that 'his father was domineering and did not believe in the Prophet Muhammed.'

The Ottomans were orthodox Sunni Muslims, as opposed to the heterodox doctrine of the Persian Shiites. Fatih had shown a leaning toward Shiite beliefs ever since his first, brief sultanate in Edirne, when the Persian dervish he had tried to protect was burned at the stake as a heretic. Fatih was also very interested in Persian literature, particularly the poetry of the Sufi mystics. This was taken as another evidence of his heterodoxy, since an old Ottoman proverb says that 'A man who reads Persian loses half his religion.'

Fatih was noted as a patron of literature, sending gifts to poets and prose stylists throughout the Islamic world, supporting thirty Ottoman writers, according to contemporary Turkish sources. Persian was the language of literature in Fatih's day, just as the language of Islamic theology was Arabic. But when Fatih himself wrote poetry it was mostly in colloquial Turkish. Writing under the pseudonym of Avni, he left a collection, known as a *divan*, of some eighty poems in Turkish, interspersed with a few Persian *gazels* that were merely paraphrases of works by the great Iranian poet Hafız.

The Ottoman court in Fatih's time was still simple in its customs, free of the ostentation and elaborate ceremonies surrounding the sultan that would develop in later times. Fatih often walked the streets of Istanbul with only a bodyguard or two when going to a mosque, where he took his place along with all of the other worshippers, as Brother George of Mühlenbach observed on a number of occasions:

I saw the ruler [Fatih], followed only by two young men, on his way to the mosque far away from his palace. I saw him going to the baths in the same way . . . I have seen the sultan at prayer in the mosque. He sat neither in a chair nor on a throne, but like the others had taken his place on a carpet spread out on the floor.

Late in the autumn of 1473 Fatih dismissed Mahmut Pasha from his post as grand vezir, replacing him with Gedik Ahmet Pasha. Mahmut was then stripped of his possessions and imprisoned in the Castle of the Seven Towers. The reasons for this are unclear, but it may have been that Mahmut had incurred the enmity of Prince Mustafa, the sultan's favourite. Mustafa was taken ill later that autumn in Karamania and died in June 1474. The reaction to his death is described by Angiolello, who was in the service of Prince Mustafa in the years 1470–4, after which he served in Fatih's court. When Fatih heard the news, he was inconsolable, weeping over the death of his beloved son for three days and nights. Angiolello writes that 'The entire city was filled with loud lamentation because Mustafa was especially beloved of his father and of all those who had dealings with him.'

The tragedy seems to have embittered Fatih against Mahmut Pasha, who he apparently felt was responsible for his son's death. After Mustafa's burial at the Muradiye in Bursa, Fatih ordered that his former grand vezir should be executed. According to the Turkish poet Meali, the sultan justified his action by saying that 'It is impossible that Mustafa's enemy should stay alive.' The orders were carried out by Sinan Bey, the bailiff of Istanbul, who on 18 July 1474 had his executioners strangle Mahmut with a bow-string in the castle. The following day he was buried in the *türbe* of his mosque on the Second Hill, in the quarter that is still known as Mahmut Pasha. It is revealing of Fatih's complex character that he declared that Mahmut Pasha's burial should be the occasion for a day of mourning.

Fatih spent all of 1479 in his new palace of Topkapı. That summer he sent out invitations to celebrate the circumcision feast of his grandson, the future Selim I, son of Prince Beyazit. One of the heads of state he invited was the doge of Venice, Giovanni Mocenigo, who politely declined. Fatih also asked the doge to send him a 'good painter', and the Venetian Senate chose Gentile Bellini, who arrived in Istanbul in September of that year, remaining until mid January 1481. Bellini painted the famous portrait of the Conqueror now in the National Gallery of London, which bears an inscription recording that it was completed on 25 November 1480. According to Angiolello, Bellini also decorated the sultan's apartments at Topkapı Sarayı with erotic paintings that he describes as '*cosa i lussuria*', objects of lechery. Angiolello was at the sultan's court at the same time as Bellini, and his description of Fatih is in good agreement with the sultan's portrait:

The emperor Mehmet, who, as I have said was known as the Grand Turk, was of medium height, fat, and fleshy; he had a wide forehead, large eyes with thick lashes, an aquiline nose, a small mouth with a round copious reddish-tinged beard, a short, thick neck, a sallow complexion, rather high shoulders, and a loud voice. He suffered from gout in the legs.

Mehmet II (1451–81) the Conqueror,
portrait by Costanza da Ferrara, c. 1480

Fatih's appearance at this time is also described by the French diplomat Philippe de Commynes in his memoirs. Commynes ranked Fatih with Louis XI and Matthias Corvinus of Hungary as the greatest rulers of the past century. But Mehmet had overindulged in '*les plaisirs du monde*'; no carnal vice had been unknown to this voluptuary, he writes, and thus from his early years the sultan had suffered from gout and other ailments brought on by his excesses. Mehmet now was suffering from a huge swelling and abscess in his leg that had first appeared in the spring of 1480. None of his physicians were able to cure or explain his malady, but they looked upon it as divine punishment for his great gluttony ('*grande gourmandise*'). Commynes goes on to say that the sultan's illness kept him confined to his palace, for he was loath to show himself in public in such a state:

Men who have seen him have told me that a monstrous swelling formed on his legs; at the approach of summer it grew as large as the body of a man and could not be opened; and then it subsided. No surgeon was able to say what it was, but it was said that his bestial gluttony had a good deal to do with it and that it must be divine punishment. Lest people notice his sorry state and his enemies despise him, he seldom allowed himself to be seen and remained secluded in his serai.

Fatih's desire for seclusion in his latter years was codified in his *kanunname*, a set of rules for imperial ceremonies and protocol. One of the new rules eliminated the banquets that Fatih had given four times a week for his vezirs after meetings of the imperial council, and thenceforth only members of the royal family would be allowed to join the sultan at his meals: 'It is my command that no one dine with my noble self except members of my family. My great ancestors are said to have eaten with their vezirs; I have abolished this practice.'

Despite Fatih's failing health he launched two campaigns in 1480. He began preparations for yet another campaign early in the spring of 1481, possibly an invasion of Egypt, which he was determined to lead himself. The grand vezir Karamanlı Mehmet Pasha was ordered to muster the army at Üsküdar, the Asian suburb of Istanbul, but otherwise the destination of the expedition was unknown.

Fatih crossed the Bosphorus to Üsküdar on 25 April and the march began the same day. A halt was made on the Gulf of Nicomedia near Gebze, where Fatih was suddenly convulsed with severe abdominal pains. One of his doctors, Hamiduddin al-Lari, apparently gave him the wrong medicine, for he immediately began to grow worse. His Jewish physician, Maestro Iacopo, who had looked after Mehmet since his childhood, now took over, but there was nothing that he could do. The sultan died the following day, 3 May 1481, 'at the twenty-second hour', according to Angiolello.

Mehmet Pasha tried to keep Fatih's death a secret so that his patron, Prince Cem, could steal a march on his older brother Beyazit and seize the throne. At the time of Fatih's death both of the brothers were serving as provincial governors in Anatolia, Beyazit in Amasya and Cem in Konya. Mehmet Pasha put Fatih's body in a sealed carriage and hurried back with it to Istanbul, telling his soldiers that the sultan had been taken ill, while in the mean time he sent a courier to inform Cem. This aroused the suspicion of the Janissaries, who supported Beyazit, and they marched on Topkapı Sarayı, demanding to see the sultan. When he failed to appear, they forced their way through the Imperial Gate and found his lifeless body being guarded by the grand vezir's servants. The Janissaries in their fury then killed Mehmet Pasha, after which they paraded through the streets of the city with his severed head held aloft on a pike, crying 'Long live Beyazit!'

Ishak Pasha had sent word to Beyazit, who arrived in Istanbul on 20 May to a tumultuous welcome from the Janissaries. Meanwhile Ishak Pasha had allied himself with the commander of the Janissaries, Sinan Ağa, and the two of them proclaimed Beyazit sultan, girding him with the sword of Osman. The following day the new sultan, now known as Beyazit II, took turns with all of the dignitaries of the empire in carrying the coffin of his father to Fatih Camii. There Fatih was buried in the tomb that he had built for himself beside his mosque, where Beyazit led twenty thousand mourners, including two thousand dervishes, in praying for the repose of his father's soul, their devotions continuing until dawn.

Nicolò Cocco, the Venetian *bailo*, or ambassador, sent word of Fatih's death to the doge, Giovanni Mecenigo. The messenger arrived in Venice on 19 May when the doge was conferring with the Signoria, the council of state, and he burst into the meeting hall and cried out, '*La grande aquila e morta!*' (The great eagle is dead.) Giovanni Sagredo, writing of this moment more than two centuries later, noted that 'It is fortunate for Christendom and for Italy that death checked the fierce and indomitable barbarian.' The doge sent a courier to Rome to inform Pope Sixtus IV, who had cannons fired and church bells rung to alert the populace there, after which he led a solemn procession to the church of Santa Maria del Popolo, followed by the college of cardinals and all of the ambassadors. As night fell there was a tremendous display of fireworks, and services of thanksgiving were held in all of the churches of the city, a scene

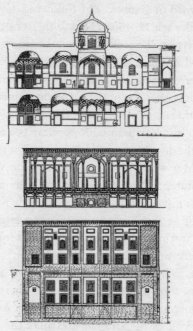

Çinili Köşk, the Tiled Kiosk

that was repeated throughout Italy and then in northern Europe as the word spread that the Grand Turk had passed from the world. Mehmet the Conqueror was dead and Christian Europe need fear him no more.

Fatih was forty-nine when he died, having reigned after his father's death for thirty years, most of which he had spent in war. As Fatih's clerk Tursun Bey wrote in his biography of the Conqueror: 'Beside the gracious gift of the Conquest of Constantinople, Fatih wrested twenty or more independent lands from the enemies of His High Estate.'

Aside from the defence walls and gateways of Topkapı Sarayı, the only building in the palace that survives unchanged from Fatih's time is Çinili Köşk, the Tiled Kiosk, which he completed in 1472. The kiosk, which is in the Persian style, stands on a terrace below the second court of Topkapı Sarayı to the west. It was designed so that Fatih could watch the palace pages as they played on the terrace at *cirit*, a game in which horsemen try to hit one another with darts. One chronicler tells of how the sultan enjoyed himself there, watching his pages having a snowball fight on the terrace. Animals from his menagerie were also brought to the terrace for him to see, and he particularly liked watching his lion-tamers at work. The dedicatory inscription in Persian compares the cupola of the kiosk, which was decorated with stars, to the dome of heaven, and the pavilion itself to the heavenly mansion that rises to the constellations. Many of the poets whom Fatih supported wrote *gazels* in praise of the kiosk, mentioning nocturnal gatherings during which the sultan drank wine under the stars with his pages, and of evenings when he was entertained there by the women of his harem, the 'virgins of paradise'. Thus did Mehmet pass his last years in this kiosk of Dar-üs Saadet, the House of Felicity.

Chapter 3

THE HOUSE OF FELICITY

Beyazit II was thirty-three when he succeeded to the throne of his father, Fatih Mehmet. He was very different from his warrior father, preferring the peace of his imperial residence at Topkapı Sarayı to the rigours and dangers of military campaigns. Beyazit was known to his people as Sufi, or the Mystic, while Western historians in modern times have referred to him as the Sedentary Sultan.

At the time of his accession, Beyazit's *birinci kadın*, or first wife, was Şirin, mother of the sultan's first son, Abdullah. When Abdullah died in 1483 the title of first wife passed to Bülbül (Nightingale), mother of Prince Ahmet, Beyazit's second son, who became the heir apparent. Besides Abdullah and Ahmet, Beyazit had six other sons, including his eventual successor, Selim I, all of them born to different mothers. Selim's mother was Ayşe Hatun, daughter of the Dulkadırlı emir Alâeddevlet Bozkurt. Beyazit also had fifteen daughters, whose mothers are identified by name only if they also gave birth to a son.

During the first year of Beyazit's reign he was involved in a war of succession with his brother Cem, who had declared himself sultan of Anatolia and rallied his army of supporters at Bursa. Cem was eventually defeated by Beyazit and fled to Rhodes, where he was given refuge by the Knights of St John, thus beginning an exile that lasted until his death in Naples on 25 February 1495. Four years later Beyazit arranged for Cem to be reburied in Bursa, where he was laid to rest in the Muradiye next to his grandfather, Murat II.

A bizarre tale about Cem's burial is told by the seventeenth-century Turkish chronicler Evliya Çelebi, writing in his *Seyahatname*, or *Chronicle of Travels*:

The corpse of Cem, together with his property, amongst which was an enchanted cup, which became brimful as soon as delivered empty into the cup-bearer's hand, a white parrot, a chess-playing monkey, and some thousands of splendid books, were delivered up to ... the Sultan ... Beyazit ordered the remains of Cem to be buried at Bursa, beside his grandfather Murat II. When they were digging the grave there was such a thunder-clap and tumult in the sepulchral chapel, that all who were present fled, but not a soul of them was able to pass its threshold till ten days had passed, when this being represented to the Sultan, the corpse of Cem was buried in his own mausoleum, near to that of his grandfather.

After Beyazit put down Cem's rebellion he set out to consolidate the empire he had inherited, developing its commerce. He built an imperial mosque complex on the Third Hill of Istanbul in 1501–6. Known as the Beyazidiye, this gave its name to the Beyazit quarter above the Covered Bazaar, and to Beyazit Square, the ancient Forum Tauri.

Beyazit left the active direction of military affairs to a succession of grand vezirs, freeing himself to take his ease in Topkapı Sarayı, where he spent the last decade of his reign secluded behind the walls of the palace. This period in Beyazit's reign is thus described by Richard Knolles in *The Lives of the Othoman Kings and Emperors*, published in 1610, the first history of the Ottoman Empire in English:

After so many troubles, Baiazet gave himself unto a quiet course of life, spending most part of his time in studie of Philosophie, and conference with learned men, unto which peaceable kind of life his owne natural disposition more enclined than to warres; albeit that the regard of his state, and the earnest desire of his men of warre, drew him oftentimes against his will into the field.

Beyazit II (1481–1512)

When Fatih first laid out his new palace he enclosed it with a line of walls that extended from the Golden Horn to the Sea of Marmara, a distance of about one and a half miles. This fortification joined up with the medieval Byzantine sea-walls along the Golden Horn and the Marmara to enclose the First Hill. The main entryway in the sea-walls was at Saray Burnu, where the Golden Horn joins the Bosphorus and the Marmara. This portal was known as Topkapı, the Cannon Gate, so called because it bristled with cannon (*top*), a name that came to be applied to the palace itself.

Fatih's land wall had twenty-eight towers and was pierced by three gates, the main entryway being Bab-ı Hümayun, the Imperial Gate. The rooms in the gateway were for the *kapıcıs*, or guards, of whom fifty were perpetually on duty. The Imperial Gate leads into the First Court of Topkapı Sarayı, an area that was not internally walled until after Fatih's time. Inside the gate to the left is the former Byzantine church of Haghia Eirene, dedicated to the Divine Peace. The church was used by the Janissaries as a storehouse for their weapons when they mustered in the First Court. The large building beyond Haghia Eirene is the Darphane, the former Ottoman Mint, which included the Outer Treasury of Topkapı Sarayı. The other buildings around the court, none of which have survived, included storerooms, workshops, the palace bakery, the infirmary, the palace waterworks, latrines, a small mosque, and barracks for artisans and domestics of the Outer Service, those whose duties did not take them into the Inner Palace.

A gate on the west side of the court leads to Çinili Köşk and Gülhane Park, formerly the lower gardens of Topkapı Sarayı, which extended around the acropolis down to the shores of the Golden Horn and the Marmara. These were first laid out and planted by Fatih, and they were cultivated throughout the nearly four centuries that Topkapı Sarayı served as the imperial residence.

A road on the right side of the court leads down to the fields where the palace pages played *cirit* and practised archery and other sports, including hunts staged by the sultan. The palace menagerie was to the left of this road at its upper end; travellers report that it housed elephants, giraffes, lions, tigers, bears, wild boars, gazelles, deer and goats. According to the sixteenth-century Turkish chronicler Lokman, the elephants and giraffes were displayed in the first court during feast days as a 'demonstration of magnificence'. Two ambassadors from the Holy Roman Emperor Ferdinand I in 1530 reported that they saw ten lions and two tigers in the first court, 'fettered with golden chains and roaring terribly'. The French traveller Louis Deshayes de Courmenin reports that the wild boars in the menagerie were used by the sultan in hunts that he held in the palace grounds, in which the prey were named for his Christian enemies: 'He gives to each wild boar the name of one of his enemies, such as the King of Spain, whom he calls the Signior of Spain, the Duke of Florence, the Grand Master of Malta, and others in this manner.'

The palace aviary was in the southeastern corner of the lower gardens, on the Marmara shore just inside the land walls of the palace. According to the seventeenth-century Armenian chronicler Eremya Çelebi, the aviary was housed in a Byzantine chapel that had been dedicated to St John the Baptist. The swans in this aviary were used to provide feathers for the arrows that the sultan used in his hunts.

Eremya also notes that on the shore just to the north of the aviary there was an imperial kiosk known as the Balıkhane Kasrı, or Fishery Pavilion, approached from within the palace grounds by a small portal known as Balıkhane Kapısı. The chief fisherman of the palace had his station here, and the sultan often came to the kiosk to watch him and his men set their nets for fish that were later served at the royal table.

There were other imperial kiosks along the shores of both the Marmara and the Golden Horn, including one built by Beyazit II. This was the Yalı Köşk, or Shore Pavilion, which stood on the shore of the Golden Horn across from Galata. The kiosk, which was rebuilt twice in the sixteenth century, was designed so that Beyazit could review the Ottoman fleet when it set off on an expedition. Once, Beyazit saw a coffin with a woman's body inside floating past the kiosk, and he demanded that an inquiry be made to see if there had been foul play. The woman's husband was arrested, but he proved that his wife had died after eating honey from a jar in which a poisonous serpent had hidden, whereupon he was 'freed from the sultan's wrath', or so the story goes.

The portal at the far end of the first court is Bab-üs Selam, the Gate of Salutations, generally known as Orta Kapı, or the Middle Gate. This was the entrance to the Inner Palace where everyone had to dismount, for none but the sultan was allowed to ride beyond this point. In the wall to the right of the gate is the Executioner's Fountain, where the executioner washed his hands and sword after a decapitation. Beside the gate there are two marble niches known as Example Stones, since they were used for the display of severed heads of notable offenders. Sometimes a head would be impaled on a pike above the gateway, as thus described by an anonymous traveller of the early sixteenth century, who mistakenly thought that this was the Gate of Felicity: 'When you go to the Seraglio you have to enter by a gate which is very richly gilded, and is called the Gate of Felicity. Sometimes you see over it, stuck upon the point of a pike, the head of a grand vezir, who has been decapitated in the morning, at the caprice of the Grand Signor.'

The rooms within the gatehouse were used to house the chief gatekeeper and his men. The room on the left side of the gate was reserved for the chief executioner, who was also the chief gardener. A cubicle beside his room housed prisoners awaiting execution.

The Middle Gate leads into the second court. This is still very much as it was when Fatih laid it out, a tranquil cloister of imposing proportions, planted with venerable cypress trees and planes; several fountains once adorned it and mild-eyed gazelles pastured on the glebe. It was also known as the Court of the Divan, the Imperial Council, which met in the domed chamber under the tower at the far left corner. The Divan and the Inner Treasury beyond it are the only buildings in the courtyard, with the remainder of the periphery consisting of colonnaded porticos. Beyond the colonnade the whole of the right side of the courtyard is occupied by the palace kitchens, while beyond the walls to the left are the Royal Stables, a mosque, and the dormitories of the halberdiers.

The Court of the Divan seems to have been designed essentially for the pageantry associated with the transaction of the public business of the empire. Here, four times a week, the Divan met to deliberate on administrative matters or to discharge its judicial functions. On such occasions the whole courtyard was filled with a vast throng of magnificently dressed officials and the corps of palace guards and Janissaries, at least five thousand people on ordinary occasions, but more than twice that many when some special ceremony was being held. Even at such times an almost total silence prevailed throughout the courtyard, a fact commented upon by the foreigners who witnessed it. The Venetian *bailo* Andrea Gritti, who

Equestrian display in the Second Court of Topkapı Sarayı

would later become doge, describes thescene that he observed in 1503, when he came for an audience with Beyazit II:

I entered into the court, where I found on one side all the Janissaries on foot and on the other side all the persons of high esteem, and the salaried officials of His Majesty, who stood with such great silence and with such a beautiful order that it was a marvellous thing not believable to one who has not seen it with his own eyes.

The Divan took its name from the low couch (*divan*) that extends around three sides of the domed council chamber. The grand vezir sat in the centre of the couch, facing the door, with the other vezirs on either side in strict order of rank. During the early years of Fatih's reign he regularly attended meetings of the Divan. But at one session a rough peasant made his way into the chamber and shouted rudely at the members of the council, saying, 'Which of you worthies is the sultan?', which so enraged Fatih that he never again attended a meeting in person. Instead he observed the occasional meeting from a grilled opening over the grand vezir's seat, a window that came to be called the Eye of the Sultan. This window looked out from a chamber under the Tower of the Divan, one of the distinctive landmarks of Topkapı Sarayı. The main entrance to the harem, the Carriage Gate, is under the tower beside the council chamber. The gate takes its name from the fact that the women of the harem passed through it in closed carriages on their rare excursions from the palace.

Beyond the three gateways in the east portico of the second court a long, narrow courtyard runs the entire length of the area. The palace kitchens open off from the east side of this courtyard, with the storerooms and the mosque of the culinary staff opposite them on the west. The earliest description of the kitchens is by Giovantonio Menavino, a Genoese who was captured by pirates and sold as a slave to Beyazit II, after which he served as a page in Topkapı Sarayı in the years 1505–14. According to Menavino, in Beyazit's time the kitchens were divided into two sections, one for the sultan and the other for the household of the palace and those who attended meetings of the Divan, staffed by about 160 cooks, bakers and other

Chief Steward

servants. The number of kitchen staff increased considerably in the century after Beyazit's reign, when the population of the palace reached its peak. The number of confectioners alone amounted to as many as six hundred in the late sixteenth century. The confectioners made up a separate branch of the kitchen service, distinguished from the other cooks by a tall white hat 'rising to a pretty height somewhat to the resemblance of a sugar-loaf', according to Jean-Baptiste Tavernier, who was with the French embassy in Istanbul during the years 1629–37. Tavernier writes of the privileged position held by the confectioners and how they abused it:

For whereas they are the only Persons who have the freedom of going in and coming out of the Seraglio, they set double the price on everything they buy. But their most considerable gain proceeds from the infamous commerce of those young Lads, whom they bring in to their Masters, and whom they cunningly slip into the Infirmary, after they had put them into habits like their own.

Ordinarily the imperial kitchens served two meals a day, but in the summer months a late supper was prepared for the sultan and the women of his harem, who dined after the last prayer, about two hours past sunset. A double line of some two hundred waiters formed between the kitchens and the sultan's quarters, with those in one row handing along the various courses as they were prepared, and those in the other passing back the empty dishes.

The portal at the far end of the second court, Bab-üs Saadet, the Gate of Felicity, is the entrance to the third court and the strictly private and residential areas of the Inner Palace, the sequestered Dar-üs Saadet, the House of Felicity. The gate was guarded by the white eunuchs, whose chiefs bore the title of *kapı ağası*, or ağa of the gate. The sultan sat enthroned under the domed canopy in front of the Gate of Felicity at the time of his accession and on the two major *bayrams*, or holidays, when he received the homage of his subjects and officials, a scene depicted in a number of paintings and engravings. The only foreigners who were permitted to pass through the Gate of Felicity were ambassadors having an audience with the

Bab-üs Saadet, the Gate of Felicity

sultan, who received them in the Audience Chamber, just inside the gateway.

Most of the other buildings in the third court were devoted to the Palace School, founded by Fatih to train promising youths for careers in the Ottoman military and civil service. The pages who attended the school at first came from the Christian minorities, recruited in the *devşirme* or taken as prisoners-of-war, and raised as Muslims, although in time Turkish youths were enrolled. The brilliant success of the Ottoman state during its early centuries derived largely from the excellence of the Palace School, whose graduates rose to the highest positions in the empire, including a number of grand vezirs. Beyazit II took great interest in the school and founded an annexe in Pera known as Galatasaray, whose name lives on today in the Galatasaray Lise.

The pages in the Palace School were supervised by the white

eunuchs, under the *kapı ağası*. Up until the last quarter of the sixteenth century the chief white eunuch was the most powerful official in the Inner Service. But thenceforth the chief black eunuch, known as the *kızlar ağası*, the ağa of the girls, was the dominant figure, a change brought about by the greatly increased size and importance of the harem, in which the women were guarded by the black eunuchs.

The building at the southwest corner of the court is Ağalar Camii, the Mosque of the Ağas, where the white eunuchs and the pages performed their prayers. The mosque could also be entered from the harem, and screened-off areas were set aside for the sultan and his favourites, as well as the *valide sultan*, or queen mother, and the chief black eunuch.

At the southwestern corner of the court a portal known at Kuşhane Kapısı, the Aviary Gate, leads into the harem. This and the Carriage Gate in the second court were the only entrances to the harem other than a private entryway from the Privy Chamber, the sultan's apartments in the *selamlık*, the men's quarters of the palace. The harem occupied the area to the west of the second and third courts, extending northward from the Tower of the Divan as far as the Mosque of the Ağas. The Privy Chamber and the rest of the *selamlık* extended from there to the northern end of the palace and the fourth court, which was really a garden with kiosks on several terraces. Virtually all of the buildings in the harem and the *selamlık* date from at least a century after the Conquest, for Fatih and his immediate successors had relatively few women in their household, and apparently the majority of them continued to live in the Old Palace. The Venetian *bailo* Alvise Sagundino reported in 1499 that only ten women lived with Beyazit II in Topkapı Sarayı, while eighty were housed outside of it, presumably in the Old Palace, where the numbers would seem to refer only to the sultan's wives and concubines, who would have had numerous women servants and ladies-in-waiting. The *bailo* Iacomo Contarini reported in 1507 on the household of Beyazit II: 'Inside his seraglio he continually keeps four aghas [eunuchs] for the guarding of his person and his house-

Fourth Court of Topkapı Sarayı

hold, who are three hundred persons, among whom there are eighty boys, and they say also some women.' Contarini adds that Beyazit occasionally visited the women in the Old Palace. Beyazit's mother, the *valide sultan* Gülbahar, lived for the last five years of her life in the Old Palace, from which she wrote to her son plaintively:

My fortune, I miss you. Even if you don't miss me, I miss you . . . Come and let me see you. My dear lord, if you are going on campaign soon, come once or twice at least so that I may see your fortune-favoured face before you go. It's been forty days since I last saw you. My sultan, please excuse my boldness. Who else do I have beside you?

Gülbahar died in September 1486, and after a period of mourning Beyazit buried her in the *türbe* next to that of her husband Mehmet II in the garden behind Fatih Camii. Gülbahar's tomb, unlike that of Fatih, has never been open to the public, and this has given rise to a number of stories and legends. One old and persistent legend, quite definitely apocryphal, has it that Gülbahar was a daughter of the King of France, sent by him as a bride for the emperor Constantine XI Dragases and captured by the Turks when they were besieging Constantinople in 1453. Evliya Çelebi recounts a version of this legend in his *Seyahatname*, where he implies that Gülbahar never embraced Islam:

I myself have often observed, at morning prayer, that the readers appointed to chant lessons from the Koran all turned their backs upon the coffin of this lady, of whom it was so doubtful whether she had departed in the faith of Islam. I have often seen Franks come by stealth and give a few aspers to the tomb-keeper to open her türbe for them, as its gate is always kept locked.

During the last decade of the fifteenth century Beyazit gave refuge to large numbers of Jews who had been expelled from Spain, resettling many of them in Istanbul, where they made a significant contribution to the commercial development of the city. Several of these Jews served as doctors in Topkapı Sarayı, continuing a tradition that dated back to Maestro Iacopo, Fatih's personal physician.

Beyazit became very ill in 1508 and was not expected to live, and though he recovered the following year he remained bedridden. Later in 1509 Istanbul was shaken by a severe earthquake, popularly called 'The Little Doomsday', which damaged the outer walls of Topkapı Sarayı as well as some of the palace buildings. Beyazit ordered the damage to be repaired, one of the restored buildings being the imperial bath. One of the rooms adjoining the bath was the *meşkhane*, or music chamber, where the palace pages were taught to sing and play musical instruments. Albert Bobovi, a Polish prisoner-of-war who served as a palace page in the mid seventeenth century, says that the palace musicians played in the imperial bath every Tuesday while the sultan was being shaved, a custom said to date from the time of Beyazit II.

Beyazit's health began to improve in the spring of 1511, though he was still confined to his bed. By then five of his sons were dead: Abdullah and Alemşah of natural causes, Şahinşah of drink, while Beyazit had done away with Mahmut and Mehmet, having had both of them poisoned in 1507 for insubordination. His remaining three sons, Ahmet, Korkut and Selim, had all been serving as provincial governors in Anatolia, and they now manœuvered to bring their forces closer to Istanbul so as to seize power when their father passed away. Selim knew that Beyazit wanted to abdicate and leave the throne to Ahmet, the oldest, and to forestall that he took his army across to Europe and camped near Edirne, raising the pay of his soldiers so that he drew recruits from his father's forces.

The following spring Beyazit was forced to submit to Selim, who entered Istanbul with his army on 23 April 1512 and took control of the city. That same day Selim met with his father, whom he had not seen in twenty-six years, and he forced Beyazit to abdicate. The next day Selim was girded with the sword of Osman and became the ninth Ottoman sultan, the third to rule in Istanbul.

Selim allowed Beyazit to retire to Demotika in Thrace, his birthplace, where he wanted to spend the rest of his days in retirement. Beyazit remained in Topkapı Sarayı for twenty days, after which he and his household departed in a caravan with all of his personal belongings and treasures. Selim accompanied his father as far as the city walls, where Beyazit with tears in his eyes blessed his son and wished him success.

The caravan never reached Demotika, for half-way there, at a village near Çorlu, Beyazit's condition suddenly worsened, and on 26 May 1512 he died in agony. A number of those in his entourage believed that he had been poisoned by his Jewish physician Hamon on the orders of Sultan Selim.

Selim arranged for his father's remains to be brought back to Istanbul to be buried in the *türbe* of the Beyazidiye, the imperial mosque complex that Beyazit had erected on the Third Hill. Evliya Çelebi notes that Beyazit's mausoleum became a place of pilgrimage: 'His tomb is now generally visited by the sick, who here find relief in their diseases, because Sultan Beyazit was a saintly monarch.'

Selim was forty-two when he became sultan, having served as a provincial governor for eighteen years in Trabzon, the Greek Trebizond. His fierce mien and cruel manner led the Turks to call him Yavuz, or the Grim. The name would seem to be merited, as evidenced by the description of Selim given by Knolles:

But in Selymus his sterne countenance, his fierce and piercing eyes, his Tartar-like pale colour, his long mustachios on his upper lip, like bristles, frild back to his necke, with his beard cut close to his chin, did so express his martial disposition and inexorable nature, that he seemed to the beholder, to have nothing in him but mischiefe and crueltie . . .

Selymus contrariwise did all things in secret, eating his meat alone without any companie, attended upon with his pages and eunuches onely, and satisfying natures want with some simple piece of meat . . . His wives he would not suffer to come to court, neither used their companie but for procreation sake, and that (as was thought) without any good countenance or famillaritie: for that being not greatly given to women, but more delighted with unnatural pleasure . . .

Shortly after his succession Selim set out to deal with his rivals to the throne. During the next year he defeated and killed his brothers Ahmet and Korkut, after which he executed six of his nephews. Selim's campaign to eliminate all possible rivals to his throne did not stop there, and on 20 December he executed three of his own sons, Abdullah, Mahmut and Murat. The reason for their execution is obscure, but presumably Selim suspected them of plotting against him.

The execution of the three princes left Selim with only a single male heir to the throne, his son Süleyman. Süleyman's mother Hafsa then became Selim's *birinci kadın*, having taken up residence in the harem of Topkapı Sarayı after Selim became sultan. Selim's mother Ayşe had died shortly before he came to the throne, so the position of *valide sultan* remained vacant during his reign. Selim also had ten daughters, five of whom were married off to pashas, including three grand vezirs.

Selim I practising archery at the Marble Kiosk

Selim may have had another son – Üveys Pasha – who was born to one of his concubines after he had given her in marriage to one of his vezirs. Selim never acknowledged him as his son, which probably saved the life of Üveys Pasha, who died of natural causes in 1546.

Selim defeated Shah Ismail of Iran at Çaldıran on 23 August 1514, adding all of eastern Anatolia to the Ottoman Empire. He then conquered the Mamluks of Egypt, capturing Cairo on 20 January 1517, thus extending the boundaries of his empire around the eastern Mediterranean. Tradition has it that at this time the caliph al-Mutawakkil transferred the rights of the caliphate to Selim and his successors in the Osmanlı line. This tradition was later revived to establish the rights of the Ottoman sultans to the title of caliph, which some of them used in support of their claim to be the leader of the Islamic world. Selim brought the sacred relics of the Prophet Mohammed back to Istanbul, where they were enshrined in a new hall of the Privy Chamber known as the Pavilion of the Holy Mantle.

Selim also built in Topkapı Sarayı a seaside pavilion known as the Marble Kiosk. Lokman notes that the Marble Kiosk was beautifully decorated and adorned with paintings, including a scene representing Selim's victory over Shah Ismail at the battle of Çaldıran. The Turkish chronicler Hoca Sadeddin, in his biography of Selim I, notes that one of the paintings was a portrait of Fatih Mehmet. When Selim first saw the painting he said, according to Hoca Sadeddin, that it was not a good likeness of Fatih, though it did evoke pleasant memories of his grandfather: 'The deceased [Fatih] used to make us sit on his blessed lap in our childhood, his noble countenance is still in our memory since he was falcon-nosed. This painter has not captured his likeness at all.'

Selim was a poet of some merit, composing verses in Turkish, Persian and Arabic. His best-known distich complains of the predicament of an all-powerful monarch who is helpless when ensnared by love:

While lions were trembling in my crushing paw
Fate made me fall prey to a doe-eyed darling.

Selim planned another campaign in 1520, but when preparations were not completed by midsummer, he postponed the expedition till the following year and decided to take a vacation in Edirne Sarayı. Selim set out from Istanbul in mid August 1520, but about half-way to Edirne, at a village near Çorlu, he became so ill that he had to interrupt his journey. This was where his father Beyazit had died a little more than eight years earlier, and now Selim met his fate here as well, and after suffering for nearly six weeks he finally passed away on 22 September 1520. Ferhat Pasha concealed Selim's death so that Süleyman, who was serving as provincial governor in Manisa, could rush to Istanbul to take control of the government and ensure his succession to the throne.

The chronicler Kemalpaşazade, who had accompanied Selim on his campaign into Egypt, wrote in a lament on the passing of the great sultan, that 'in a brief space of time he had achieved much, and, like the setting sun, had cast a long shadow over the face of the earth.'

The news of Selim's death occasioned services of thanksgiving throughout Christian Europe, where there had been fear that he was about to embark on another campaign of conquest, perhaps against the Hungarian capital at Buda. As Paolo Giovio wrote of the reaction of Pope Leo X on hearing the news of Selim's death: 'When he had heard for a surety that Selimus was dead, he commanded that the litany of common prayers be sung throughout all Rome, in which men should go barefoot.' Selim had not divulged his plans to anyone, for he always kept his own counsel, as the *bailo* Bartolomeo Contarini remarked in one of his reports: 'He reflects constantly; no one dares to say anything, not even the pashas who are there with him; he governs alone, on the basis of his own thinking.' And now Selim had taken his last secret to the grave, as Christian Europe rejoiced. An anonymous commentator remarked that 'Selim the Grim died of an infected boil and thereby Hungary was spared.'

Soon after his accession Süleyman decided to build an imperial mosque complex in honour of his father on the Fifth Hill. Selim was reburied there in a *türbe* behind the mosque, which was dedicated as the Selimiye. The huge catafalque of Selim the Grim stands alone in the centre of the domed tomb, with the enormous turban that the sultan wore in life at its head, just as it is described by Evliya Çelebi:

There is no royal sepulchre that fills the visitor with so much awe as Selim's. There he lies with the turban called Selimiye on his coffin like a seven-headed dragon. I, the humble Evliya, was for three years the reader of hymns at his tomb.

Chapter 4

SÜLEYMAN
THE MAGNIFICENT

Süleyman was nearly twenty-six when he came to the throne. Foreign observers found him to be more pleasant than his grim father, and they were hopeful that his reign would bring better times, as Bartolomeo Contarini wrote just before Süleyman's succession:

He is twenty-five years of age, tall but wiry, and of a delicate complexion. His neck is a little too long, his face thin, and his nose aquiline. He has a shadow of a mustache and a small beard; nevertheless he has a pleasant mien, though his skin tends to pallor. He is said to be a wise lord, and all men hope for good from his reign.

Süleyman was born on 6 November 1494 in Trabzon, the former Trebizond. His father, Selim I, had at the time just taken up his appointment as provincial governor there. Süleyman's mother, Hafsa Hatun, who was seventeen at the time of his birth, may have been a daughter of Mengli Giray, *khan* of the Crimean Tartars.

Süleyman twice served as provincial governor under his grandfather Beyazit II, first at Bolu in western Anatolia in 1509 and then at Caffa in the Crimea in 1509–12, after which he governed at Manisa throughout the reign of his father Selim I. He had also twice served briefly as his father's regent in Edirne when Selim was off on campaign.

The courts of the Ottoman princely governors were modelled on the imperial court, rivalling it in opulence. Registers show that in the latter years of Süleyman's governorate in Manisa his household numbered 673, which included 17 women in his harem. The women comprised his mother Hafsa, six concubines, six ladies-in-waiting, two laundrywomen, a scribe and a doctor. The only concubine whose name is known was Mahidevran, identified variously as an Albanian or Circassian, who in 1515 gave birth to a son, Mustafa. At that time Süleyman already had another son, Mahmut, born in 1512, and then in 1519 he fathered a third son, Murat, neither of whose mothers are known. Murat died in 1521 and Mahmut passed away the following year. The records show that a daughter of Süleyman died in 1521, and that another of his daughters married the admiral Ali Pasha. Neither of these daughters nor their mothers are identified.

When Süleyman succeeded to the throne his mother Hafsa became *valide sultan*. After the death of his brother Mahmut, Prince Mustafa was the heir apparent and his mother Mahidevran became Süleyman's *birinci kadın* and *haseki*. But by then she already had a rival, for by the time of his succession or soon after Süleyman had a new favourite, Haseki Hürrem (Joyous One), better known in the West as Roxelana.

Roxelana is thought to have been born in the western Ukraine, which was then part of Poland. Polish tradition has it that she was Aleksandra Lisowska, daughter of a Ruthenian priest, and that she was taken captive by Tartars and sold in the Istanbul slave market. The name Roxelana was believed by Europeans to mean 'the Russian woman', but it is now thought to be a Polish term meaning 'Ruthenian maiden'. During the first five years of Süleyman's reign Roxelana bore him five children: a son Mehmet in 1521; a daughter Mihrimah in 1522; and then three sons, Abdullah, Selim and Beyazit. Abdullah died in 1526, succumbing to one of the many plagues that ravaged the harem.

Soon after his accession Süleyman and his grand vezir Piri Pasha began making preparations for a campaign into Europe. Süleyman's objective was Belgrade, the gateway to all of the lands along the middle Danube, which he captured on 29 August 1521. When word

*Süleyman the Magnificent (1520–66)
and his wife Roxelana*

reached the doge of Venice he wrote to his ambassador in England, saying that 'This news is lamentable, and of importance to all Christians.'

After the capture of Belgrade, Süleyman grew a beard, a traditional sign of maturity among the Turks. He is first depicted with a beard in the *Süleymanname* of Arifi, the court historian, illustrated by an unknown master, in a painting representing his victorious return to Istanbul after the triumph at Belgrade.

The following year Süleyman replaced Piri Pasha as grand vezir with Ibrahim Pasha, who had long been his intimate friend. Ibrahim, the son of a Greek fisherman, had been captured by the Turks as a child and sold as a slave to the imperial household in Istanbul, where he was trained in the Palace School. He served as a page in Topkapı Sarayı, where he and Süleyman soon became close friends, the two of them being the same age. When Süleyman became sultan he first made Ibrahim his chief falconer and then chief of the royal bedchamber. Then, after appointing Ibrahim as grand vezir, Süleyman gave him a palace on the Hippodrome, a huge edifice that was far larger than any of the buildings in Topkapı Sarayı. The following year Ibrahim was married to Süleyman's sister Hadice. Their marriage was celebrated with a festival in the Hippodrome that lasted for fifteen days, according to the sixteenth-century Turkish historian Ibrahim Peçevi, who writes that 'spread before the eyes was such an abundance and merriment as had never before been observed at the wedding of a princess.'

Ibrahim was the only person outside of the imperial household who was ever allowed to enter the Inner Palace at Topkapı Sarayı, where he often slept in a bedroom that was kept for him near that of Süleyman.

Early in the spring of 1526 Süleyman led a campaign into Hungary, with Ibrahim Pasha in command. The campaign climaxed on 29 August of that year at the battle of Mohacs, where the Ottomans utterly defeated the Hungarians in a battle that lasted less than two hours. Most of the Hungarian soldiers died in the battle or were executed by Süleyman, who ordered that no prisoners be taken. As Süleyman noted in his diary for 31 August, writing in the third person: 'The sultan, seated on a golden throne, receives the homage of the vezirs and beys; massacre of 200 prisoners, the rain falls in torrents.' Then in another entry on 2 September: 'Rest at Mohacs; 20,000 Hungarian infantry and 4,000 of their cavalry are buried.'

Immediately after the battle Süleyman had his scribes send letters announcing his victory to all the provincial capitals of the empire. He himself wrote a letter giving the news to his mother Hafsa, the *valide sultan*, who at the time is described by the *bailo* Pietro Bragadin as being 'a very beautiful woman of 48, for whom the sultan bears great reverence and love'. He also wrote to Roxelana, whose ability to read and write was at that time limited, so that she was forced to use a scribe in corresponding with Süleyman. In one

Scribe in Topkapı Sarayı

of her early letters to him she wrote, 'My sultan, you wrote that if I were able to read what you write, you would write at greater length of your longing for me.' But later she was able to write on her own, eloquently, as in a personal note telling Süleyman how much she and her children missed him:

My sultan, there is no limit to the burning anguish of separation. Now spare this miserable one and do not withhold your noble

*letters. Let my soul gain at least some comfort from a letter ...
When your noble letters are read, your servant and son Mir Mehmet
and your slave and daughter Mihrimah weep and wail from missing
you. Their weeping has driven me mad, and it is as if we were in
mourning. My sultan, your son Mir Mehmet and your daughter
Mihrimah and Selim Khan and Abdullah send you many greetings
and rub their faces in the dust at your feet.*

Many of their letters were written as poems, such as one from
Süleyman to Roxelana beginning with this verse:

*My very own queen, my everything,
    my beloved, my bright moon;
My intimate companion, my one and all,
    sovereign of all beauties, my sultan.*

One of the poems that Roxelana wrote in response to Süleyman
begins with these lines, telling of her longing for him:

*Go, gentle breeze, tell my sultan, 'She weeps and pines away;
Without your face, like a nightingale, she moans in dismay.
Don't think your power can heal her heartache in your
    absence:
No one has found a cure for her woes,' that's what you should
    say,
'The hand of grief pierces her heart with its painful arrow;
In your absence, she is sick and wails like that flute, the ney.'*

A description of Süleyman at that time is given by Bragadin in a
letter dated 9 June 1526:

*He is thirty-two years old, deadly pale, with an aquiline nose and
a long neck; of no great apparent strength, but his hand is very
strong, as I observed when I kissed it, and he is said to be able to
bend a stiffer bow than anyone else. He is by nature melancholy,
much addicted to women, liberal, proud, hasty, and yet sometimes
very gentle.*

After his victory at Mohacs Süleyman led his army back to Istanbul, where he remained for six months before setting off on his next campaign into Europe, with Ibrahim Pasha once again in command. The goal of the expedition was Vienna, which Süleyman's forces besieged unsuccessfully. After suffering heavy losses Süleyman was forced to raise the siege on 15 October 1529, so as to march his army back to Istanbul before the winter began.

This was the first reverse suffered by Süleyman, and he tried to save face by pretending that he had invaded Austria only to protect his vassal John Zapolya against the archduke Ferdinand of Habsburg. Süleyman also tried to distract the attention of his subjects from the failure of his campaign, and on 27 June 1530 he celebrated the circumcision of three of his sons – Mustafa, Mehmet and Selim – with a lavish festival in the Hippodrome that lasted for three weeks.

Mustafa, the heir apparent, was then fifteen, and was already showing remarkable promise. Six years earlier Bragadin had remarked of him that 'he has extraordinary talent, is much loved by the Janissaries, and performs great feats.' The *bailo* also noted that Mustafa was the 'whole joy' of his mother Mahidevran, who was still Süleyman's *birinci kadın*, though she had been supplanted as *haseki* by Roxelana. Bragadin reported in 1526 that Süleyman no longer paid attention to Mahidevran, but lavished all of his affection on Roxelana, whom he described as 'young but not beautiful, although graceful and petite'. Never before had a sultan restricted his attention to one woman, and this amazed Süleyman's subjects, who thought that Roxelana had cast a spell over him, which made them hate her and call her a witch.

Then in 1531 Roxelana bore Süleyman another son, Cihangir, but she was disappointed when she saw that the child was a hunchback. Nevertheless Süleyman doted on Cihangir, who became his constant companion.

Süleyman's preference for Roxelana led Mahidevran to attack her rival one day in the harem, scratching her face and pulling out tufts of her hair, an incident reported by the *bailo* Bernardo Navagero. Roxelana retired to her room and refused to come out when the chief black eunuch summoned her to Süleyman's apartment, saying that Mahidevran's assault had left her in no fit condition to be seen by her sultan. When Süleyman learned of this he banished Mahidevran to the Old Saray, leaving Roxelana supreme in the harem.

Another incident is reported by Bragadin. When Süleyman's mother Hafsa presented him with a new concubine for his harem, a 'beautiful Russian maiden', Roxelana 'became extremely unhappy and flung herself to the ground weeping'. Süleyman sent the girl away 'because his wife would have perished from sorrow if these maidens – or even one of them – had remained in the palace.'

Navagero's report indicates that Süleyman married Roxelana around 1533, the first instance in Ottoman history of a slave-concubine being made the legal wife of a sultan. The marriage between Süleyman and Roxelana was all the more remarkable in that he put all of his other women aside for her and had no other wives for the rest of his days. Their wedding took place in Topkapı Sarayı and was followed by a week-long festival in the Hippodrome.

Roxelana had by this time moved from the Old Palace on the Third Hill into the harem of Topkapı Sarayı. Süleyman did extensive building and restoration in Topkapı Sarayı during the early years of his reign, much of it undoubtedly connected with Roxelana's move into the harem.

Early in 1532 Süleyman mounted another expedition against Vienna under Ibrahim Pasha, but his army penetrated only as far as the Austrian frontier. After the Ottoman army returned to Istanbul, Süleyman once again held a celebration to mark what his subjects were told was another successful campaign. As Süleyman wrote in his diary at the time: 'Five days of feasts and illuminations . . . The bazaars remain open all night, and Süleyman goes to visit them incognito.'

Süleyman's mother, the *valide sultan* Hafsa, passed away in March of 1534, so Roxelana now ruled supreme among the women in the harem. She was also the power behind the throne, according to Navagero, who remarked at the time that Roxelana 'has the bridle of the Sultan's will in her hands'.

Süleyman now turned his attention to his eastern frontiers, and in the spring of 1534 he led his army in an invasion of Iran and Iraq, capturing Tabriz and Baghdad. Süleyman spent the winter in Baghdad, constantly exchanging letters with Roxelana, as he always did while on campaign. While in Baghdad he received a letter from Roxelana complaining bitterly about her plight in the harem:

My lord, your absence has kindled in me a fire that does not abate. Take pity on this suffering soul and speed your letter, so that I may find in it at least a little consolation . . . When I read your letters, your son Mehmet and your daughter Mihrimah were by my side, and tears streamed from their eyes. The tears drove me from my mind . . . You ask me why I am angry with Ibrahim Pasha. When – God willing – we are together again, I shall explain, and you will learn the cause.

Ibrahim had by that time reached the peak of his power, and this was undoubtedly the source of Roxelana's unhappiness. Just a year or so before, Ibrahim had boasted to a European envoy of the great authority that he wielded, unsurpassed even by that of Süleyman. The Venetian interpreter Ludovico Gritti, quoting a similar statement by the grand vezir, was led to remark that 'if Süleyman should send one of his cooks to kill Ibrahim Pasha, there would be nothing to prevent the killing.'

Ibrahim apparently fell from favour after the campaign of 1534–5, when Süleyman seems to have suspected him of disloyalty or even of treason. Ibrahim met his end on the night of 14–15 March 1536, when he was invited by Süleyman to have dinner with him in the imperial apartments at Topkapı Sarayı. What happened that evening is a mystery, but the common belief is that Süleyman sent his mutes to strangle Ibrahim while he slept. Ibrahim seems to have put up a struggle, because for long afterwards bloodstains could still be seen on the walls of the room in which he had been sleeping.

After Ibrahim's death Süleyman ordered all of his possessions to be confiscated by the state, including the grand vezir's palace on the Hippodrome. He then appointed Ayas Pasha to be his new grand vezir.

Coffin of Ibrahim Pasha being removed from
Topkapı Sarayı

On the occasion of Roxelana's birthday in 1538, Süleyman surprised her with the gift of a mosque complex that he had built in her name on the Seventh Hill. This was Haseki Hürrem Camii, designed by the architect Sinan. Sinan had been trained in the Palace School and served as a military engineer in four of Süleyman's campaigns, after which he was appointed chief of the imperial architects.

Late in the autumn of 1539 Süleyman and Roxelana marked the circumcision of two of their sons, Beyazit and Cihangir, with a celebration in the Hippodrome that lasted for fifteen days. At the same time they also celebrated the marriage of their daughter Mihrimah to Rüstem Pasha, who at the time was governor of Diyarbakır in southeastern Anatolia. Rüstem came to be known as Kehle-i-Ikbal, the Louse of Fortune, a nickname that he acquired when he married Mihrimah. It seems that Rüstem's enemies had tried to prevent him from marrying the princess by spreading the rumour that he had leprosy. But when the palace doctors examined Rüstem they discovered that he was infested with lice; consequently they declared that he was not leprous, for accepted medical belief had it that lice never inhabit lepers. Thus Rüstem was allowed to marry Mihrimah, whereupon Süleyman appointed him second vezir. Five years later he was appointed grand vezir, beginning the first of his two terms of office under Süleyman, during which time he became the wealthiest and most powerful of the sultan's subjects. Thus it was that Rüstem Pasha came to be called Kehle-i-Ikbal, from the old Turkish proverb that 'When a man has his luck in place even a louse can bring him good fortune.'

An epidemic of smallpox in 1543 took the life of the *şehzade* (prince) Mehmet, eldest son of Süleyman and Roxelana, who was twenty-one when he died. Süleyman was heartbroken at the death of his beloved son, and he sat beside Mehmet's body for three days before he would permit the burial to take place. Süleyman decided to commemorate Mehmet by erecting a huge mosque complex on the Third Hill called Şehzade Camii, the Mosque of the Prince, completed by Sinan in 1548.

Two years later the sultan commissioned Sinan to build a vast mosque complex, to be known as the Süleymaniye. The mosque of the Süleymaniye, whose great dome and clustering semi-domes are framed by four lofty minarets, rose to dominate the skyline of the old city from the ridge of the Third Hill above the Golden Horn. The complex includes the imperial mosque itself as well as four *medreses* and their preparatory school, a school for reading the Kuran, a school of sacred tradition, a primary school, a medical college, a hospital, an insane asylum, a public kitchen, a market street, a public bath and two tombs, one for Süleyman and the other for Roxelana. The Süleymaniye was finally completed in 1557, and on the day of its dedication, according to Evliya Çelebi, the architect Sinan said to Süleyman: 'I have built for thee, O emperor, a mosque

*The Süleymaniye, the mosque complex of Süleyman
the Magnificent*

which will remain on the face of the earth till the day of judgment.'

By this time all four of Süleyman's surviving sons were serving as provincial governors, with Mustafa in Amasya, Selim in Manisa, Beyazit in Konya, and Cihangir in Aleppo. Ogier Ghiselin de Busbecq, ambassador of Charles V, reports that Roxelana had been for some time plotting with her son-in-law Rüstem Pasha to eliminate Mustafa, the heir apparent, so that one of her sons, either Selim or Beyazit, would be first in line to succeed Süleyman, Cihangir being considered ineligible. Mustafa, who was described by the Frenchman Guillaume Postel as 'marvelously well-educated and prudent and of the age to reign', was idolized by the Janissaries and everyone fully expected that he would eventually succeed his father. Navagero wrote in 1553, when Mustafa was thirty-eight, that 'It is impossible to describe how much he is loved and desired by all as successor to the throne.' Busbecq writes that Mustafa 'was then in the prime of his life and enjoyed a high repute as a soldier'.

Süleyman mounted a campaign against the Safavids of Iran in the spring of 1553. While the Ottoman army was still in central Anatolia, the grand vezir Rüstem Pasha convinced Süleyman that Mustafa was conspiring with the Safavids to usurp the Ottoman throne, supported by the Janissaries whom he commanded as provincial governor. Late in October of that year Süleyman summoned Mustafa to his camp at Ereğli in Karaman, where the prince arrived on 6 November. According to Busbecq, when Mustafa came to Süleyman's tent he was strangled by his father's mutes, while the sultan looked on from behind a screen, urging the assassins to get on with their work.

The Janissaries were outraged by Mustafa's execution and were on the point of revolting, but Süleyman appeased them with a large increase in their salary and by dismissing Rüstem Pasha as grand vezir, replacing him with Kara Ahmet Pasha. When the news of Mustafa's death reached Prince Cihangir in Aleppo, he was so overcome with grief that he took sick and died on 27 December of that year. His body was brought back to Istanbul for burial, and Süleyman commissioned Sinan to build a mosque in Cihangir's memory, erecting it on the European shore of the lower Bosphorus in the quarter that still bears his name.

After the execution of Mustafa, Süleyman resumed the campaign. In November 1555 he led his army in pomp into Aleppo, a colourful spectacle witnessed by the English traveller Anthony Jenkinson. After listing the various units that preceded the sultan in the parade, including 12,000 'men of armes . . . 16,000 Janizaries . . . and 1,000 pages of honour . . .', Jenkinson describes the passage of Süleyman and his entourage:

Immediately after them came the Great Turke himselfe, with great pompe & magnificence, using in his countenance and gesture a wonderfull majestie, having onely on each side of his person one page clothed with cloth of gold: he himselfe was mounted upon a goodly white horse, adorned with a robe of cloth of gold, embroidered moste richly with the most pretious stones, and upon his head a goodly white tuck, containing in length by estimation fifteene yards, which was of silke and linen woven together, resembling something Callicut cloth, but is much more fine and rich, and in the toppe of his crowne a little pinnacle of white Ostrich feathers, and his horse most richly apparelled in all points correspondent to the same.

After him followed six goodly young Ladies, mounted upon fine white hackneis, clothed in cloth of silver, which were of the fashion of mens garments, embrodered very richly with pearle, and pretious stones, and upon their heades caps of Goldsmiths worke, having large flackets of heare hanging out on each side, every of them having two eunuches on each side, and little bowes in their hands, after an Antike fashion.

Roxelana passed away on 15 March 1558, after which she was buried in the tomb that had been built for her behind the Süleymaniye mosque. The chroniclers are strangely silent on her death, and there is no testimony recording Süleyman's reaction to the loss of his beloved wife. His enduring love for the woman he called the Joyous One is recorded in a poem that he wrote after the death of Roxelana:

I languish on sorrow's mountain
  where night and day I sigh and moan:
Wondering what fate awaits me
  with my beloved gone.

After Roxelana's death her sons Selim and Beyazit began to make war on one another, each trying to eliminate the other so as to establish himself as the sole heir to Süleyman's throne. Beyazit's rebellious behaviour had by then alienated Süleyman, who sent Selim an army of Janissaries and Sipahis, or cavalry knights, under the command of Sokollu Mehmet Pasha. Selim defeated his brother in a battle near Konya in May 1559, after which Beyazit was forced to flee to the court of Shah Tahmasp in Persia. After lengthy negotiations Süleyman persuaded Tahmasp to execute Beyazit and four of his sons who had accompanied him into exile. Beyazit had a fifth son, a three-year-old who had remained behind in Bursa with his mother, and so Süleyman sent orders for him to be executed too. Marcantonio Donini, secretary to the Venetian *bailo*, reports on Süleyman's reaction to the news that the executions had been carried out:

On hearing of their death, it is said, he looked up to heaven with joined hands and spoke after this fashion, 'God be praised that I have lived to see the Moslems freed from the miseries which would have come upon them if my sons had fought for the throne; I may now pass the rest of my days in tranquility, instead of living and dying in despair.

Busbecq writes of how Süleyman had now become increasingly religious and superstitious, apparently concerned about the fate that awaited him beyond the grave:

The Sultan is becoming day by day more scrupulous in his religious observance, in a word, more superstitious. He used to enjoy listening to a choir of boys who sang and played to him; but this has been brought to an end by the intervention of some sibyl (that is to say, some old woman famous for her profession of sanctity), who declares that penalties awaited him in a future life, if he did not give up this entertainment. He was thus induced to break up and commit to flames all the musical instruments, even though they were orna- mented with fine work in gold and studded with precious stones. He used to eat off a service of silver plate, but some one found such fault with him for this that he now only uses earthenware.

Süleyman's appearance and state of health at the time are thus described by Donini:

His Majesty during many months of the year was very feeble of body, so that he lacked little of dying, being dropsical, with swollen legs, appetite gone, and face swelled and of a very bad colour. In

Süleyman praying at the shrine of Eyüp

the month of March last, he had four or five fainting fits, and he has had one since, in which his attendants doubted whether he was alive or dead, and hardly expected that he would recover from them. According to the common opinion his death must occur soon, in spite of the strong remedies resorted to by his physician . . .

Despite the sultan's failing health he was still very much in command, and all of Christian Europe lived in fear of the man they had come to call Süleyman the Magnificent. (Süleyman is known to the Turks as Kanuni, or the Lawgiver, because he was the first ruler of the Ottoman Empire to codify civil law and to reconcile it with religious law.) Busbecq remarks on the awesome power of Süleyman at the end of his last letter from Turkey, in the autumn of 1562:

Soleiman stands before us with all the terror inspired by his own successes and those of his ancestors; he overruns the plain of Hungary with 200,000 horsemen; he threatens Austria; he menaces the rest of Germany; he brings in his train all the nations that dwell between here and the Persian frontier. He is at the head of an army equipped with the resources of many kingdoms; of the three continents into which our hemisphere is divided, each contributes its share to achieve our destruction. Like a thunderbolt he smites, shatters, and destroys whatever stands in his way; he is at the head of veteran troops and a highly trained army, which is accustomed to his leadership; he spreads far and wide the terror of his name. He roars like a lion along our frontier, seeking to break through, now here, now there . . .

Süleyman launched a major expedition in 1565 against the fortress of the Knights of St John on Malta, but the campaign was a catastrophic failure. Süleyman attributed the Ottoman defeat to the fact that he himself had not been in command at Malta, leading him to remark that 'Only with me do my armies triumph!'

Ali Pasha, who had been grand vezir since the death of Rüstem Pasha in July 1561, died later in 1565. He was succeeded as grand vezir by Sokollu Mehmet Pasha, who immediately began preparations for a new campaign into Hungary. Süleyman had not led his army in the field for more than a decade, and he was determined to erase the memory of the failure at Malta by one more triumph of Ottoman arms under his own leadership. He could no longer ride a horse, and when the army prepared to leave Istanbul on 1 May 1566 Süleyman had to be helped into his carriage.

The principal objective of the campaign was to capture Sziged in southern Hungary, held by Count Nicholas Zrinyi. The Ottoman army reached Sziged on 5 August and put it under siege, forcing Zrinyi to retreat to the citadel. The fortress finally fell on 7 September 1566, after Zrinyi led out his surviving troops in a desperate sortie

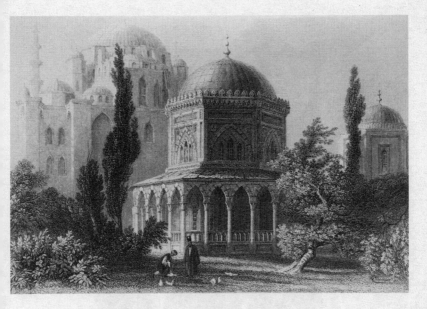

Tombs of Süleyman the Magnificent (left) *and Roxelana* (right) *at the Süleymaniye*

against the Turks, who captured him and then blew off his head with a cannon-ball.

Süleyman did not live to see the capture of Sziged, for he died in his tent of a heart attack on the night of 5–6 September. The only ones present at the time were Süleyman's physician and Sokollu Mehmet Pasha, who told no one of Süleyman's death. After Süleyman's corpse was embalmed Sokollu did away with the doctor for fear that he would reveal the secret. He then sent a courier with the news to Selim at Kütahya in Anatolia, where the prince had been serving as provincial governor, advising him to meet the army on its homeward march so that he could take control as soon as possible. Meanwhile Sokollu shared the news only with his trusted secretary, Feridun Bey, and the sultan's sword-bearer, Cafer Ağa. All others were barred from the royal tent, while operations continued through

Burial of Süleyman at the Süleymaniye

written orders forged in Süleyman's hand by Cafer Ağa. Orders were given for the army to begin its homeward march to Istanbul via Belgrade. Süleyman's corpse was transported in a carriage, with Sokollu Mehmet Pasha riding directly behind, a scene depicted in the illustrated manuscript of the Sziged campaign written by Feridun Bey. At each stopping-place Süleyman was carried in a litter to his tent and enthroned there, after which Sokollu made a show of calling on the sultan as if he were making his daily report and receiving orders.

Selim finally met up with the army near Belgrade, and only then did the soldiers learn of Süleyman's death. When the army reached

Istanbul the Janissaries mutinied, demanding higher pay and other privileges, to which Selim acceded. The following day, after returning to Topkapı Sarayı, Selim buried his father at the Süleymaniye.

Süleyman was laid to rest in the beautiful *türbe* that Sinan had built for him behind the mosque, next to the tomb of his wife Roxelana, Selim's mother. A couplet from one of Süleyman's love poems to Roxelana comes to mind in the presence of their tombs, which stand side by side in the shade of spectral cypresses, the Trees of Paradise:

All of a sudden, my glance fell upon her:
  Like a cypress she was standing slender . . .

Chapter 5

THE SULTANATE OF WOMEN

Selim II was forty-two years old when he succeeded his father Süleyman to the throne. He was the eleventh sultan in the House of Osman and the fifth of his line to rule in Istanbul.

When Selim began his term as governor in Manisa in 1543, at the age of nineteen, he set up his harem there, living with his favourite Nurbanu, who became his first wife. Nurbanu was born Cecelia Venier-Baffo, the illegitimate daughter of two noble Graeco-Venetian families. She was captured by the Turks on the Aegean

Selim II, the Sot (1566–74)

*The harem of Topkapı Sarayı with the outer gardens and
pavilions, including the Shore Pavilion, 1581–2*

island of Paros in 1537, when she was twelve years old. She was
then brought to Istanbul and became a slave in Topkapı Sarayı,
being given the name Nurbanu when she was chosen for the harem
of Prince Selim. Nurbanu bore Selim four children in a little over
three years. The first three were girls – Hace Geveri, Esmahan and
Şah Sultan – followed by Selim's first son, the future Murat III,
born in Manisa on 4 July 1546.

Selim was called the Sot (*sarhoş*), the name by which he is still
known today. According to Knolles: 'He was but of a mean stature,
and of an heavie disposition; his face rather swolne than fat, much
resembling a drunkard.'

Selim reappointed Sokollu Mehmet Pasha as grand vezir, giving
him full charge of the government. The sultan believed that he was
meant to enjoy his pleasures in the harem undisturbed by any concern
for affairs of state, as noted by the *bailo* Lorenzo Bernardo:

Sultan Selim . . . initiated the following opinion: That the true felicity of a king or emperor did not consist in military toils and in operations of bravery or glory, but in idleness and tranquility of the senses, in the enjoyment of all comforts and pleasures in palaces filled with women and buffoons, and in the fulfillment of all desires for jewels, palaces, loggias, and stately constructions.

Philippe du Fresne-Canaye, a member of the French embassy in 1573, noted that during the three months that he was in Istanbul the sultan left the palace only twice to attend the Friday noon-prayer. Except for occasional excursions to Edirne Sarayı, Selim lived in Topkapı Sarayı throughout the year, spending most of his time in the harem. The *bailo* Costantino Garzoni reports that Selim used to enter 'this seraglio of women each night for his pleasure, from a gate in his gardens'. According to Garzoni, about one hundred and fifty women lived in the harem there, including servants, as well as the sultan's wives and concubines and their ladies-in-waiting.

The women of the harem were organized into two distinct classes. The lower class was that of the *cariyeler*, or servants, who were assigned most of the routine housework of the harem. These women were classified according to their skill and seniority as *çırak* (apprentice), *kalfa* (qualified worker) or *usta* (superintendent). The slave girls worked their way up through the ranks and often retired with comfortable incomes. These women rarely came into intimate personal contact with the sultan, although there was always the chance that they might catch his eye and share his bed.

The highest class of women in the harem was that of the *gedikiler*, or privileged ones. The *gedikiler* were chosen for their beauty and talent, usually as musicians, singers and dancers. These girls were first apprenticed to one of the older women of the harem, the *kaya kadın*, who instructed and dressed them in preparation for their introduction to the sultan. If the sultan noticed one of them and chose her as a possible concubine she was designated as *gözde*, which means, literally, 'in the eye'. Thereupon the girl was set up in an apartment of her own and was prepared for her appointment with the sultan by the Keeper of the Bath, the Mistress of the Robes and the Keeper of the Treasury. If, after her first night with the sultan, she remained in his favour, she became an *ikbal*, or royal concubine, known in the West as an odalisque, from the Turkish 'oda', or 'room', in this case referring to the sultan's bedroom. If the sultan's favourite, the *haseki*, bore him a child, and if this was the sultan's eldest living son, she became the *birinci kadın*. If her son succeeded his father to the throne then she became the *valide sultan*, the titular head of the harem.

A detailed account of life in the harem of Topkapı Sarayı is given by Ottaviano Bon, Venetian *bailo* in the years 1605–7. Bon tells of how the young non-Muslim women taken into the sultan's harem were converted to Islam, after which 'they go to school, to learn to speak and read, if they will, the Turkish tongue, to sew also, and to play upon divers instruments.' He notes that several hours every day were 'allowed them for their recreation, to walk in their gardens, and use such sports as they familiarly exercise themselves withall'.

Selim's harem was headed by Nurbanu, who, as mother of his eldest son and heir Murat, held the title of first wife. She was Selim's *haseki*, his favourite, and he loved her dearly, as the *bailo* Jacopo Soranzo wrote in 1566: 'The Chassechi . . . is said to be extremely well loved and honoured by His Majesty both for her beauty and for being unusually intelligent.' Nurbanu bore Selim no more children after their daughter Fatma was born in 1559. Selim added several additional concubines to his harem after he became sultan, and they bore him eight more children, including six sons. Nevertheless, Nurbanu was still his favourite, as the *bailo* Andrea Badoara remarked of her in 1573: 'She is called the Chassechi and is much loved by His Majesty.'

The Old Palace on the Third Hill, Eski Saray, was known as the 'Palace of Tears', since it housed the women from the harems of departed sultans, as well as their children. Those women who had been the wives or concubines of a sultan usually remained in the Old Palace for the rest of their days, though others who had not been odalisques were sometimes married off to Ottoman officials.

Mute assigned to the Inner Palace

According to Bon, the sultan maintained an apartment there, which he used when he came to visit the women of his family who had been relegated to the Old Saray.

The women of the sultan's harem were very closely supervised, Bon notes, describing how they were punished if they broke the rules:

The women of the Seraglio are punished for their faults very severely, and extreamly beaten by their overseers; and if they prove disobedient, incorrigible, and insolent, they are by the king's order, and express command, turned out and sent into the old Seraglio, as being utterly rejected and cast off, and the best part of what they have is taken from them: but if they shall be culpable of witchcraft, or any such like abominations; they are bound hand and foot, and put into a sack, and in the night cast into the sea.

Bon concludes his chapter on the women of the harem with a section entitled 'Prevention of Lust':

Now it is not lawful for any to bring aught into them, with which they may commit the deeds of beastly and unnatural uncleanness, so that if they have a will to eat radishes, cucumbers, gourds, or such like; they are sent in unto them sliced, to deprive them of the means of playing the wantons: for they are all young, lusty and lascivious wenches, and wanting the society of men . . .

The women in the harem of Selim II were guarded by eighteen black eunuchs. From the time of Murat III the chief black eunuch, the *kizlar ağası*, became the most powerful official in the Inner Service. All of the eunuchs under his charge lived in a three-storey barracks just inside the Carriage Gate, the main entrance to the harem from the Second Court. The chief black eunuch had a private apartment just inside Kuşhane Kapısı, the Aviary Gate, the entrance to the harem from the Third Court. The young princes were tutored here by him before going off to the Palace School when they reached the age of puberty.

The eunuchs were taken into the palace as youths, having been castrated after they were bought in slave markets, the blacks generally coming from Nubia and the whites from Circassia. Bon notes that both black and white eunuchs were educated in the Palace School along with the other students. He also remarks on the names given to the black eunuchs: 'They are named by the names of flowers, as Hyacinth, Narcissus, Rose, Gillyflower, and the like. For that, serving the women, and being always near about them, their names may be answerable to their virginity, sweet and undefiled.'

There are occasional references to a very few of the black eunuchs retaining some sexual potency after their emasculation. A story to this effect is told about the black eunuchs by the eighteenth-century Turkish chronicler Ali Seydi Bey, who claimed that he heard it from one of his companions-in-arms in a unit of the palace guards:

I am a witness to the fact that these black infidels are so traitorous that they may fall in love with one of the odalisques and spend all that they earn on them. At every opportunity they meet secretly and make love. You might ask, do the odalisques who establish relations with these black eunuchs find pleasure in them? It is notorious in Istanbul that the odalisques find such pleasure. Two halberdiers of our unit who married odalisques from the imperial palace divorced them within the week when the odalisques told their husbands: 'We do not enjoy relations with you as we did with the black eunuchs.'

The sultan also employed a staff of 'inferior persons, as Buffons, Mutes and Musicians', as Bon describes them:

There are also Buffons, and such as shew tricks, musicians, wrestlers, and many Mutes both old and young, who have liberty to go in and out of the King's gate, with leave only of the Capee Agha. It is worth the observation that in the Seraglio both the Grand Seignor, and divers that are about him, can reason and discourse with the Mutes of any thing, as well and as distinctly . . . by nods and signs, as they can with words; a thing well befitting and suiting the gravity of the better sort of Turks, who cannot endure much babbling. Nay, the Sultanas also, and many others of the King's women do practise it, and have many dumb women and girls about them for that purpose.

Bon goes on to say that the sultan sometimes used these mutes to dispose of any of his vezirs who fell from favour with him, in which case 'he makes but a sign unto them, and they presently fall upon him, and strangle him, and so draw him by the heels out of the gate.'

The reign of Selim II began a period in Ottoman history known as Kadınlar Sultanatı, the Sultanate of Women, in which a series of powerful and determined women in the harem exercised considerable influence over affairs of state. Nurbanu was the first of these strong-willed women to dominate the harem, acting as the power behind the throne throughout Selim's reign and during the early years of her son Murat's rule. She carried on a correspondence with

The valide sultan, or queen mother

Catherine de' Medici, the queen mother and regent for King Henry III of France, promoting good relations between the French and Ottoman courts.

Sokollu Mehmet Pasha's principal rival in the court was Joseph Nasi, originally known as Joao Miquez, a wealthy Portuguese Jew who had first come to Istanbul during the latter years of Süleyman's reign. Nasi soon became a bosom friend to Selim, who was then serving as provincial governor in Kütahya, presenting him with a wealth of gold and jewels. As soon as Selim succeeded to the throne he made Nasi Duke of Naxos, one of the Aegean isles that the Turks had taken from Venice. Nasi never went to Naxos to claim his duchy, for he had far more important matters to deal with in Istanbul, where his intimacy with Selim gained him a monopoly on the wine trade of the empire. Nasi always presented Selim with his finest wines, as noted by an unidentified Venetian *bailo*: 'His Highness drinks much wine and . . . Don Joseph sends him many bottles of it from time to time, together with all manner of other delicacies.'

Even before Selim became sultan Nasi had persuaded him that the Ottomans should take Cyprus from the Venetians, for the riches of the island included its famous wines. Selim promised Nasi that if he did conquer the island he would make him King of Cyprus.

Early in the spring of 1571 Selim ordered his forces to attack Cyprus, although Sokollu Mehmet Pasha was totally opposed to the idea. The expedition was a success, and the last Venetian fortress on the island surrendered on 1 August 1571, beginning an Ottoman occupation that was to last for more than three centuries. But Nasi's hope of becoming King of Cyprus never materialized, for Sokollu eventually won Selim over to his side and persuaded him to abandon his Jewish favourite, who died a disappointed man in 1579.

Selim in his last years spent much of his time with his former wet-nurse, or *daye hatun*, the mother of Şemsi Ahmet Pasha. As the *bailo* Garzoni wrote in 1573: 'The sultan spends the greater part of his time playing chess with the mother of Ahmet Pasha, an elderly woman who was formerly his nurse.'

The imperial wet-nurse, also known as *süt anne*, or milk-mother, often held a revered place in the harem. Fatih's nurse, known only as Daye Hatun, became very wealthy after he came to the throne and endowed several mosques. She outlived Mehmet by nearly five years, dying in Istanbul on 14 February 1486.

Selim took great pleasure in planting flowers in the palace gardens. As he wrote in 1574 to an Ottoman official in Aleppo: 'I need about 50,000 tulips for my royal gardens. To bring these bulbs I send you one of the chiefs of my servants. I command you in no way to delay.'

Selim was a poet of some merit, and a number of his *gazels* have survived. Most of them celebrate the pleasures of love and wine, as in the closing lines of his best *gazel*:

O dear one, give Selim thy wine-hued liplet,
Then by thine absence turn my tears to wine, love.
Make my tears red, like wine, and turn them to tears of blood.

Selim died in the harem of Topkapı Sarayı on 15 December 1574, having fallen in his bath while drunk. He was in his fifty-first year and had reigned for eight years and three months. Evliya Çelebi, in noting the passing of Selim the Sot, writes that 'He was a sweet-natured sovereign, but much given to pleasure and wine.'

Nurbanu, aided by Sokollu Mehmet Pasha, kept Selim's corpse in an icebox to conceal his death until her son Murat could be summoned from Manisa, where he had been serving as provincial governor. Murat finally arrived in Istanbul twelve days after Selim's death. He went first to the throne room in the third court of the palace, where he was proclaimed as sultan by Sokollu, whom he immediately reappointed as grand vezir.

That night Murat had his five surviving younger brothers strangled to eliminate them as rivals to the throne, justifying his murders by the Ottoman code of fratricide. The following day he buried his father Selim in the garden beside Haghia Sophia, commissioning the architect Sinan to build a splendid tomb over the grave. Selim's huge catafalque now lies under the dome of his tomb, surrounded by the smaller coffins of his five murdered sons, the princes Abdullah, Cihangir, Mustafa, Osman and Süleyman. Süleyman was only an infant when he was executed, torn from the breast of his mother, who committed suicide when he was strangled by the chief executioner.

Murat was midway through his twenty-ninth year when he became sultan, having served as provincial governor at Akşehir for three years and then at Manisa for thirteen years.

During the first years of his reign Murat commissioned the architect Sinan to build a number of structures in Topkapı Sarayı, including the palace kitchens, which had been badly damaged by a fire in 1574. Among the new chambers created by Sinan were two of the most splendid in Topkapı Sarayı, the Imperial Hall, which served as the throne room in the Inner Palace, and the Salon of

Murat III, where the sultan took his ease with his favourite concubines and pages.

Murat also built new baths in the harem, which in his reign
increased greatly in population. The *hamam* was the centre of the
harem's social life, and the rituals of bathing there would have been
the same as they were in women's public baths in Istanbul. These
baths are described by Luigi Bassano da Zara, an Italian who served
as a page in Topkapı Sarayı in the mid sixteenth century:

*Most of the women go to the baths in parties of twenty at a time
and wash each other in a friendly manner – one neighbour with
another, and sister with sister. But it is common knowledge that as
a result of this familiarity in washing and massaging women fall
very much in love with each other. And often one sees a woman in
love with another one just like a man and woman. And I have
known Greek and Turkish women seeing a lovely young girl, seek
occasion to wash with her just to see her naked and handle her . . .*

Murat left all affairs of state in the capable hands of Sokollu
Mehmet Pasha, who was now serving as grand vezir under his third
sultan. Sokollu Mehmet Pasha finally met his end on 12 December
1579 at a meeting of the imperial council, when he was assassinated
by a Sipahi whom he had dismissed from his holding. After his
death Murat changed grand vezirs ten times in sixteen years. The
frequent shifts in government were part of the general instability in
the Ottoman government that followed the passing of Sokollu
Mehmet Pasha, evidence of a decline in the empire that he had held
in check while he was in office. As the *bailo* Maffeo Venier remarked
in his report to the doge: 'With Sokollu Mehmet, Turkish virtue
sank into the grave.'

When Murat came to the throne he had only one wife, an Albanian
woman named Safiye whom he had married in 1563. She was the
mother of his first son, the future Mehmet III, born on 26 May
1566, and of his first daughter, Ayşe. Safiye was considered a rival
by Murat's mother Nurbanu, the *valide sultan*, who until then had
been the supreme power in the harem. Nurbanu, aided by her

Murat III (1574–95)

daughters, sought to diminish Safiye's influence over Murat by encouraging him to take other women into his harem, but to no avail, as noted by the *bailo* Gianfrancesco Morosini: 'Although surrounded by lovely women presented to him as gifts by various people, he ignored his mother and sisters when they urged him to consort with other women ... He loved her [Safiye] so much that they could not change his mind.'

During the summer of 1582 Murat celebrated the circumcision of his eldest son, Prince Mehmet, with a festival in the Hippodrome that lasted for fifty-two days. The actual circumcision was performed privately in the harem on the thirty-seventh day of the festival. With his father looking on, Mehmet was circumcised by Cerrah ('the Surgeon') Mehmet Pasha, who then presented to the *valide sultan* Nurbanu the knife with which the operation was performed, while the prince's mother, the *haseki* Safiye, received the foreskin on a golden plate.

Nurbanu continued to rule in the harem as *valide sultan* until her death in December 1583. Paolo Contarini, in a report to the doge written shortly before her death, wrote that Nurbanu was the person in the Ottoman court on whom Murat relied most for guidance: 'He bases his policies principally on the advice of his mother, it appearing to him that he could have no other advice as loving and loyal as hers, hence the reverence which he shows toward her and the esteem that he bears for her unusual qualities and many virtues.' Just before she died Nurbanu gave her son some final words of advice, which were, according to Gianfranceso Morosini, 'the most judicious and present caution as regards this government that could have come from a good, intelligent, and consummate statesman'. Her advice to Murat concerned three matters: that he should render swift and impartial justice to his subjects, restrain his natural greed for gold and above all keep a close watch on his son Mehmet. When Nurbanu died Morosini noted her passing in a dispatch to Venice, concluding with the statement that 'All universally admit that she was a woman of the utmost goodness, courage, and wisdom.'

Murat was devastated by his mother's death, and he honoured her with a funeral of unprecedented pomp and ceremony. After the funeral Murat ordered Sinan to build a mosque complex in honour of Nurbanu. Known as Atik Valide Camii, the mosque was erected atop the highest hill in Üsküdar, a monument rivalling the Süley-maniye in its splendour.

Morosini, in a report written in 1585, describes Murat's appear-ance at that time and tells how the sultan occupied himself in the palace:

The sultan is very small but well formed – perhaps a bit fat. He has large, pale eyes, an aquiline nose, good skin color, and a big blond beard. He looks good when seated on horseback, wearing his turban, because then his smallness is not so obvious, but when he is seen standing on his own feet he looks almost dwarfish. His facial expression does not suggest an evil character. His health is rather delicate, and his life is not likely to be long . . . He is almost always secluded in his seraglios in the company of eunuchs, pages, dwarfs, mutes, and slave girls . . . There is no worthwhile person for him to talk to, since except for a few of the women everyone in the seraglios is less than thirty years old and belongs to one of the types I mentioned . . . If it is a council day he gives an audience to the aga of the janissaries, the cadi-askers, and finally the pashas . . . When the vezirs after another short time depart, most of the time he returns to the women, whose conversation delights him extremely, and when he remains outdoors, he returns to some parts of his gardens to practice archery and to play with his mutes and buffoons. He frequently has noisy instruments played, and enjoys artificial fireworks very much . . . He also frequently has comedies acted . . . Then he always re-enters the harem for dinner with the approach of night, both in the summer and winter.

Morosini goes on to tell of how Murat, after two decades during which his only wife was Safiye, came to enlarge his harem considerably. It seems that he succumbed to the charms of a slave girl presented to him by his sister Hüma, and this led him to take other women into his harem. Safiye tried to prevent this by using 'charms and spells to keep him tied to her with love and make him impotent with other women'. When Murat learned of this he lost all respect for Safiye and became even more promiscuous, as Morosini writes:

He tried out many other beautiful young girls, whom everyone brought to him, and in this way began the life he now leads. This is very different from his old ways; he is now not satisfied with one or two but has relations with more than twenty. Every night he sleeps with two, and often with three. Since their religious laws require a man who has been with one woman to wash before going to another, he often bathes two or three times a night. This is a real danger to his life because his health is weak, and he suffers from epilepsy; he could easily drop dead without warning.

The sultan presiding at a reception at the Shore Pavilion

Harem archives credit Murat with twenty-four sons and thirty-two daughters, a record for the Osmanlı dynasty. The record is all the more impressive in that fifty-four of these children were born in the last twelve years of Murat's life, when he seems to have done little other than serve as the royal stud.

Safiye retained her position as *birinci kadın*, acting as the power behind her husband's throne. The *bailo* Giovanni Moro wrote of her in 1590 that 'with the authority she enjoys as mother of the prince, she intervenes on occasion in affairs of state, although she is much respected in this and is listened to by His Majesty, who considers her sensible and wise.' Safiye continued the pro-Venetian policy of Nurbanu, though she expected to be rewarded for her efforts. The *bailo* Lorenzo Bernardo remarked of Safiye in a report in 1592 that 'I always consider it wise to retain her good will by presenting her on occasion with some pretty thing that might invite her gratitude.'

Like Nurbanu, Safiye maintained an extensive foreign correspondence, most notably with Queen Elizabeth of England. This had grown out of diplomatic exchanges concerning the establishment by English merchant-adventurers of the Levant Company, who in 1580 were given a seven-year charter by Murat III, enabling them to set up trading stations in Istanbul and Izmir.

Murat seldom emerged from Topkapı Sarayı during the latter years of his reign. Lorenzo Bernardo, who had quoted the remark of Selim II that the palace was where a king should spend his time and not the battlefield, observed that Murat III had outdone his father in this respect. 'In these thoughts of Sultan Selim the present Sultan, Murat, his son, has followed, but much more so, since the former used to go out of his palace at times to hunt, as far as Edirne, but the present Grand Seignior . . . almost never goes out.' Bernardo goes on to describe the hunts that Murat staged in the gardens of Topkapı Sarayı:

He holds hunts in his garden, having first stocked it not only with deer and goats but also wild boar, bears and lions, and standing at a window he watches his novices hunt. He also has birds of every kind brought there, and riding a horse in his garden he watches them fly; and in short all the pleasures of the hunt that other princes have in the countryside, he has within his seraglio and enjoys them at his convenience.

During the latter part of his reign Murat did not leave Topkapı Sarayı to attend Friday services for two years, according to Venetian diplomatic reports. Giovanni Moro remarked in 1590 that Murat went to the Friday prayer only because the grand vezir advised him 'to comfort with his appearance the ignorant masses, who, while they are displeased with him, nevertheless flock in great numbers to see him'.

Musical performances and other entertainments were held in the Imperial Hall, the magnificent chamber that had been built for Murat by the architect Sinan. The women of the harem also gathered here on holidays to offer their greetings to the sultan. The ceremony is described by Domenico Hierosolimitano, a Jewish doctor who served in the court of Murat III:

Then the Grand Signor gets up and goes to give holiday greetings to the female sultanas, who are all gathered in a large room waiting for him, and on his arrival they all stand up and make him a humble bow; saluting him with a cheerful expression, they wish him happy holidays, and he without answering looks at them with a smile and turns to a eunuch who carries as many jewels, all similarly made, as there are women, and equally to each of them he gives one with his own hands, together with a bag of gold coins, so that they have money to give to their slaves.

Although secluded in the Inner Palace, the women of Murat's harem could take the air in the extensive gardens that stretched down to the shores of the Golden Horn, the Bosphorus and the Sea of Marmara. The English diplomat John Sanderson writes of a dramatic incident that took place one day when Nurbanu and Safiye were walking in the gardens with other ladies of the harem. They saw a number of boats on the Bosphorus filled with wailing women, and when Nurbanu made inquiry she was told that they were prostitutes who were about to be drowned by the chief black eunuch. Thereupon Nurbanu sent orders for the eunuch to desist, threatening that otherwise she would tell Murat and have him executed.

The grand vezir Koca Sinan Pasha built a pavilion for Murat called Incili Köşk, the Kiosk of the Pearl, set above the sea-walls on the Marmara shore. During the last five years of Murat's life it was his habit to visit Incili Köşk several times a week to watch the passing ships, which always saluted him as they sailed by.

During the autumn of 1594 Murat became increasingly ill with the kidney ailment that had long troubled him, compounded with epilepsy, and early in 1595 he felt that his death was near. As Murat's end approached he asked to be taken to Incili Köşk, so that he could look out upon the passing ships for the last time. He summoned the palace musicians to perform for him, and while they played a melancholy Persian song he mouthed the words, 'Come and keep watch with me tonight, O Death.' Two galleys of the Ottoman fleet passed the kiosk, and knowing that the sultan was therein, fired a salute, whose blast shattered the windows of the pavilion, scattering shards of glass around the room and reducing Murat to tears. 'Once the salvoes of my entire fleet would not have broken those windows, but now . . .', he moaned, heaving a deep sigh. 'Such is the kiosk of my life.' His attendants then carried him back to his apartment in the Inner Palace, where he died three days later, on 16 January 1595, in his forty-ninth year.

News of Murat's death was kept secret by his widow Safiye, who wanted to give her son Mehmet time to return to the capital from Manisa. Safiye confided only in the grand vezir Ferhat Pasha, who proposed sending another vezir to fetch Mehmet. According to the *bailo* Marco Venier, Safiye and the other royal widows disagreed, for 'the Sultanas declared that this sudden departure would awaken suspicion. Accordingly they resolved to send the chief gardener, in the middle-sized caique, as he was accustomed to go every day to fetch water for the Sultan's use.'

During the time that it took for Mehmet to be informed and brought back to Istanbul, news of Murat's death leaked out, causing great concern among the populace, who feared that the Janissaries and other unruly elements would take advantage of the situation to sack the city, as they had several times in the past. Marco Venier reports on the situation eleven days after Murat's death:

The rumor of the Sultan's death has spread down to the very children; and a riot is expected, accompanied by a sack of shops and houses as usual . . . In the eleven days which have elapsed since the death of Sultan Murad, several executions have taken place in order to keep the populace in check. Inside the seraglio there has been a great uproar, and every night we hear guns fired – a sign that at that moment some one is being thrown into the sea.

Mehmet reached Istanbul on 28 January and proceeded straight to Topkapı Sarayı. According to Rabbi Salomone, author of a report prepared for the English ambassador, Mehmet went directly to the harem to call on his mother Safiye, whom he had not seen in the twelve years since he had left Istanbul. She took him to see the body of his dead father, which presumably had been preserved in the same icebox in which the corpse of Selim II had been kept twenty-one years before. He then went to the Throne Room, where Ferhat Pasha and all of the other vezirs and notables filed in to offer their obeisance and kiss his hand, after which he was raised to the throne as Mehmet III.

The following day Murat was buried next to the tomb of his father Selim in the garden of Haghia Sophia, where Mehmet directed that a splendid *türbe* be erected by the architect Davut Ağa. Salomone notes that 'His tomb will be made and adorned with the richest marbles like that of the other kings.' He then tells of how Mehmet dealt with the other surviving sons of Murat III, his half-brothers:

That night his nineteen young brothers were conducted to the king Sultan Mehmet. They were the male children then living of his father by several wives; they were brought to kiss his hand, so that he should see them alive, the oldest of them was eleven. Their king brother told them not to fear, as he did not wish to do them any harm; but only to have them circumcised, according to custom. And this was a thing that none of his ancestors had ever done, and directly they had taken his hand they were circumcised, taken aside, and dexterously strangled with handkerchiefs. This seemed a terrible and cruel thing, but it is the custom and people are used to it.

Shakespeare mentions this fratricide in 2 *Henry IV*, act V, scene 2, referring to Murat III as Amurath, where he has the newly crowned Henry V greet his younger brothers thus:

Brothers, you mix your sadness with some fear:
This is the English, not the Turkish court;
Not Amurath an Amurath succeeds,
But Harry Harry.

Salomone goes on to describe the funeral of the nineteen princes, who were buried in the garden of Haghia Sophia around their father:

On Saturday these innocent princes were washed and got ready according to custom, one after another according to age, and were laid in cypress coffins, and placed in the piazza of the Divan and shewn to the king dead. For it is the custom that he should first see them alive and then dead and with the blood of his brothers establish the foundations of his kingdom. From that place, accompanied by the like mourning of the day before and twice the number of people, the remains of the poor princes were carried . . . They were buried according to age, around the tomb of their father amidst the tears of all the people.

Salomone notes that Murat left a number of his wives pregnant when he passed away, and that 'two male children have been born since his death and were quickly drowned.' Knolles, after describing Mehmet's slaughter of his brothers, tells of how he then did away with all of his late father's concubines who might possibly be with child: '. . . and at once to rid himselfe of the feare of all competitors (the greatest torment of the mightie) he the same day (as is reported) caused ten of his fathers wives and concubines, such as by whom any issue was to be feared, to bee all drowned in the sea.'

After the funeral of his brothers, Mehmet moved into the imperial apartment of Topkapı Sarayı, where his mother Safiye now took her place in the harem as *valide sultan*. The surviving wives and concubines of Murat III were then sent off to Eski Saray, the Old Palace, along with their twenty-seven daughters, their nursemaids and other servants and eunuchs, including the departed sultan's dwarfs and mutes, a pathetic scene described by Salomone:

Directly after these poor princes, who people said possessed great beauty, had been buried, the populace waited at the gate to witness the departure from the Seraglio of their mothers and all the other wives of the king [Murat III], with their children and their goods. All the carriages, coaches, mules, and horses of the court were employed for this purpose. Besides the wives of the king and the 27 daughters, there were 200 others, consisting of nurses and slaves, and they were taken to the Eschi Seraglio, where the wives and daughters of the [departed] king reside, with their Aghas, that is eunuchs, who guard and serve them in royal fashion. There they can weep as much as they like for their dead sons, a thing that was forbidden at the other Grand Seraglio, under penalty of capital punishment . . . All the nurses and tutors of his dead brothers were also sent away together with a large number of eunuchs and a great crowd of mutes and dwarfs who were there for the diversion of the Sultan's father. It is said that they were sent off from the Seraglio, because the king has not much liking for such folk.

Fynes Moryson, who arrived in Istanbul two years after the accession of Mehmet III, noted that the wives and concubines and daughters of the late Murat III were still living in Eski Saray, the 'Palace of Tears'. He was told that the most beautiful women of the imperial household were in the harem of Topkapı Sarayı with Mehmet III, 'for the fairest and dearest to him were taken to live in his court.'

Chapter 6

AN ORGAN FOR THE SULTAN

Mehmet III was twenty-nine when he succeeded to the throne, prior to which he had served for twelve years as provincial governor in Manisa, his birthplace. He was the last sultan to have served as governor, for after his time the princes remained in Topkapı Sarayı.

When Mehmet was appointed provincial governor in 1583, he left Istanbul for Manisa with an entourage numbering some two thousand. He set up his harem in the royal palace in Manisa, where in the next twelve years his concubines gave birth to four sons: Mahmut, Selim, Ahmet and Mustafa. After he became sultan Mehmet fathered two more sons, Süleyman and Cihangir, both of whom died young. Mehmet also fathered seven daughters, the first being Sevgilim, the only one whose name is known.

Immediately after Mehmet's accession the Janissaries mutinied and demanded higher pay and other privileges. Mehmet gave in to these demands, but then another and more general mutiny broke out among the townspeople in Istanbul, which was put down only after the vezir Ferhat Pasha cleared the streets by bringing out his artillery and blowing away the mutineers.

The year after his accession Mehmet decided that he would personally lead his army in a campaign against the Habsburgs. Mehmet had been led to take the field by his tutor, Sadeddin Hoca, who persuaded him, with difficulty, of 'the necessity of conquests for sultans and the virtues of holy war', particularly since the

Ottoman army had suffered a series of defeats at the hands of the Christians.

The *valide sultan* Safiye was vehemently opposed to having her son go off to war, and she persuaded Mehmet's favourite concubine to beg him to change his mind. But this cost the girl her life, as Marco Venier noted in a report dated 6 June 1596:

It has been found impossible to delay much further the departure of the sultan for the war. The sultana mother, enraged at seeing him leave her, persuaded a girl of singular beauty, with whom he is desperately in love, to beg of him as a favour that he would not go. She did so one day when they were together in a garden, but the sultan's love suddenly changed to fury, and drawing his dagger, he slew the girl. Since then no one has dared to approach the subject.

Mehmet was accompanied on the campaign by Edward Barton, the English ambassador to the Sublime Porte, the name by which the Ottoman court was referred to in diplomatic circles. Barton, through the intercession of Safiye, had established a warm relationship with the sultan, who brought him along on the campaign for possible use as a negotiator with the Habsburgs.

The Ottoman army captured the fortress of Erlau in northern Hungary on 12 October 1596, and two weeks later they met the main Habsburg army, who were well entrenched on the plain of Mezo Keresztes. Mehmet lost his nerve at that point and was on the point of deserting his army and heading back to Istanbul, but the vezir Sinan Pasha persuaded him to remain. When the two armies met the following day, 26 October, Mehmet became terrified and was about to flee. But Sadeddin Hoca wrapped the sacred mantle of the Prophet Mohammed about the sultan and persuaded him to join in the battle, which soon resulted in an unexpected victory for the Ottomans. This earned Mehmet the title of *Gazi*, and the chronicler Hasan Kafi el-Akhisarı praised him as 'the world-conquering emperor, Sultan Gazi Mehmet Khan'.

After his triumphal return Mehmet never again led his army into battle. The *bailo* Girolamo Capello noted that 'The doctors have

Mehmet III (1595–1603)

declared that the sultan cannot leave for war on account of his bad health, produced by his excesses in eating and drinking.'

The following spring Mehmet executed his second son, Prince Selim, perhaps for rebellion, though the Ottoman sources are strangely silent on the incident. The only mention of the prince's death is by Capello, in a report dated 10 May 1597, where he mistakenly refers to Selim as the sultan's eldest son: 'The sultan's eldest son is dead, and the sultan is grown so fat they say he will make no more.'

The only other incident noted in 1597 is by the chronicler Selaniki, who writes that in October of that year Mehmet moved to the Eski

Saray on the Third Hill. He notes that the sultan went there in 'perfect splendour and magnificence', spending a month at the Old Palace in search of 'tranquility and repose' after a spectacular display of fireworks in which 'the resounding echo of dreadful crashing caused commotion to the farthest point in the heavens.'

Barton had been petitioning his superiors in England to send a present to Mehmet to mark his succession to the throne. Writing on 27 July 1595 to Sir Thomas Heneage, Vice-Chancellor and Privy Councillor, Barton suggested that the queen should send 'a clock in the form of a cock, which I hear Her Highness hath in one of her palaces or some other princely gift'. But by the end of 1597 the present still had not arrived, though Barton had made repeated requests for it to the Levant Company, whose merchants would be the principal beneficiaries of the sultan's good will. On 28 September 1597 he wrote to his secretary John Sanderson, who had been posted back to England, telling him of his frustration concerning the royal gift: 'We heare so smalle comfort of the present . . . I cannot write to the Company more than I have thereuppon . . .' Three months later Barton was dead, succumbing to a sudden attack of dysentery in his thirty-fifth year.

The merchants of the Levant Company had already agreed to commission a present from Queen Elizabeth to Sultan Mehmet. Influenced by Barton's suggestion, they decided that the present should be an elaborate organ with an ingenious clock mechanism. This is described in a document first published in *The Illustrated London News* of 20 October 1860 as 'a new instrument of extraordinary kind, and endowed with various motions, both musical and of other special use, such as for the rarity and art therein used may render it fit to be sent from her Majesty to any Prince or potentate whatever'.

Thomas Dallam, a member of the Blacksmiths' Company in London, was commissioned to make the organ. Dallam completed the organ in little more than a year, and on the evening of 14 November 1598 he demonstrated it for Queen Elizabeth at the Palace of Whitehall. Elizabeth was apparently impressed, for in her papers there is a letter dated 31 January 1599, with this sentence: 'Here is a great and curious present going to the Great Turk which no doubt wilbe much talked of, and be very scandalous among other nations specially the Germanes.'

Dallam's commission required that he go to Istanbul with the organ and install it in the sultan's palace. He and his three assistants dismantled the organ and loaded it aboard the *Hector*, an armed merchantman chartered by the Levant Company. They were accompanied by John Sanderson, who was returning to Istanbul to serve as consul under Henry Lello, Barton's replacement as ambassador.

The *Hector* set sail on 13 February 1599 and reached Istanbul on 15 August, dropping anchor off the Castle of the Seven Towers. The case containing the organ was unloaded and taken to the courtyard of Lello's house in Pera, where Dallam and his assistants unpacked it. The organ proved to have been damaged during the voyage, and Dallam spent two weeks repairing it, noting finally in his diary for 30 August 1599 that 'The 30th daye my worke was finished, and made perfitt at the imbassaderes house.'

The organ was dismantled again for shipment across the Golden Horn to Topkapı Sarayı on 11 September. Dallam writes of how he and his men were escorted through the Imperial Gate and on into the Third Court, where they were to install the organ, an area that normally would be off-limits to outsiders. Dallam's account indicates that he set up the organ in the porticoed garden of the Privy Chamber.

At this point Dallam interrupts his narrative to note that Queen Elizabeth's present to the *valide sultan* Safiye, a sumptuous coach that had actually cost more than the organ, had been that day delivered to her by the ambassador's secretary, Paul Pindar, a handsome and charming young man who apparently found great favour with the queen mother.

Dallam and his men then began to set up the organ, guarded by two *acemoğlans*, or apprentice guards, with whom they soon became very friendly, conversing through their *dragoman*, or interpreter. At the end of the day they went back to Pera and then for the next

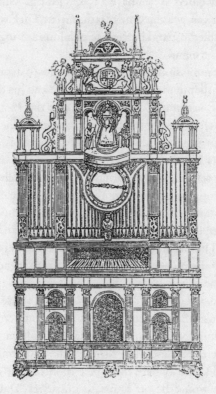

Organ made by Thomas Dallam for the sultan, from the
Illustrated London News *of 20 October 1860 and said there*
to be taken from the original specifications

month Dallam returned to Topkapı Sarayı daily to check on the organ, as he writes: 'The 15th I finished my worke in the Surraliao, and I wente once everie daye to se it, and dinede Thare almost everie Daye for the space of a monthe; which no Christian ever did in there memorie that wente awaye a Christian.'

The day chosen for the presentation of the organ to the sultan was Tuesday 25 September, when Mehmet returned from his mother's summer palace on the Bosphorus. At nine-thirty in the morning, as

Dallam and his party watched from the garden portico of the Privy Chamber, the sultan landed from his *pazar caique*, or royal barge, powered by eighty oarsmen. Dallam made the final adjustments on the organ, setting it to begin playing at ten o'clock, and as the time approached he could hear the voices of the crowd that had assembled in the adjacent chamber to await the sultan's arrival. Dallam was forced to wait in a side chamber, while the sultan entered and sat on a throne facing the organ, after which the crowd of courtiers took their places on the other three sides of the hall. Dallam writes that 'The Grand Sinyor beinge seated in his Chaire of estate commanded silence,' whereupon the organ, which he calls the 'presente', began to play, with two figures on its second storey sounding silver trumpets:

Than the muzicke went of, and the orgon played a song of 5 partes twyse over. In the tope of the orgon being 16 foute hie, did stande a holly bush full of blacke birds and thrushis, which at the end of the musick did singe and shake their wynges. Divers other motions thare was which the Grand Sinyor wondered at.

The sultan asked the *kapıcıbaşı*, or head gatekeeper, if the organ would play again. Dallam was summoned to reset the organ and was suddenly confronted with the sight of the sultan and his court, which he says included 200 pages, 100 dwarfs and 100 mutes, the latter making signs to him to indicate the motions they had seen on his organ. After Dallam had the organ play a second time he bowed to the sultan and prepared to depart, escorted by the *kapıcıbaşı*:

When the company saw me do so theye semed to be glad, and laughed. Then I saw the Grand Sinyor put his hande behind him full of goulde, which the Coppagaw Received, and broughte unto me fortie and five peecis of gould called chickers [sequins] and then was I put out againe wheare I came in, beinge not a little joyfull of my good suckses.

Five days later Dallam was summoned to Topkapı Sarayı to make some adjustments on the organ. He writes that while there the two *acemoğlans* whom he had befriended asked him to stay on permanently in the palace, saying that the sultan would set him up there with two women for his own harem.

Those jemoglanes, my ould acquaintance which kept that house, and had bene appointed by the Grand Sinyor to perswade me to staye thare allwayes, as indeed theie had done diveres times and diveres wayes, now they thoughte that I would staye in deed, theye imbraced me verrie kindly, and kiste me many times . . .

Dallam politely declined, as he notes in his diary:

I answered them that I had a wyfe and Childrin in Inglande, who did expecte my returne. Than they asked me how long I had been married, and how many children I hade. Though in deede I had nether wyfe nor childrin, yeat to excuse my selfe I made them that Answeare.

Dallam was summoned to Topkapı Sarayı once again, on Friday 12 November, this time to be given a tour of the sultan's own apartments and other parts of the *selamlık*, which continued on the following Sunday and Monday. During the course of his tour, which was conducted by one of the *acemoğlans*, Dallam was allowed a brief glimpse into the sultan's harem, and his account of what he saw is one of the very rare eyewitness descriptions of the royal concubines within the House of Felicity:

When he had showed me many other thinges which I wondered at, than crossinge throughe a litle squar courte paved with marble, he poynted me to goo to a graite in a wale, but made me a sine that he myghte not goo thether him selfe. When I came to the grait the wale was verrie thicke, and graited on bothe the sides with iron verrie strongly; but through that graite I did se thirtie of the Grand Sinyor's Concubines that weare playinge with a bale in another courte. At the first sighte of them I thoughte they had bene yonge men, but when I saw the hare of their heades hange doone on their backes, platted together with a tasle of smale pearle hanginge in the

*lower end of it, and by other plaine tokens, I did know them to be
women, and verrie prettie ones in deede.*

*Theie wore upon theire heades nothinge bute a little capp of clothe
of goulde, which did but cover the crowne of her heade; no bandes a
boute their neckes, nor anythinge but faire cheans of pearle and a jeull
hanginge on their breste, and juels in their ears; their coats weare like
a soldier's mandilyon [cloak], som of reed sattan and som of blew,
and som of other collors, and grded like a lace of contraire collor; they
wore britchis of scamatie, a fine clothe made of coton woll, as whyte
as snow and as fine as lane [muslin or lawn]; for I could desarne
the skin of their thies throughe it. These britchis cam doone to their
mydlege; som of them did weare fine cordevan buskins, and som had
their leges naked, with a goulde ringe on the smale of her legg; on her
foute a velvett panttoble [a shoe] 4 or 5 inches hie. I stood so longe
loukinge upon them that he which had showed me all this kindnes
began to be verrie angrie with me. He made a wrye mouthe, and
stamped with his foute to make me give over looking; the which I was
verrie lothe to dow, for the sighte did please me wondrous well.*

The following Tuesday Dallam was informed that the sultan
wanted the organ moved to another location, which turned out to
be the Incili Köşk. Accompanied by his interpreter, Dallam was
taken there by the two *acemoğlans*. Dallam goes on to tell of how
he reassembled the organ in the Incili Köşk, but a page of his diary
is missing at this point, and when the manuscript resumes he notes
that the *acemoğlans* had suddenly fled:

*. . . By chance I caled to my drugaman and asked him the cause of
theire runinge awaye; then he saide the Grand Sinyor and his
Conquebines weare cominge, we muste be gone in paine of deathe;
but they run all away and lefte me behinde, and before I gott oute
of the house they weare run over the grene quit out at the gate, and
I runn as fast as my leggs would carrie me aftere, and 4 neageres
or blackamoors cam runinge towardes me with their semeteris
[scimitars] drawne; yf they could have catchte me theye would have
hewed me all in peecis with their semeteris . . . Now, as I was runinge*

for my life, I did see a litle of a brave show, which was the Grand Sinyor him selfe on horsebacke, many of his conquebines, som ridinge and some on foute, and brave fellowes in their kind, that weare gelded men, and keepers of the conquebines; neagers that weare as black as geate [jet], but verrie brave; by their sides great semeteris; the scabertes seemed to be all gould, etc.

Dallam, his work completed, departed from Istanbul on 28 November 1599, never to return. Nothing more is heard of Dallam's organ in the last years of the reign of Mehmet III. But the coach presented by Elizabeth to Safiye was often in evidence as the *valide sultan* drove about town on her excursions from Topkapı Sarayı. Safiye was very popular with the ordinary people of Istanbul, but the army and the *ulema*, the ruling body of Muslim jurists, became increasingly resentful of her power over the sultan, as Henry Lello noted in a report at the time: 'She [Safiye] was ever in favour & wholly ruled her sonne: notwithstanding the Mufti & souldiers had much compleyned of her to ther king for misleading & Ruling him.'

Safiye's power was evident in the new mosque complex that she commissioned in 1597, the edifice now known as Yeni Cami. The site chosen for the mosque was on the shore of the Golden Horn in the quarter of the Karaite Jews, a schismatic sect who had split from orthodox Jewry in Byzantine times. Safiye resettled the Karaim on the other side of the Golden Horn, after which she had their houses demolished to make way for her mosque.

The *valide sultans* had carried out their financial dealings through a series of Jewish women known collectively as *kira*, who acted as commercial agents for the sequestered women in the harem. Safiye's *kira* was Esperanza Malchi, who amassed an enormous fortune acting as agent for the *valide sultan*. Paul Rycaut, secretary to the English embassy in the 1660s, writes of the great power held by the *kira*, whom he calls Mulki Kadın, attributing her influence over Safiye to the fact that she and the *valide* were lovers:

For in the time of Sultan Mahomet [Mehmet III] . . . when the whole government of the Empire rested in the hands of one Mulki

Carriage of the valide sultan

Kadın, a young audacious woman, by the extraordinary favour and love of the Queen Mother (who, as it was divulged, exercised an unnatural kind of carnality with the said Queen) so that nothing was left to the counsel and order of the Visier and grave Seniors, but was first to receive approbation and authority from her; the black Eunuchs and Negroes gave laws to all, and the cabinet councels were held in the secret apartments of the women; and there were prescriptions made, Officers discharged, or ordained as were most proper to advance the interest of this Feminine Government ...

Mehmet's health was visibly declining, and he had several fainting fits and spells in which he appeared to be out of his senses, as in an incident noted by the *bailo* Capello on 29 July 1600: 'The Grand Signor has retired to Scutari, and public rumour has it that for three days he had been subject to one of his fits of idiocy, with lucid intervals.'

The imperial cavalry, the Sipahis, rose up in revolt in 1600 because of the debasement of the coins with which they were paid. Their fury was directed against Esperanza Malchi, whom they blamed for the inflation, and they brutally killed her and her eldest son, who had been appointed head of the customs office. Mehmet pacified the rebel Sipahis by telling them, according to Selaniki, that 'he would counsell his mother and correct his servants.'

The Janissaries revolted early in 1603, and when they approached Topkapı Sarayı they did battle with the Sipahis before order was restored, but only after many on both sides had been killed. Knolles reports that this led the sultan to ban wine in Istanbul, for he attributed the insurrection of the Janissaries to their excessive consumption of alcohol:

The Mufti commanded all such as had any wine in thir houses in Constantinople or Pera, upon paine of death to bring it out and to stave it, except the embassadours of the Queene of England, the French king, and of the State of Venice; so that (as some report) wine for a space ran downe the channels of the streets in Constantinople, as if it had been water after a great shower of raine.

The Janissaries rose up in arms again later that year. They protested that all the disorders in the empire were due to the fact that the sultan was completely under the influence of his mother and the *kapı ağası*, the chief white eunuch, whose head they demanded, otherwise they would depose Mehmet in favour of his eldest son Mahmut. Mehmet gave in to their demands, and let the Janissaries behead the chief white eunuch and some other palace officials. He also banished his mother Safiye to the Old Saray. But she soon returned to the harem of Topkapı Sarayı, as the *bailo* Agostino Nani noted in one of his reports, mentioning that the *valide sultan* was forced to halt the construction of her new mosque. Nevertheless Safiye had her way, at least for the time being, for John Sanderson noted a few months later, referring to Safiye's mosque as a church, that 'The Great sultanaes church goeth up apace, and she rayneth as before.'

The threat by the Janissaries that they would depose the sultan in favour of his son Mahmut alarmed Mehmet. Mahmut, who was then about twenty-one, was very popular with the Janissaries, according to Peçevi. Mehmet, by contrast, was grossly fat and so physically unfit that his physician had warned him against going on another campaign, as the *bailo* Capello noted in one of his reports. Mehmet was further alarmed when Safiye intercepted a letter from a religious seer to Mahmut's mother, in which he predicted that the sultan would die within six months and be succeeded by her son. This led Mehmet to eliminate Mahmut and his mother, who were executed on 7 June 1603. The incident is recorded by Henry Lello in his report to the Crown, where he writes that Prince Mahmut was 'strangled & most basely & obscurely buried'.

The first part of the seer's prediction was correct, to within two weeks, for Mehmet III died on 12 December 1603, apparently of a heart attack. He was then midway through his thirty-eighth year, having reigned for almost nine years. Knolles writes of Mehmet's death, after which he gives his low opinion of the late sultan's character:

. . . the great Sultan Mahomet in the middest of all his pleasures and delights, died in his imperiall palace at Constantinople . . . He was a man of no great spirit, and yet exceeding proud, which was the cause, that hee was both the lesse beloved and feared of his subjects in generall, but especially of his Janizaries and other of his soldiours and men of warre, who scorning his loose government, and grieved to see even the greatest affaires of state not only imparted to women, but by them managed and overruled also (as by his mother, the Sultanesse his wife, and others) not only rebeled against him, but were ofttimes in their rages about to have deposed him. He was altogether given to sensualitie and voluptuous pleasure, the marks whereof he still carried about him, a foule, swoln, unweldie, and overgrowne bodie, unfit for any princely office or function; and a mind thereto answerable, wholly given over unto idlenesse, pleasure, and excesse, no small meanes for the shortening of his dayes, which he ended with obloquie, unregarded of his subjects, and but of few or none of them lamented.

Incili Köşk, the Kiosk of the Pearl

Mehmet was succeeded by his son Ahmet I, who was then aged thirteen years and eight months. Despite his youth Ahmet was very much his own man, and on his accession he insisted on girding himself with the sword of his ancestor Osman Gazi, rather than having it done by the *şeyhülislam*. Nor did he wait for the vezirs to enthrone him, but sat himself on the throne without hesitation. Shortly after his enthronement Ahmet consulted with his vezirs and paid a large sum of money to the Janissaries and the other soldiers in Istanbul, as was expected of a new *padişah*, or sultan, after which he rode through the streets of the city to receive the acclaim of his subjects.

The only other son of Mehmet III then alive was Mustafa, aged nine. Mustafa was mentally deranged, which may be why he was spared by his brother Ahmet, so that for the first time in three generations of the Ottoman dynasty there was no slaughter of princes on the accession of a sultan. But Mustafa may have been spared because he was the only male left in the Osmanlı line other than his brother Ahmet, who was as yet too young to have shown his ability to father a son and successor.

The day after his accession Ahmet presided at the funeral of his father, who was buried in the garden beside Haghia Sophia. Ahmet commissioned a splendid *türbe* for his father, the third of the three imperial mausolea beside Haghia Sophia, the last resting-place of the three sultans who in turn succeeded Süleyman the Magnificent, all of them buried there with their many wives and concubines and their numerous children.

During the second year of his reign Ahmet rid himself of an unwanted inheritance from his father, the wondrous mechanical organ that Thomas Dallam had installed in the Incili Köşk. Like his father, Ahmet I often went there to perform his devotions at the *namazgah*, the outdoor place of prayer, in the kiosk. The sultan's *imam*, Mustafa Safi, writes in his chronicle that Ahmet, who was much more pious than his father, was offended by all the figural representations on the organ, which were better suited to a heathen temple and could 'not be tolerated in a place of prayer and mansion of the caliphate'. Thus in 1605 Ahmet ordered that the organ be demolished and removed from the palace.

Chapter 7

REGICIDE

When Ahmet I succeeded to the throne he sent his grandmother Safiye to the Old Saray on the Third Hill, where she lived until her death fifteen years later. Safiye was thus forced to halt construction of the mosque that she was building on the shore of the Golden Horn, so the half-finished building soon began to fall into ruins.

Ahmet's mother Handan, now the *valide sultan*, never attained the prominence and power of her predecessor, for she had little influence on her headstrong son. Handan died on 26 November 1605, on the eve of Ahmet's departure on a campaign to put down a rebellion in Anatolia. The following day Handan was buried next to her husband Mehmet III in his *türbe* beside Haghia Sophia. Ahmet refused to postpone his departure from Istanbul for the customary seven days of mourning, and marched off with his army immediately after his mother's funeral. This led to rumours that Ahmet had done away with Handan because of her interference with his rule. Sir Thomas Sherley, an English traveller who was imprisoned in Istanbul in the years 1602–5, writes that Ahmet, wanting to dispense with Handan's unwanted advice, 'spared not his owne mother but poysoned hir in Auguste 1605'.

Ahmet also rid himself of his younger brother Mustafa, sending him and his mother (her name is unknown) to live in the Old Saray. Soon after his accession Ahmet was stricken by smallpox and almost died, whereupon some of the vezirs suggested that Mustafa should

Ahmet I (1603–17)

be brought out of the Old Saray to succeed his brother. This proved to be unnecessary when Ahmet recovered, whereupon he dismissed the vezirs who had suggested that Mustafa might succeed him.

Aside from Mehmet II in his first, brief reign, Ahmet was the first sultan to succeed to the Ottoman throne without having fathered a male heir to the throne. He took little time to produce one, however, for his first son, the future Osman II, was born on 3 November 1604, ten and a half months after Ahmet's accession. The boy's mother was Mahfiruz, also known as Hadice, a concubine who may have been of Greek origin.

Within the next year two other concubines, whose names are unknown, gave birth to Ahmet's second son, Mehmet, and his first daughter, Geverhan. During the decade that followed Ahmet fathered at least fifteen more children, including ten sons and five daughters.

During the second year of Ahmet's reign a new concubine entered his harem, a young Greek girl named Anastasia, daughter of an Orthodox priest of the Aegean isle of Tinos, who had been captured by the Turks and sold as a slave in the Istanbul slave market. She was the first in a group of new concubines brought into the harem at that time, and so Ahmet called her Kösem, the Leader of the Flock. Later she was also known as Mahpeyker. Kösem soon became Ahmet's favourite, and in 1605 she gave birth to his second daughter, Ayşe. During the next ten years Kösem bore Ahmet two more daughters and four sons, including the future sultans Murat IV, born on 29 August 1609, and Ibrahim, born on 9 November 1615.

Kösem became Ahmet's *haseki*, displacing Mahfiruz, who seems to have been relegated to the Old Saray, while her son Osman remained in Topkapı Sarayı. Kösem looked after Osman, and she often took the young prince in her carriage when she made excursions into Istanbul. The reports of the Venetian *bailos* note that on these excursions Osman enjoyed throwing handfuls of coins to the passers-by who flocked to see the young prince, while his stepmother Kösem remained concealed behind a curtain. The *bailos* also noted that Ahmet was totally devoted to Kösem, who became the power behind the throne. Cristoforo Valier wrote that 'she can do what she wishes with the King and possesses his heart absolutely, nor is anything ever denied to her.' Simon Contarini describes her as a woman of:

beauty and shrewdness, and furthermore ... of many talents, she sings excellently, whence she continues to be extremely well loved by the king ... Not that she is respected by all, but she is listened to in some matters and is the favourite of the king, who wants her beside him constantly ... She restrains herself with great wisdom from speaking too frequently of serious matters and affairs of state.

All doubts of his potency now having been dispelled, Ahmet seems to have regretted his decision to spare his brother Mustafa, who continued to be confined in the Old Saray with his mother. According to Simon Contarini, writing in 1612, the sultan twice gave orders for his brother to be strangled, but on both occasions he changed his mind, first because he was suddenly stricken with severe stomach pains, and the second time because a violent thunderstorm frightened him badly. Contarini believed that it was really Kösem who saved Mustafa, her motive being 'to see if it was possible that this mercy which she displayed at present to the brother [Mustafa] might also be employed later toward her son [Murat]'.

During the autumn of 1606 the Jewish quarter of Istanbul was ravaged by a fire. Sultan Ahmet took the lead in fighting the blaze, according to Knolles, who writes that the sultan was injured in the process: 'In which tumult and noise of the people running to and fro, and quenching of the fire the great Sultan having a fall from his horse, was thereof for a while sicke.'

Ahmet quickly recovered from his injury. That same year he decided to build an imperial mosque complex on the First Hill, appointing the architect Mehmet Ağa to design and build it on the east side of the ancient Hippodrome. Tradition has it that Ahmet was so enthusiastic about his mosque that he often pitched in himself, working alongside the labourers and craftsmen, whom he himself paid when their salaries were due, rewarding those who had made an extra effort.

Ahmet commissioned a number of new structures in Topkapı Sarayı, including two baths, one in the *selamlık* and the other in the harem, and a beautiful little library adjoining the Salon of Murat III in the imperial apartments. The French diplomat, Henry de Beauvau, who visited the palace in 1605, describes the men's bath, remarking that 'Nowadays the king does not use it any longer, instead he uses the one for the women.'

Ahmet also built a kiosk in the terraced gardens of what is now known as the Fourth Court. This kiosk, which has now vanished, was used by the sultan to entertain the ladies of his harem with 'comedies of voice and instrument', according to the French diplomat Julien Bordier, who notes that the performances were given by the Jews and Jewesses who were the court players of the day.

The French diplomat Gilles Fermanel noted that Ahmet erected

One of the sultan's favourites

'a very pretty little building' in the First Court. This housed a special bakery, now vanished, that was used, according to its dedicatory inscription, 'For the baking of the purest bread in the palace'. The flour for this bread was made from wheat grown in Bithynia, in northwestern Asia Minor, mixed with goat's milk supplied by a herd of goats kept in a grove in the palace grounds. This superfine white bread was reserved for Sultan Ahmet and the few favourites upon whom he bestowed it. One of these was the palace physician Domenico Hierosolimitano, who writes of the bread in his memoir:

A fine white flour was reserved, and every day was made 120 loaves of four pounds each, which were given only to the favourites of the Grand Turk, or to one of the six doctors of his person, as was the third doctor Domenico Hierosolimitano, who by the grace of God, finds himself now a Christian in Rome, supporting great poverty for the love of our Saviour.

Ottaviano Bon, who visited the palace during Hierosolimitano's time, describes how the women in Ahmet's harem were examined by the sultan's physician when they became ill:

But if she, which is sick, be the Queen or one of the Sultanas with whom the Grand Seignor hath lain, then her arm and hand, which she holdeth out of the bed for the physician to hold her pulse, is covered with a fine piece of white silk or Taffata sarcenet, for her flesh may not be seen or touched bare; neither may the doctor say any thing in her hearing, but, being gone out of the chamber, prescribeth what medicine he thinks fit; which for the most part, according to the knowledge and common custom of the Turks, is but only some kind of loosening and refreshing Sherbit, for they seldom use any other physick; nor do I hold their skill sufficient to prepare medicines for every malady. But in case the party deceased [i.e. diseased] should have need of a Chirugeon [surgeon]; she then must do as she may, and suffer without any scruple. For there is no remedy to conceal her skin and flesh from him.

Bon was one of the few foreigners ever to see the Inner Palace of Topkapı Sarayı, taking advantage of the absence of Sultan Ahmet on a hunting expedition to make a tour with the assistant of the *bostancıbaşı*, the head gardener. The first part of the palace that Bon saw was the porticoed garden of the Privy Chamber, where he describes a lake used by Sultan Ahmet to play with his mutes and buffoons:

And in the lake there is a little boat, the which (as I was informed) the Grand Seignor doth oftentimes go into with his Mutes, and Buffoons, to make them row up and down, and to sport with them, making them leap into the water; and many times, as he walks along with them above upon the sides of the lake, he throws them down into it, and plunges them over head and ears.

Knolles ends his history of the Ottoman Empire in 1610, the seventh year of Ahmet's reign, concluding with a description of the sultan and a judgement of his character:

This great Sultan Achmat, of whom we now speake, and who now reigneth, was, as before said) about fifteene years old when he came to the Empire, and is now about the age of two and twentie yeares, round and full face, and withal well favoured, but that the signes of the small Poxe are yet in his face somewhat to be seene. His beard being but little, is of a brown chestnut colour, growing in little tuffes in foure severall places, on each cheeke and each side of his chinne one ... He is of a good and just stature, well complectioned, and enclined to be fat, as was his father Mahomet: strong and well limmed, and withall active ... He is much given to sensuality and pleasure, wherein there is some hope, that he will at length burie himselfe, so as did his father Mahomet before him ... He hath by these his concubines foure children, two sonnes and two daughters, his eldest sonne being about five yeares old. He is exceedingly much delighted also with the pleasures of the field, as with hawking and hunting.

Knolles goes on to write of Ahmet's hobby of making horn rings, which he learned in keeping with the Ottoman policy of teaching every young prince a handicraft:

Everie one of the Turkish Emperours is bound by the laws of their religion, once every day to use and practice some manuall or handie craft trade or occupation: and therefore Sultan Mahomet [Mehmet III] the last Grand Seigniour, gave himself to the making of arrowes: and this his sonne Achmat, to the making of horne rings, which all the Turkes wear upon their thumbs, to draw their bowes therewithall when they shoot. Which custome of making of such horne rings, this Great Sultan religiously observeth little or much everie morning after his devotions ended.

During the ninth year of his reign Ahmet organized an extravagant festival to celebrate the wedding of his eldest daughter, Geverhan

Sultan, then only eight years old, to the captain Kara Mehmet Pasha, who was fifty-five. The festivities are described by Paul Rycaut in his history of the Ottoman Empire, published in 1680:

The Marriage Day being come, the Bride was Conducted to her Husband's Lodgings: First Marched the Janizaries, as before, then follow'd the Grand Provost and other Officers, the Emirs to the number of Eighty came next, then the Judges, afterwards the Veziers, and Grand Vezier, with the Mufti on his Left Hand, the Musick consisting of Thirty Drums and Hautboys came next, being followed by Eight Egyptians, who carred Biscain Tabors, and did a Thousand Apish Tricks: These were succeeded by Forty Musicians, Marching two and two, some playing on Cittarus, others on Harps, and some on Lutes, after the Turkish manner a Fool (held to be a Saint amongst them) being Muffled with a Cap and a Cloak, covered with Mutton Bones, Danced and Sang with these Instruments: the Chief Officers of the Arsenal Marched after them, and 30 Men with Hammers and other Iron Instruments, to break down whatever advanced too far in the Streets, and might obstruct the passage of 2 Trees of an immense height, laden with divers sorts of Fruits, all of Wax, carryed by many Men, and supported from the Top and Middle with Ropes: Then came Twenty Officers belonging to Ackmet Basha, the High Treasurer, God-Father to the Bride, and he himself alone Richly attired, and Proudly Mounted, after whom came two great Torch Lights, carry'd by Many Slaves, and a third Torch of a vast bigness, all covered with Plates of Gold, and more shining with Precious Stones than the Flames that burnt it: The Kaisler Aga [chief black eunuch] with Fifty of the Princess's Officers, followed those Lights, and after them was carryed a great Canopy of Crimson Velvet, and then another greater one, Covered with Gold Plates, whose Curtains being shut on all sides, hung down to the Ground: under this Canopy was the Princess on Horse-back, with some of her Black Eunuchs, her Caroch followed, cover'd with Cloth of Gold, and drawn by Four great White Horses of a wonderful Beauty: Then came Eight Caroches more, wherin were a great many other Bride-maids with divers Gelded Negroes; and Lastly, Twenty Five Virgin Slaves, chosen from among the Fairest, all on Horse-back, having their Hair confusedly hanging on their shoulders ...

The day after the wedding Sultan Ahmet assaulted the bride's mother, beating and stabbing her in his fury because she had strangled one of his favourites. Paul Rycaut gives a vivid description of the incident:

But not withstanding all this Pomp and Magnificence, the Sultan the day after the Marriage, cruelly beat his Sultana, this Daughters Mother, now Marry'd to the Captain Basha, and Stabbed her with his Dagger through the Cheek, and Trod her under his Feet, because she had Strangled a Favourite of his, which was one of his Sisters Slaves, and with whom he had fallen in Love, and sent for her: And if this made him somewhat uneasie, the Plague that furiously raged in Constantinople forced him to his Country Palace, called the Seraglio of Dorut [Davut] Basha, to avoid the Danger; but while here, when he went to the Stately Mosque he caused to be Built there, a Dervish threw a great Stone at him.

Five months later Ahmet married off the princess Ayşe Sultan, his first daughter by Kösem, to the grand vezir Nasuh Pasha. Ayşe was only seven years old, while her husband was middle-aged. Two years later Sultan Ahmet executed Nasuh Pasha, leaving the Princess Ayşe a widow at the age of nine. Ayşe went on to marry five more pashas in turn, two of them killed in battle, one assassinated and two dying of natural causes. The last of her husbands was Haleb Ahmet Pasha, who died in 1644, leaving Ayşe a widow for the sixth time at the age of thirty-nine.

Such serial marriages of a royal princess occurred frequently in the Osmanlı dynasty in the century after Süleyman, allowing the royal family to establish a network of alliances with the most powerful of the pashas. Kösem, in particular, used her daughters to help maintain herself in power for nearly half a century. As she wrote to the grand vezir Hafiz Ahmet Pasha in 1626, a few months

Mosque of Ahmet I from the Hippodrome

before he became her daughter Ayşe's third husband: 'Whenever you're ready, let me know and I'll act accordingly. We'll take care of you right away. I have a princess ready. I'll do just as I did when I sent out my Fatma.'

During the thirteenth year of his reign Ahmet dedicated the imperial mosque that he had founded beside the Hippodrome. Tradition has it that when the mosque was dedicated Ahmet wore a turban shaped like the foot of the Prophet Mohammed, in token of his humility.

Ahmet had little time to enjoy his mosque, for he died the year after it was completed, on 22 November 1617, aged twenty-seven years and eight months. The cause of his death is believed to have been typhus. Sultan Ahmet was buried in the large *türbe* beside the mosque that bears his name.

Ahmet's death led to a crisis concerning the question of his successor, for his eldest son, Prince Osman, had just turned thirteen. During the first three centuries of the Osmanlı dynasty the succession had been from father to son, the throne almost always passing to the eldest, through fourteen generations. But now, because of Osman's youth, the imperial council decided that the throne should go to Ahmet's brother Mustafa, who was then twenty-five years old, having been sequestered in the Old Saray during the fourteen years of his brother's reign. Peçevi, who was a contemporary observer of the event, gives his explanation for the change in the succession:

His [Ahmet's] sons being still young but his brother Sultan Mustafa being older and having reached the age of manhood, he ascended the imperial throne . . . It was thought that, because bringing a child prince to the throne when there was a full grown prince available would cause public rumour and would create numerous potential dangers, the times required that the throne of the sultanate, by way of succession, be Sultan Mustafa's. Otherwise they would be the target of all the people's arrows of censure and reviling.

Peçevi implies that the change in the law of succession was engineered by the chief black eunuch Mustafa Ağa, 'to whose management all affairs of state had been committed during the reign of Ahmet Khan'. As the *bailo* Simon Contarini suggested, it is possible that Kösem used her influence to have Prince Mustafa chosen as Ahmet's successor, hoping that he would be more inclined to spare her sons Murat and Ibrahim than would Osman, whom she feared might be inclined to use the bloody code of fratricide to eliminate his younger brothers.

After Mustafa's succession the women and children of Ahmet I were relegated to the Old Saray, including Kösem and her four sons, the eldest of whom was Murat. Kösem continued to receive her regular stipend of 1,000 aspers a day during the time she was in the Old Saray, retaining her status as *haseki* even though her husband was deceased.

Mustafa's mental condition had not been generally known until he became sultan, but then it became obvious to all who came in contact with him that he was insane and incapable of ruling on his own. His mother, who now assumed the role of *valide sultan*, was appointed regent, as the scholar Kâtip Çelebi noted in his *Fezleke*: 'When signs of mental and physical illness became apparent in the illustrious sultan, he was committed to the care of doctors . . . and the conduct of government was delegated to his honoured mother.' The *valide* was urged by the leaders of the *ulema* to dismiss Mustafa Ağa, who was gathering support among the vezirs to depose Sultan Mustafa. But, as Naima writes, the *valide* was 'deceived by his weeping eyes and his sweet tongue', and so she allowed him to remain as chief black eunuch. Mustafa Ağa then persuaded the *ulema* to issue a *fetva*, an official opinion, stating that Sultan Mustafa's mental incapacity made him unfit to rule. This done, Mustafa was deposed on 26 February 1618, ending a reign that had lasted only ninety-six days. He was then confined to an apartment in the Inner Palace of Topkapı Sarayı known as the Kafes, or Cage, which would become infamous in the history of the Osmanlı dynasty.

The same day that Mustafa was deposed his nephew succeeded to the throne as Osman II, aged thirteen years and four months. His mother Mahfiruz seems to have remained in the Old Saray, for there is no record that she took her place as *valide sultan* in Topkapı Sarayı. She died in 1620, two years after Osman's accession, and she was buried unceremoniously in Eyüp. At the time of Osman's accession Mustafa's mother was sent to the Old Saray. There the stipend of 3,000 aspers a day that she had received as *valide sultan* was reduced to 2,000 aspers. The old *valide sultan* Safiye, mother of Mehmet III, was still living in the Old Saray, where she continued to receive a stipend of 3,000 aspers a day. Safiye died in 1618, after which she was buried beside her husband in his *türbe* in the garden of Haghia Sophia. Kösem, who continued to receive her stipend of 1,000 aspers a day as *haseki* of the departed Ahmet I, remained in the Old Saray with her sons Murat and Ibrahim. Through her efforts they had been spared from the bloody code of fratricide by Osman, along with seven other sons of Ahmet I, the eldest of whom was Prince Mehmet, who was nearly thirteen.

Three months after his accession Sultan Osman wrote to James I of England, explaining why the rule of succession in the Osmanlı dynasty had been changed when his uncle Mustafa I came to the throne:

This paternall Empire and Monarchicall Kingdome hath almost untill this present blessed time been alwaies hereditarie, from Grandfather to Father, from Father to Sonne, and so cursively in that manner: but having regard unto the age and yeeres of Our Great and Noble Uncle, Sultan Mustafa, hee was preferred and honoured to sit on the Ottoman throne.

By that time Osman had already dismissed those who had been responsible for changing the rule of succession in order to enthrone Mustafa rather than himself, and in a decree to the army he referred to his uncle's brief reign as a wrongful break with 'ancient tradition'.

During the third year of Osman's reign a brilliant sword-shaped comet made its appearance in the evening sky, and the court astrologers agreed, according to Demetrius Cantemir, that this was 'a sign of victory and increase of Empire to the Othmans'. A year later the Bosphorus froze over, and Cantemir reports that the same astrologers considered this to be a bad omen.

It was imperative that Osman produce an heir to the throne, and on 20 October 1621 his concubine Meylişah finally gave birth to a son, Emir, but the boy died in January of the following year. Other concubines soon afterwards gave birth to his second son, Mustafa, and his daughter Zeynep, but both of them also died in infancy. His failure to sire an heir made Osman fear that he might be deposed in favour of his brother Mehmet, whom he decided to eliminate before a campaign into Poland. Mehmet was executed on 12 January 1621, the fratricide sanctioned in a *fetva* issued by the chief justice of Rumelia, who said that it was necessary in order to prevent a possible war of succession.

The following year Osman took the highly unusual step of marrying a beautiful Turkish girl of distinguished lineage, a break with the tradition of having slave concubines of non-Turkish origin.

His bride was Ukayle, daughter of the *mufti* Esat Efendi, and great-granddaughter of Süleyman the Magnificent. The marriage, which was held on 7 February 1622, was very unpopular among both the Muslim civilian population and the army. This is mentioned in a letter by Sir Thomas Roe, the English ambassador to the Sublime Porte:

About 12 daies since, contrary to the counsell and will of all his ministers, the Grand Signor hath married the grandchild of a sultana, wife to Pertav Bassa, only for her bewty, without any pomp, which is ill interpreted here; his successors of late yeares not usually taking wives, especially of a Turkish race, for respect of kindred. This and other inconstancies, with extreme avarice, hath made him odious with the soldiers; and his daily haunting the streets on foot, sometymes disguised, with a page or two, pryeing into houses and taverns, like a petty officer, encreasing his contempt even in the city.

Osman's unpopularity led to a revolt on 18 May 1622, in which the soldiers in Istanbul were joined by most of the populace of the city. Their rebellion was sanctioned by the *şeyhülislam*, who issued a *fetva* condemning the grand vezir Dilaver Pasha and others for corrupting the sultan. The mob then ran amok through the streets of Istanbul and forced their way into the first court of Topkapı Sarayı, where they seized the grand vezir and tore him to pieces. Osman's advisors convinced him that his only hope was to make a personal appeal to the rebels, who were led, though secretly, by Kara Davut Pasha, the deposed sultan Mustafa's brother-in-law. Osman rode to the mosque of the Janissaries beside their head-quarters in Beyazit, accompanied by his advisors, and pleaded with the rebels for mercy, but they paid no heed and massacred all of those who accompanied him. Thus Osman was left alone to face his fate, as the rebels took him in a cart to Yedikule, the Castle of the Seven Towers, where he was imprisoned. Davut Pasha now feared that a counter-revolution might restore the deposed sultan, and so he issued orders for Osman to be executed immediately.

Janissary under arms

Evliya Çelebi describes the execution in his account of Osman's last hours:

From the mosque they carried him in a cart to the Seven Towers, where he was barbarously treated, and at last most cruelly put to death by Pehlevan [the Wrestler]. Kafir Agha cut off his right ear, and a Janissary one of his fingers, for the sake of the ring on it. The former brought the ear and the finger to Davut Pasha, who rewarded the bearer of such acceptable news with a sum of money.

The following day Osman was unceremoniously buried beside his father in the *türbe* of the mosque of Sultan Ahmet. He is known to the Turks as Genç (Young) Osman, because he was only seventeen and a half when he died. Osman was the first Ottoman sultan to be assassinated by his own people, which some foreign observers took

Entrance to Yedikule, the Castle of the Seven Towers

to be an omen of the decline of the Ottoman Empire. As Sir Thomas Roe wrote in a letter to England when he heard the news of Osman's execution:

At this instant I am advised, that the newe great vizier Daout bassa, by the command of the newe emperour, hath strangled Osman, sent to prison butt fower howers agoe: The first emperour that they ever laid violent hands on; a fatal signe, I think, of their declynation.

Chapter 8

THE PROCESSION OF
THE GUILDS

During the insurrection that overthrew Osman II, his uncle Mustafa was taken from Topkapı Sarayı by the rebels, who brought him first to the Old Saray and then to the quarters of the Janissaries in order to protect him. Mustafa was then brought to Topkapı Sarayı and enthroned, beginning his second reign as sultan on 19 May 1622.

The following day Mustafa's mother received Osman's severed ear from Davut Pasha, proof that the deposed sultan was dead and that her son's rule was now secure. She thus began her second term as *valide sultan*, once again acting as her mad son's regent, rewarding Davut Pasha for his execution of Osman by appointing him grand vezir.

Davut Pasha had married the *valide's* daughter, Mustafa's sister, who subsequently bore him a son named Süleyman. According to Sir Thomas Roe, the *valide* and her son-in-law concocted a plot to have all of the surviving sons of Ahmet I murdered, so as to leave Davut's son Süleyman as the only living male in the Osmanlı line other than Sultan Mustafa, who had fathered no children and resisted all attempts to introduce concubines into his harem. Thus the *valide's* grandson would inherit the throne, or at least she and Davut Pasha so hoped.

The *valide's* henchman, the chief white eunuch, led a group of his men into the Old Saray to kill the young princes, but they were stopped by the palace pages. The pages alerted the Janissaries and Sipahis on duty around the palace, who apprehended the would-be assassins and hanged the chief white eunuch in the Hippodrome as a public spectacle. The soldiers demanded justice, and as a result Davut Pasha was dismissed as grand vezir, though the *valide* escaped punishment because of her privileged position as the mother of Sultan Mustafa, whose madness led the populace to consider him a saint. Soon afterwards the Janissaries did away with Davut Pasha, strangling him in the same chamber of the Castle of the Seven Towers where, on his order, they had killed Osman.

The empire was now in a state of chaos, revolts having broken out in Anatolia, while the troops in Istanbul were on the verge of insurrection because their wages were overdue, the imperial treasury being empty. Sultan Mustafa's mother, acting as regent for her son, changed grand vezirs six times during the course of the year. None of the grand vezirs could bring order to the chaotic regime, and eventually all parties agreed that Mustafa must be deposed and replaced by his nephew Murat, Kösem's eldest son. The end came on 10 September 1623, when representatives of all factions confronted Mustafa and convinced him that he must give up his throne in favour of his nephew, who ascended the throne as Murat IV.

Murat was aged fourteen years and twelve days when he came to the throne, after having been confined to the Old Saray since the death of his father Ahmet I nearly six years before. The day after his accession Murat sent his uncle Mustafa to the Old Saray, where the deposed sultan was confined for the rest of his days. Mustafa's mother was presumably sent to the Old Saray too, but her fate is uncertain. She was replaced as *valide sultan* by Kösem, who now returned to the harem of Topkapı Sarayı, where she would act as regent for her son Murat during the early years of his reign. Her other sons, Süleyman, Kasım and Ibrahim, who ranged in age from twelve to eight at the time of their brother Murat's accession, stayed with their mother in the harem of Topkapı Sarayı until they reached the age of puberty. Each of them in turn then moved into the *selamlık* along with Prince Beyazit, the only other surviving son of Ahmet I, where they were educated together with the royal pages. Later, when they were old enough to be a threat to the throne, they were confined in the Cage by Murat, who eventually murdered all but one of them.

Murat set up his own women in the harem of Topkapı Sarayı after his accession. His first *haseki*, Ayşe, gave birth to a son, Ahmet, in 1627, and other concubines bore him four more sons in the next eight years. None of Murat's five sons survived their childhood, four of them dying of the plague in 1640. Murat also fathered twelve daughters, six of whom died in infancy, the other six being married off at a young age to pashas, several of whom were or became grand vezirs, the marriages being arranged by his mother Kösem.

During the early years of Murat's reign Kösem, acting as regent, corresponded frequently with the various grand vezirs, none of whom she identifies by name in the seven extant letters, which are undated. In one of her letters she expresses her worries about the situation in Yemen and her son's health:

Letters have come from Egypt – apparently to you too – which describe the situation there. Something absolutely must be done about Yemen – it's the gate to Mecca. You must do whatever you can. You'll talk to my son about this. I tell you my mind is completely distraught over this ... It is going to cause you great difficulty, but you will earn God's mercy through service to the community of Muhammed. How are you getting along with salary payments? Is there much left? With the grace of God you will take care of the obligation and then take up the Yemen situation. My son leaves in the morning and comes back at night, I never see him. He won't stay out of the cold, he's going to get sick again ... I tell you, grieving over the child is destroying me. Talk to him, when you get a chance. He must take care of himself. What can I do – he won't listen. He's just gotten out of a sickbed and he's walking around in the cold. All this has destroyed my peace of mind. All I wish for him is to stay alive. At least try to do something about Yemen. May God help us in the situation we are in ...

Throughout this time Murat lived under the constant threat of being deposed and killed by the Janissaries, who were now almost totally out of control, resentful of the fact that they had renounced their usual payment when he became sultan. While the grand vezir was off on campaign the government was effectively under the control of four brothers-in-law of the sultan, three of them married to daughters of Kösem. Rycaut comments on this in a section entitled 'The disorders in the Ottoman State':

The Government was at that time chiefly in the hands of the four Brothers-in-law, who had married four Sisters of the Grand Signior's, and for that reason were powerful, and employed in the principal Offices of State ... besides the violences daily practiced by the Brothers, the extravagant humors in the Sultan himself added to the disorders of State, and increased the discontents and dissatisfactions of the people ...

Rycaut goes on to write of the excesses of Murat, who completely neglected his responsibilities as sultan and spent his time carousing with his courtiers, including 'Buffoons, Players upon the guitar, and Eunuchs', ruining his health and disgracing himself in public, while in the absence of authority the empire faced collapse. Then in September 1631 Murat was so terribly frightened by a stroke of lightning, which nearly killed him, that he was led to abstain from wine, for a time, and to reform his conduct in thanksgiving to God for having spared his life.

The Janissaries and Sipahis revolted on 18 November 1631 and threatened to depose Murat in favour of his brother, unless he gave them the grand vezir Hafız Ahmet Pasha, Kösem's son-in-law, so that they could take their vengeance on him. Murat was forced to give them Hafız Ahmet and fifteen other members of his court, including his favourite page Musa, all of whom were slaughtered by the soldiers. Murat bided his time and the following year he took his revenge on the rebels, executing them in large numbers, so that 'many bodies were found swimming in the Bosphorus', according to Rycaut.

The following year Murat closed all of the coffee-houses in

Istanbul, on the grounds that they were centres of sedition (the coffee-houses were closed on numerous occasions and usually reopened soon afterwards), and even went so far as to ban the smoking of tobacco as well as opium. But at the same time he issued an edict legalizing the selling and drinking of alcohol, even for Muslims, a startling law without precedent in Islamic history. Cantemir refers to this law in writing about Murat's addiction to drink, which he acquired through his friendship with an alcoholic named Bekri (the Drunkard) Mustafa:

But he [Murat] is much more remarkable for his drunkenness, in which he exceeded all his predecessors that were given to that vice. Led to it by Becri Mustapha, he was not content to drink wine in private, but compelled even the Muftis and Cadiulaskers [kadıaskers, or chief judges] to drink with him, and also by a publick edict, mention'd before, allow'd wine to be sold and drunk by men of all orders and degrees. As an immoderate lover of wine, so was he a mortal enemy to opium and tobacco, forbid both on pain of death, and with his own hand kill'd several, whom he found either eating opium, or smoking or selling tobacco.

Cantemir tells the story of how this Bekri Mustafa led Sultan Murat to begin drinking wine. It seems that Murat was wandering through the market quarter in disguise one day when he came upon Bekri Mustafa 'wallowing in the dirt dead drunk'. Murat was intrigued by the drunkard and brought him back to the palace, where Mustafa introduced the sultan to the joys of wine, showing him that the best cure for a hangover is more of the same. Bekri Mustafa soon died of drink, leaving Murat bereft, as Cantemir writes:

At his death the Sultan order'd the whole Court to go into mourning, but caus'd his body to be buried with great pomp in a tavern among the hogsheads. After his decease the Emperor declar'd he never enjoy'd one merry day, and whenever Mustapha chanc'd to be mention'd, was often seen to burst out into tears, and to sigh from the bottom of his heart . . .

Murat IV (1623–40)

Murat's addiction to wine eventually made him realize how dangerous it was for the stability of the state, and in 1634 he banned the sale and drinking of alcohol and closed all of the taverns in Istanbul and elsewhere in the empire. Rycaut writes of this in his description of the increasingly tyrannical rule of Murat, whose drinking led to episodes of insane fury and cruelty that made the populace dread his approach:

Murat being greatly addicted to Wine, was sensible of the ill effects of it himself, and that the heat of debauchery inclined him to violence and cruelty, and from hence collecting how dangerous this humor

[127]

*of drunkenness was in his people, especially in his Souldiery, for
that much of the late Seditions might be attributed thereunto, he
published a most severe Edict against Wine, commanding all Taverns
to be demolished, the Butts to be broken, and the Wine spilt. It was
the common custom of the Grand Signior to walk the streets in
disguise, when meeting any drunken person he would imprison him,
and almost drub him to death. It was his fortune to meet a deaf
man one day in the streets, who not hearing the noise of the people,
nor the rumor of his approach, did not readily shift out of the way,
as was consistent with the fear and dread of so awful an Emperour,
for which default he was strangled immediately, and his body thrown
into the streets.*

Murat personally led a campaign into Persia against the Safavids
in 1635, capturing the city of Revan (Erivan). Murat sent news of
his success back to Istanbul, with instructions to have his brothers
Beyazit and Süleyman executed during the victory celebration, so
that their deaths would pass unnoticed.

Murat returned to Istanbul at the head of his triumphant army
on 29 December 1635. He was the first sultan since Süleyman to
have led his army personally in a victorious campaign, leaving aside
the accidental triumph of Mehmet III at Mezo Keresztes in 1596.
Thus the entire populace of the city turned out to give Murat a
hero's welcome, a scene described by Evliya Çelebi:

*On the 19th of Rajab 1045 [29 December 1635] the illustrious
emperor made his entry into Istanbul with a splendour and magnificence which no tongue can describe nor pen illustrate ... The
windows and roofs of the houses in every direction were crowded
with people, who exclaimed, 'The blessing of God be upon thee, O
conqueror! Welcome, Murat! May thy victories be fortunate!' ...
The sultan was dressed in steel armour, and had a threefold aigrette
in his turban, stuck obliquely on one side in the Persian manner: he
was mounted on a Noghai steed, followed by seven led horses of
the Arab breed, decked out in embroidered trappings set with jewels.
Emirgüneh, the khan of Erivan, Yusuf Khan, and other Persian*

khans walked on foot before him, while the bands with cymbals, flutes, drums, and fifes, played the airs of Afrasiab. The emperor looked with dignity on both sides of him, like a lion who has seized his prey, and saluted the people as he went on, followed by three thousand pages clad in armour. The people shouted 'God be praised!' as he passed. The merchants and tradesmen had raised on both sides of the way pavilions of satin, cloth of gold, fine linen, and other rich stuffs, which were afterwards distributed amongst the . . . servants of the Sultan . . . During this triumphant procession to the sarai all the ships at Seraglio Point, Kiz Kule, and at Tophane, fired salutes, so that the sea seemed in a blaze. The public criers announced that seven days and nights were to be devoted to festivity and rejoicing.

Evliya, who was then twenty-four, had been present at the capture of Erivan, having gone on the campaign in the company of his father Derviş Mehmet Ağa, chief of the guild of goldsmiths. Evliya's maternal uncle Melek Ahmet Ağa (later Pasha) was at the time Murat's sword-bearer and intimate companion, and soon after their return from the Erivan campaign he arranged for his nephew to meet the sultan. The meeting took place in 1635 on Kadır Gecesi, the Night of Power, which commemorates the Prophet Mohammed's visit to heaven. That evening Evliya was serving as *müezzin* in Haghia Sophia, when, in the sultan's presence, he recited the entire Kuran from memory. This so impressed Murat that he sent Melek Ahmet and another aide to fetch Evliya and bring him to the royal *loge*. There, before the entire congregation, they placed a golden crown on Evliya's head and led him by the hand into the sultan's presence. As Evliya writes:

On beholding the dignified countenance of Sultan Murat I bowed and kissed the ground. The emperor received me very graciously, and after the salutations, asked me in how many hours I could repeat the whole of the Kuran. I said, if it please God, if I proceed at a quick rate I can repeat it in seven hours, but if I do it moderately, without much moderation of the voice, I can accomplish it in eight hours. The Sultan then said, 'Please God! he may be admitted into the number of my intimate associates in the room of the deceased Musa.' He then gave me two or three handfuls of gold, which altogether amounted to 623 pieces.

That very evening Evliya was brought into Topkapı Sarayı, where Murat had him enrolled among the pages in the Inner Service, those who waited on the sultan himself. He was then dressed in the costume of a page and escorted to the Has Oda, the great domed hall known as the throne room within, where Murat soon made his appearance, as Evliya writes:

The emperor now made his appearance, like the rising sun, by the door leading to the inner harem. He saluted the forty pages of the inner chamber and all the Musahib [favourites], who returned the salutation with prayers for his prosperity. The emperor having with great dignity seated himself on one of the thrones, I kissed the ground before it, and trembled all over. The next moment, however, I complimented him with some verses that most fortunately came into my mind. He then desired me to read something. I said, 'I am versed in seventy-two sciences, does your majesty wish to hear something of Persian, Arabic, Romaic, Hebrew, Syriac, Greek, or Turkish? Something of the different tunes of music, or poetry in various measures?'

Evliya recited some verses, after which he matched wits with the sultan and his favourites, played upon the tambourine, danced like a dervish before the throne, and then sang a plaintive love song about the deceased Musa that reduced Murat to tears. When Murat recovered his composure he immediately directed that Evliya be admitted into the company of his *musahibs*. The gathering broke up when the call for the evening prayer was heard, whereupon, as Evliya writes, 'the emperor ordering me to assist the *müezzin*, I flew like a peacock to the top of the staircase and began to exclaim, "Ho to good works!"'

Soon afterwards Evliya began his studies in the Palace School,

The sultan with his scribe

receiving instruction in Persian and Arabic in addition to his regular courses in music, writing, grammar and in the reading and recitation of the Kuran. During the course of his studies Evliya only occasionally came into contact with Murat, as he remarks in telling of his time at the Palace School, where one of his teachers was his old mentor and namesake Evliya Efendi:

Thus three times a week I read the Kuran with Evliya Efendi, and also had lessons in Arabic, Persian and writing. In this way it was but seldom that I could attend in the service of the emperor, but whenever I came into his presence he was always delighted, and treated me so graciously, that I never failed to show my wit and pleasantry . . . versed as I was in every branch of science, I enjoyed the greatest favour of the Sultan, who liked a joke and a laugh as well as any plain dervish . . .

Evliya goes on to tell of Murat's great strength and athletic ability, of which he had a dizzying demonstration one day in the gymnasium near the sultan's bath:

One day he came out covered with perspiration from the bath in the Has Oda, saluted those present, and said, 'Now I have had a bath.' 'May it be to your health,' was the general reply. I said, 'My emperor, you are now clean and comfortable, do not therefore oil yourself for wrestling today, especially as you have already exerted yourself with others, and your strength must be considerably reduced.' 'Have I no strength left?' said he, 'let us see'; upon which he seized me as an eagle, by my belt, raised me over his head, and whirled me about as children do a top. I exclaimed, 'Do not let me fall, my emperor, hold me fast!' He said, 'Hold fast yourself,' and continued to swing me about, until I cried out, 'For God's sake, my emperor, cease, for I am quite giddy.' He then began to laugh, released me, and gave me forty-eight pieces of gold for the amusement I had afforded him.

During the time that he spent in the palace Evliya observed how Murat scheduled his various activities during the winter months, when he was not off on campaign:

During the winter he regulated his assemblies as follows: On Friday evening he assembled all the divines, Sheikhs, and the readers of the Kuran, and with them he disputed till morning on scientific subjects. Saturday evening was devoted to the singers who sang the Ilahi, the Na't and other spiritual tunes. Sunday evening was appropriated to the poets and reciters of romances . . . On Monday evening he had the dancing boys . . . and the Egyptian musicians . . . The assembly sat until daybreak, and resembled the musical feast of Hüseyin

Bukhara. On Tuesday evening he received the old experienced men who were upwards of seventy years, and with whom he used to converse in the most familiar manner. On Wednesdays he gave audiences to the pious saints; and on Thursdays to the Dervishes. In the mornings he attended to the affairs of the Moslems. In such a manner did he watch over the Ottoman states, that not even a bird could fly over them without his knowledge. But were we to describe all his excellent qualities we should fill another volume.

The Persians recaptured Revan in 1636, whereupon Murat began preparations for another campaign against the Safavids. He began his planning for this crusade by ordering that all the guilds of Istanbul pass in parade before the Alay Köşkü, the Kiosk of the Processions, a review pavilion built into the outer defence walls of Topkapı Sarayı.

Evliya devotes more than a third of one volume of his *Seyahatname* to this procession, giving an account 'Of all the Guilds and Professions, Merchants and Artisans, Shops and Occupations in this vast town of Constantinople, with the Regulations handed down to them by their Sheikhs or Ancients'. The parade lasted for three days, with the sultan and his court looking on from the Alay Köşkü. Evliya writes of the marchers that 'They were distributed into fifty-seven sections and consist altogether of a thousand and one guilds', although the number of guilds that he actually describes is just seven hundred and thirty-five. Representatives of each of the guilds paraded in their uniforms or in bizarre costumes, exhibiting on floats or on foot their various crafts or trades, trying to outdo one another in entertaining or astounding the sultan and the other spectators, who included the entire populace of the city other than those actually marching in the procession. Evliya describes them as they pass, telling the number in each guild and how many shops they have, giving their rallying cries and identifying their sheikhs and their patron saints:

All these guilds pass in wagons or on foot, with the instruments of their handicraft, and are busy with great noise at their work ...

The Bakers acknowledge for their first patron Adam ... Gabriel taught Adam to grind the corn to make flour and to bake it into bread, of which he ate when it was yet warm; it is from this circumstance that Adam became the patron of the bakers ... The bakers having a great number of assistants, they form a considerable troop. They have nine hundred and ninety-nine shops. They figure at the public processions on wagons, and represent their business, by some of them kneading, some baking and throwing small loaves of bread among the crowd. They also make for this occasion immense loaves, the size of the cupola of a hamam covered with sesamum and fennel; these loaves are carried on litters and wagons, each weighing fifty quintals, or on rafts made of poles which are dragged along by from seventy to eighty pair of oxen. No oven being capable of holding loaves of so large a size, they bake them in pits made for that purpose, where the loaf is covered from above with cinders, and from the four sides baked slowly by fire ...

The Carpenters prepare wooden houses, the Builders raise walls, the Woodcutters pass with loads of trees, the Sawyers pass sawing them, the Masons whiten their shops, the Chalk-Makers crunch chalk and whiten their faces, playing a thousand tricks ... The Toy-Makers of Eyüp exhibit on wagons a thousand trifles and toys for children to play with. In their train you see bearded fellows and men of thirty years of age, some dressed as children with hoods and bibs, some as nurses who care for them, while the bearded babies cry after playthings or amuse themselves with spinning tops or sounding little trumpets ...

According to Evliya, there were several disputes concerning precedence in the imperial procession, all of which were settled by Sultan Murat. The first of these quarrels was between the Butchers and the Captains of the White Sea (Mediterranean). Murat settled the dispute in favour of the Captains, issuing this imperial edict:

Indeed, beside the fact that they supply the capital with provisions, they have also taken Noah for their protector. They are a respectable guild of men, who militate in God's ways against the Infidels, and

[134]

Procession of the guilds: the Bakers

*are well-skilled in many sciences. They may also pass in great
solemnity, and then be followed by the Butchers.*

Thus the Captains of the White Sea were moved up in the imperial
procession, whereupon they put on one of the most spirited performances seen during the festivities, as Evliya describes it:

*The Captains of the Caravellas, Galleons and other ships, having
fired from them a triple salute at Saray point, pour all their men on
shore, where they place on floats some hundred small boats and*

drag them along with cables, shouting 'Aya Mola!' In their boats are seen the finest cabin boys dressed in gold doing service to their masters, who make free with drinking. Music is played on all sides, the mast and oars are adorned with pearls and set with jewels, the sails are of rich stuffs and embroidered muslin, and on top of each mast are a couple of boys whistling tunes of Silistria. Arriving at the Alay Köşkü they meet five or ten ships of the infidels, with whom they engage in a battle in the presence of the emperor. Thus the show of a great sea-fight is represented with the roaring of cannon, the smoke covering the sky. At last, the Muslims emerging victorious, they board the ships of the infidels, take booty and chase the fine Frank boys, carrying them off from the old bearded Christians, whom they put in chains. They upset the crosses of the Christian ships, and dragging the captured vessels astern of their own ships, they cry out the universal Muslim slogan of 'Allah, Allah!' Never before the time of Murat IV was there seen so brilliant a union of mariners.

After the Captains of the White Sea passed the Alay Köşkü the Butchers attempted to join the line of march, but their place was disputed by the guilds of the Egyptian Merchants. The two groups assembled before the kiosk, where once again Murat decided against the Butchers, 'to the great delight of the Egyptian Merchants, who leaping for joy, passed immediately after the Captains of the White Sea'. The Egyptian Merchants were organized in eight separate guilds, of which the most popular among the spectators was that of the Merchants of Musk-Sherbets. As Evliya describes them, 'They pass exposing to public view in china vases and tankards every kind of sherbet made of rhubarb, ambergris, roses, lemons, tamarinds, etc., of different colours and scents, which they distribute among the spectators.'

Then finally the Butchers were allowed to take their place in the procession, marching at the head of the tenth section before the Men of the Slaughter-House and the Jewish Meat-Merchants:

The Butchers, who were almost all Janissaries, pass clad in armour on wagons, exposing to public view in their shops, adorned with rich stuffs and flowers, fat sheep of Karamania weighing from forty

Two Ottoman marines

to fifty occas. They trace on their white flesh figures with saffron, gild their horns, cut them up with their large knives, and weighing them in yellow-coloured scales, cry, 'Take the occa for an asper, take it my soul, it is an excellent roast dish!'

Evliya writes of another quarrel that Murat had to settle regarding the order of march in the procession of the guilds, a dispute between the Fish-Cooks and the Helvacıs, or Sugar-Bakers, the latter being allowed to go first. The Helvacıs were divided into five separate guilds, the first of whom to pass in the procession were the Imperial Confectioners and the last the Helvacıs of Galata, who put on the best display, according to Evliya:

They produce at this public exposition trees of sugar, with fruits upon them, an admirable show! Behind them walks the Chief Confectioner of the Saray, and of the town, with their troop of confectioners in pointed caps and with their eightfold Turkish music.

The Fish-Cooks followed in the fourteenth section, along with thirteen other guilds of fishermen and fishmongers, most of whom were Greeks, according to Evliya's account:

The Fishermen adorn their shops on litters with many thousand fish, amongst which many monsters of the sea are to be seen. They exhibit dolphins in chains, sea-horses, otters, whales, and other kind of fish of great size, which they catch a couple of days before the public procession, and load wagons with them drawn by seventy-eight buffaloes. A great number of these fishermen are Greeks ... They pass, crying 'Hai' and 'Hui' to the great amazement of the beholders ... The Fish-cooks are nine hundred men, with five hundred shops. They are all infidel Greeks, who catch fish in different ways ... In the public procession they pass singing songs and making jests. They are a comical set of people, and make the emperor laugh much, who was of a merry temperament.

Evliya writes of still another quarrel over precedence that took place in the twenty-eighth section, where Murat was called upon to adjudicate between the Fur-Makers and the Tanners:

There was a wonderful contest between the Fur-Makers and Tanners, about the precedency of rank. At length the emperor decided in favour of the first, because all the first men of the state dress in fur ... The Greek fur-makers of the marketplace of Mahmut Pasha form a separate procession, with caps of bear-skin and breeches of fur. Some are dressed from head to foot in the skins of lions, leopards and wolves, with kalpaks of sable on their heads. Some dress again in skins, as wild men and savages, so that those who see them are afraid, each one being tied by six or sevenfold strong chains, and led by six or seven people. These wild men assailing their leaders and keepers, spread amongst the people a noise and confusion, which is beyond all description. Some are dressed as strange figures, with their feet turned to the sky apparently, while they walk with their real feet on the ground. Others, clad in the skins of lions, leopards and bears, represent these animals walking on all fours and dragged with chains. Every time they grow mutinous they are beaten by their guards. Some representing swine, apes and other animals, not dangerous, follow in crowds without chains. Others assail them with dogs and hounds, representing the show of a hunting party with halberds in their hands.

The parade came to an end when the last of the marchers passed the Alay Köşkü at sunset on the third day, 'after which the guilds accompanied their officers to their lodgings and everyone returned home'. As Evliya writes of the parade's end:

The procession of the imperial camp began its march at dawn and continued the whole day until sunset. On account of this parade all work and trade in Constantinople were stopped for three days, during which time the riot and confusion filled the town to such a degree which is not to be described by language, and which I, the humble Evliya, only dared to describe. Nowhere else has such a procession been seen or shall be seen; it could only be carried into effect by the imperial orders of Sultan Murat IV ... Amen! By the Lord of all the Prophets: God be praised that I have overcome the task of describing the guilds and corporations of Constantinople!

Chapter 9

THREE MAD SULTANS

Murat spent the better part of two years preparing for his new campaign in Persia, his object being the reconquest of Baghdad. While the preparations were underway his rule became increasingly tyrannical, as his bouts of drunkenness led him into acts of cruelty so frightful that it was feared that he had gone mad. Those whom he oppressed hoped that his excesses would soon lead to his death, as Rycaut notes in describing Murat's behaviour at the time:

The Pashas of greatest note and riches he put to death, and confiscated their Estates to his Exchequer; and whereas avarice and cruelty were equally predominant in his nature, there was scarce a day wherein he made not some demonstration of these dispositions . . . He took a singular delight to sit in a Chiosk by the Sea-side, and from thence to shoot at the people with his Bow and Arrow, as they rowed near the Banks of the Seraglio, which caused the Boat-men afterwards to keep themselves at a distance from the Walls of the Seraglio. And as he likewise took pleasure to go from one Garden to another on the Bosphorus, so if he observed any so bold, as to put forth his head to see him pass, he commonly made him pay the price by a shot from his Carbine.

Another story about Murat's psychotic behaviour at this time is told by Evliya Çelebi. In describing the imperial summer pavilion at Dolmabahçe, on the European shore of the lower Bosphorus,

Evliya writes that 'Sultan Murat IV happened once to be reading here the satirical work *Sohami* of Nefi Efendi, when the lightning struck the ground near him; being terrified, he threw the book into the sea, and then gave orders to Bayram Pasha to strangle the author.'

Murat's preparations for the campaign were complete by the beginning of 1638. His preparations had been delayed by an outbreak of plague in the summer of 1637, which, according to Rycaut, 'took away the only Son of the Grand Signior of two or three years old'.

The death of Murat's only surviving son left just two males of the Osmanlı line besides Murat, namely his brothers Kasım and Ibrahim, both of whom were confined in the Cage. Kasım, the elder of the two, was thus the heir to the throne, unless Murat fathered another son. Kasım was terrified of arousing any suspicion that he had designs on the throne. Thus he was all humility when he presented himself before Murat to pay his respects and wish him success on his expedition to reconquer Baghdad. Murat accepted Kasım's best wishes, and then later that same day, 17 February 1638, he had his brother strangled.

Baghdad surrendered to Murat on 22 December of that year after a five-week siege in which the Turks lost 100,000 men. After the defenders laid down their arms Murat ordered his men to slaughter all of the surviving garrison and populace of the city. He then led his army back to Istanbul, making his triumphal entry into the city of 12 June 1639, a scene described by Rycaut:

The Grand Signior, in his own Person appeared in the Persian habit, with a Leopards skin thrown over his shoulders ... having his Stirrup attended with twenty two of the chiefest Nobles, whom he had reserved at Bagdat purposely to lead in Triumph when he made this Entry.

While Murat had been away on campaign his uncle, the deposed Sultan Mustafa, had finally passed away, dying of unknown causes on 20 January 1639 to the Old Saray, where he had been confined since his second deposition from the throne more than fifteen years

Baghdad Kiosk, built by Murat IV in 1638

before. According to Evliya Çelebi, Mustafa was buried in the former baptistery of Haghia Sophia, since 'all the funeral monuments were then crowded with Sultans and princes.'

Mustafa's death left Ibrahim as the only captive prince in the Kafes, or Cage, the apartment in the Inner Palace that from 1618 on had been used to confine the younger brothers of a reigning sultan. The Kafes was probably a two-storeyed building hidden away in the *selamlık*; it was originally surrounded by a high wall, but this was demolished in the mid eighteenth century, when more windows were opened up in the building. The only companions of the captive princes were the mutes who served them and the few barren women who formed their harem. The only education they had was what they might have acquired in the harem or the Palace School before they were confined to the Cage, after which they were totally cut off from the outside world, leaving those who succeeded to the throne ill prepared to rule.

After his capture of Baghdad Murat spent all of his time carousing with his favourites, who now included the captured Persian prince Emirgüneh. Demetrius Cantemir writes of how Murat's drinking made him behave like a homicidal madman, terrifying his subjects:

He thirsted after innocent blood, breath'd nothing but slaughter, and seem'd as if it were to be nourish'd by it. Very often at midnight he stole out of the women's apartments through the private gates of the palace with his drawn sword, and running through the streets barefooted with only a loose gown about him, like a madman, kill'd whoever came in his way. Frequently from the windows of the higher rooms, where he us'd to drink and divert himself, he shot with arrows such as accidentally pass'd by. In the day time he ran up and down in disguise, and did not return till he had kill'd some unfortunate wretches for little or no cause. So great terror did he strike into the whole City, that no man dar'd even mention his name within his walls . . .

Murat's drinking had by now completely undermined his health. Rycaut's description of the sultan indicates that he had an advanced case of cirrhosis of the liver, and a drunken banquet with Emirgüneh early in February 1640 finally did him in:

This dissolute repast became fatal to the Grand Signior; for a fire being kindled in his veins and bowels, he fell into a violent and continued Feaver. The Physicians being called, were fearful to administer Remedies, lest proving unsuccessful, their lives should pay for this ineffectual operation: at length they agreed to let him bleed, but this hastened his death. For he died the fourth day of his Feaver, being the 8th [actually the 9th] of February, in the seventeenth year of his Reign, and the one and thirtieth of his Age, having ruled in the height of all disorders and irregular excesses, which his youthful years enabled him to support.

During Murat's last illness he decided to kill his brother Ibrahim so that the Osmanlı line would end when he himself died, in which case the sultanate would pass to the Tartar Khans. As Rycaut writes of Murat's last wish:

*He left no Son, for though he had divers, they died in their infancy,
notwithstanding which his kindred were so detested by him, that
he wished that he might be the last of the Ottoman Line, that the
Empire of that Family might end with him, and devolve unto the
Tartar.*

Ibrahim was saved by his mother Kösem, who persuaded the
grand vezir Kara Mustafa Pasha and the other members of the
imperial council that he was the rightful successor. Ibrahim had
spent the past four years imprisoned in the Cage, living in constant
terror that at any moment he would be killed by his murderous
brother. Thus he was at first too terrified to open his door to the
vezirs when they brought him the news of Murat's death and his
own succession to the throne. Only when Kösem had Murat's corpse
brought before the door of the Cage did Ibrahim believe that his
brother was dead, whereupon he at last emerged from his cell,
shouting in glee, 'The butcher is dead, the butcher is dead!'

That same day, 9 February 1640, Ibrahim was raised to the throne,
and on the day following Murat was buried beside his father in the
türbe of the Sultan Ahmet mosque. Evliya Çelebi writes thus of his
patron's passing:

*Sultan Murat, being obedient to the call, 'Return to thy lord', bade
farewell to this perishable world and embarked on his journey to
the everlasting kingdom. The whole of the Mohammedan nation
was thrown into the deepest affliction, and lamented his loss. Horses
hung with black were let loose in the Hippodrome, where his Majesty
was buried close to Sultan Ahmet ... I have since heard from the
pearl-shedding lips of my lord, Kara Mustafa, that had God spared
Murat but six months longer, the whole of the infidels would have
been reduced to the capitation tax.*

Soon afterwards Ibrahim was girded with the sword of Osman
at Eyüp, receiving the congratulations of the populace as he rode
back through the city, though, as Rycaut remarks, 'whether it were
for want of practice, or by reason of a posture natural unto Fools,

Sultan Ibrahim the Mad (1640–8)

he sate so ridiculously on his Saddle, as moved rather the Laughter than the Acclamation of the People.'

Rycaut gives an unflattering description of the new sultan, who was known as Deli (Mad) Ibrahim:

Ibrahim was in his own nature of a gentle and easy temper, of a large Forehead, of a quick and lively Eye, and Ruddy Complexion, and of a good proportion in the Features of his Face; but yet had something in the air of his Countenance, that promised no great abilities of mind.

Ibrahim was twenty-four when he succeeded to the throne, having been a prisoner for all but the first two years of his life, first in the Old Saray, then in the harem of Topkapı Sarayı, where for the four years prior to his accession he was locked up in the Cage. This confinement, added to his mental illness, made him totally unfit to rule on his own. Thus power fell to his mother Kösem, who was once again *valide sultan*, working together with Kara Mustafa Pasha, who was reappointed as grand vezir. The *bailo* Alvise Contarini reported that the *valide* and the grand vezir were often at odds, each trying to overthrow the other.

Kösem's power enabled her to amass enormous wealth, which she used to endow a number of charities, one of which was to care for orphaned girls and to provide them with dowries which would enable them to marry. She also endowed a mosque in Üsküdar, known as Çinili Camii, and a huge caravanserai in the market quarter of Istanbul called the Valide Hanı.

When Ibrahim first came to the throne it was thought that he might be impotent. Since he was the only surviving male in the imperial Ottoman line, there were fears that the dynasty would come to an end, as Rycaut notes:

The continual apprehensions that he entertained of Death during his Imprisonment, had so frozen his constitution with a strange frigidity towards Women, that all the dalliance and warm embraces of the most inflaming Ladies in the Seraglio, could not in a whole Years time thaw his coldness; which was the occasion at first of that report, which spoke him to be impotent.

Kösem took it upon herself to remedy this by finding beautiful concubines for Ibrahim's harem, which were supplied to her from the slave market by a confidant named Pezevenk, or the Pimp. But when her son at first showed no interest in these women she consulted the sultan's tutor and confidant, Cinci Hoca, who dosed Ibrahim with aphrodisiacs and brought him illustrated pornographic books to stimulate both his body and his imagination. The treatment worked, and Ibrahim soon began enjoying the company of his concubines as well as the other pleasures of life that had been denied to him during the years that he had been secluded or imprisoned. Rycaut writes of this in his account of the first year of Ibrahim's reign:

The Sultan in this interim had little regard unto the Government both for want of Capacity, and by reason of his luxurious Appetite,

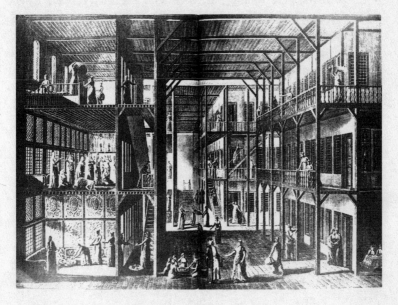

Harem of Topkapı Sarayı

to which he indulged in the highest excess of sensuality; for having been accustomed to a Prison, and restraint, he knew not how to enjoy the freedome he had recovered, but by subjecting it to the imperious servitude of his Lusts. This humour the Vizier and great Ministers cherished in him, by continual Banquets, Feasts and Entertainments, in which he always took high content and satisfaction. His other Recreations were, Horse-races, and Shooting with the Bow, rewarding the most dextrous Archers . . . The year 1641 being now entered, the Sultan now passed a most Luxurious Life in his Seraglio, consuming an immense Treasure on his Women . . .

Rycaut goes on to tell of how later in that year Ibrahim was stricken by a serious illness. This renewed fears that the Ottoman line might come to an end, since he had not yet sired a successor to the throne despite his newly aroused interest in the women of his harem, where it was rumoured that he was still impotent.

These fears were finally put to rest on 2 January 1642, when Ibrahim's concubine Hadice Turhan gave birth to a son, the future sultan Mehmet IV. Within the next fourteen months two more of Ibrahim's concubines presented him with sons, the future sultans Süleyman II and Ahmet II. Ibrahim's concubines eventually bore him a total of eighteen children, nine boys and nine girls, all born within a period of fewer than seven years. During this time he had a total of nine *hasekis*, of whom the names of only four are known: Hadice Turhan, Saliha Dilaşub, Hadice Muazzez and Hümaşah. The first three of these are known because they were the mothers of future sultans, Hadice Turhan of Mehmet IV, Saliha Dilaşub of Süleyman II and Hadice Muazzez of Ahmet II. Hümaşah was Ibrahim's last *haseki*, the favourite of his final years; she was known as 'Telli Haseki', because of the silver and gold threads (*tels*) that are traditionally used to adorn a bride's hair. The chronicler Naima writes of the curious circumstances surrounding the marriage of Ibrahim and Hümaşah, which was celebrated with an elaborate state ceremony:

In accordance with the imperial command, the vezirs of the imperial council each gave the gift of a moon-faced slave girl bedecked with jewels. Then they escorted [the bride] in a well-ordered procession from the gardens of Davutpasha to the imperial palace. The ceremonial was performed with the chief black eunuch acting as proxy for the bride and the grand vezir for the sultan. Robes of honour were bestowed on the vezirs and the ulema, *and others received honours according to custom.*

Ibrahim erected several structures that still survive in Topkapı Sarayı. One of these is the Kiosk of the Circumcisions, a handsome tiled pavilion that he erected at the southern end of the marble terrace near the Privy Chamber. The kiosk takes its name from the tradition that the circumcisions of Ibrahim's sons were carried out there. Ibrahim also rebuilt the pool and fountain on the inner side of the terrace, and on its outer side he erected a bronze gazebo known as Kasrı Iftariye, projecting above the lower gardens of the

Accouchement in the harem

palace. The gazebo took its name from the fact that Ibrahim sat there to have his *iftar*, the meal that is taken after sundown during the holy month of Ramadan. He also sat there watching his favourites swimming in the pool and playing on the terrace, often joining in the fun by throwing them into the water along with his buffoons, mutes and dwarfs, according to the French diplomat François de la Croix, who noted that 'representations of comedies, marionettes, and other diversions occur in front of this basin.'

The grand vezir Kara Mustafa Pasha and Kösem continued to direct the affairs of government throughout the first four years of

Ibrahim's reign. The rivalry between the *valide sultan* and the grand vezir grew stronger as time went on, and early in 1644 Kösem finally persuaded Ibrahim to have Kara Mustafa executed.

The new grand vezir was Sultanzade Mehmet Pasha, a great-great-grandson of Süleyman the Magnificent. His appointment was largely due to the influence of the sultan's favourite, Cinci Hoca, who had been Ibrahim's tutor and only companion during the years that he had been confined to the Cage. The new grand vezir now became a puppet of Cinci Hoca, whose great influence over Ibrahim forced Kösem into the background, so that she was no longer the power behind the throne.

After Hadice Turhan presented Ibrahim with an heir, the chief black eunuch Sümbül (Hyacinth) Ağa arranged for one of his own female slaves to serve as a wet-nurse to the prince. Sümbül Ağa had purchased this girl from a Persian slave dealer in the belief that she was a virgin, but when she turned out to be pregnant he sent her to the house of his steward, where she gave birth to a son. Sümbül was so taken by the boy that he adopted him, and arranged for him to be raised in the imperial harem when the slave girl became Prince Mehmet's wet-nurse. Ibrahim also took a deep affection for the boy, who was much better looking than his own son, and took great delight in playing with him, while he ignored Prince Mehmet. This aroused the jealousy of Hadice Turhan, who one day vented her fury on the nurse and her son. Ibrahim was so enraged by her behaviour that he took Mehmet out of Hadice Turhan's arms and threw him into a cistern, where the child would have been drowned had the harem servants not gone to the rescue. As it was Mehmet suffered a cut to his head, resulting in a scar that he bore for the rest of his days.

This so alarmed Sümbül Ağa that he begged Ibrahim to allow him to retire, and when his request was granted he took the slave girl and her son and set sail from Istanbul, having announced his intention of making the pilgrimage to Mecca. Contrary winds forced them to put in at Rhodes, where they were boarded by Maltese pirates who killed Sümbül Ağa and captured the slave girl and her son. The pirates carried their captives and booty to Crete, which was still held by the Venetians. They believed the child to be the son of Sultan Ibrahim, and at first they thought that they could ransom him for a great fortune, but to no avail. The boy was raised as a Christian and in time became a Dominican friar, known to all as Padre Ottomano, since many believed he was the heir to the Ottoman throne.

When news of Sümbül Ağa's murder reached Ibrahim he was furious, and his first thought was to mount an attack against Malta. But his advisors persuaded him that Malta was impregnable, and so he decided to invade Crete, thus seeking revenge on the Venetians for having allowed the pirates to take refuge there. Thus Ibrahim launched an expedition against Crete in the spring of 1645, masking it as an attack on Malta to give the Ottoman forces the advantage of surprise.

Otherwise Ibrahim spent all of his time in the harem, where his orgies reached epic proportions, according to Cantemir:

As Murad was wholly addicted to wine, so was Ibrahim to lust. They say, he spent all his time in sensual pleasures, and when nature was exhausted with the frequent repetition of venereal delights, he endeavour'd to restore it with potions and art. Every Friday, which is the Turkish Sabbath, he dedicated to Venus, and commanded a beautiful Virgin richly habited to be brought to him by his Mother, Prime Vizir, or some other Great man. He cover'd the walls of his chamber with looking glass, that his love-battles might seem to be acted in several places at once. He order'd his pillows to be stuffed with rich furs, that the bed destin'd for the imperial pleasure might be the more pretious. Nay, he put whole sable skins under him, in a notion that his lust would be inflam'd, if his love-toil were render'd more difficult by the glowing of his knees. In the palace garden call'd Chas, he frequently assembled all the virgins, made them strip themselves, and himself naked, neighing like a stallion, ran among them, and as it were ravish'd one or another kicking and struggling by his order. Happening once to see by chance the privy parts of a wild heifer, he sent the shape of them in gold all over the Empire, with orders to make enquiry, whether a woman made just in that manner could be found for his lust. At last they say, such a one was found and receiv'd into the women's apartment. He made a collection of great and voluminous books of pictures, expressing the various ways of coition, whereby he invented some new and before unknown postures.

The heifer-like woman described by Cantemir was an Armenian from the village of Arnavutköy on the Bosphorus, who is said to have weighed three hundred and thirty pounds. Rycaut writes that Ibrahim became so enamoured of his new favourite that he could deny her nothing, which led to her undoing, for she incurred the enmity of Kösem: 'By these particulars the Queen Mother becoming jealous, one day inviting her to Dinner, caused her to be Strangled, and perswaded Ibrahim that she died suddenly of a violent Sickness, at which the poor Man was greatly afflicted.'

Evliya Çelebi writes of the sultan's capricious ways in appointing the lowliest of his favourites to the highest offices in the realm:

He was a most prodigal sovereign, and lavished his treasures on the lowest men and on his favourite women. He raised a bath-keeper to the charge of general of the Janissaries with the rank of pasha with three tails [the equivalent of a three-star general]; and to please Sheker Para his favourite lady, he made the son of a rice-dealer an Agha of the Janissaries. The same dignity he would have conferred on Ahmet Kuli, a gypsy by extraction, who was a celebrated wrestler and juggler, with whose skill he was much pleased. The juggler answered, 'Gracious Sovereign, since the time of the Pharaohs, by whom we wandering gypsies were expelled from Egypt, not one of my ancestors has been either a minister or a vezir; and such ideas came only into Pharaoh's head, when he was near his fall.' Thus saying, he most prudently declined the offered dignity, and begged leave to go to Mecca on a pilgrimage.

The favourite mentioned by Evliya was Şeker Para, or 'Piece of Sugar'. According to Rycaut, Şeker Para served as Ibrahim's procuress in obtaining beautiful women for his harem. She also served as his go-between when he fell in love with one of the widows of his departed brother Murat. But the woman spurned him, and when he tried to rape her she drew her dagger and threatened to stab him if he persisted. Their struggle was overheard by Kösem, who reprimanded Ibrahim and allowed the woman to escape. This so infuriated Ibrahim that he banished his mother from the harem and confined her in the Old Saray.

At the same time Ibrahim humiliated his sisters Ayşe, Fatma and Hanzade, as well as his niece Kaya, subordinating them to his concubines, to whom he gave their land and jewels. He also made his sisters and niece serve his wife Hümaşah, forcing them to work as her maids. This outraged Kösem and turned her against Ibrahim, changing her maternal love for him to a hatred that would seal his doom. As she wrote to the grand vezir Ahmet Pasha at the time about Ibrahim: 'In the end he will leave neither you nor me alive. We will lose control of the government. Have him removed from the throne immediately.'

Ibrahim now fell in love with a daughter of the *mufti*, whose charms had been described to him by Şeker Para. The *mufti* was well aware of Ibrahim's depraved character and did not want to give up his beloved daughter to him. But out of fear he disguised his feelings and said that he did not want to force his daughter into marriage, though he would try to persuade her to wed the sultan. Ibrahim was satisfied with this, but the *mufti* returned the following day to say that his daughter was not willing to go through with the marriage. Şeker Para was then sent to persuade the *mufti's* daughter, bringing with her an enormous diamond as a present from the sultan, but the girl persisted in her refusal. Ibrahim's patience was exhausted and he ordered the grand vezir Ahmet Pasha to seize the girl and bring her to the harem. He enjoyed her for a few days, but her tears and reluctance took the edge off his pleasure, so he eventually returned her with scorn to her father. The outraged *mufti* complained to Sofu Mehmet Pasha, a member of the Divan, and also to Murat Ağa, the commander of the Janissaries, who agreed that the time had come to depose Ibrahim and also to eliminate his grand vezir, a conspiracy in which they were joined by Kösem. The conspirators were soon joined by the two *kadıaskers*, the chief justices of Rumelia and Anatolia, after which they decided to make their move.

The revolt began on 7 August 1648, when Murat Ağa, accompanied by the *kadıaskers* and other ministers, led the Janissaries into Topkapı Sarayı and forced Ibrahim to speak with them, demanding that he dismiss Ahmet Pasha in favour of Sofu Mehmet Pasha. Ibrahim was forced to agree, whereupon Sofu Mehmet Pasha was appointed grand vezir and Ahmet Pasha fled to the house of the *mufti*, thinking that he would find a haven there. But the Janissaries dragged him from the house and killed him, throwing his body in front of the mosque of Sultan Ahmet. The body of the deposed grand vezir was hacked to bits by the mob in the Hippodrome, so that thenceforth he was referred to as Hezarpara Ahmet, or Ahmet of the Thousand Pieces. Cinci Hoca and Pezevenk suffered the same fate, according to Evliya Çelebi, who notes that Şeker Para was exiled to Egypt.

The following day the Janissaries assembled before the *mufti* and obtained from him a *fetva* deposing Ibrahim for being 'a Fool and a Tyrant and Unfit for Government'. When the *fetva* was presented to Ibrahim he tore it up in disdain and threatened the *mufti*, who thereupon issued a second *fetva* declaring that anyone who did not obey the law of God 'was an Infidel and automatically fallen from his throne'. When the second *fetva* was given to Ibrahim he tore it to pieces and ordered the *mufti* to be executed. But Ibrahim had now lost all authority and his command was ignored, whereupon the Janissaries rioted in front of the Gate of Salutations to demand his deposition. Ibrahim then lost his nerve and fled into the arms of his mother Kösem, whom he had reluctantly allowed back into the harem, begging her to protect him. Kösem persuaded him to abdicate, whereupon the Janissaries raised Ibrahim's eldest son to the throne as Mehmet IV.

Ibrahim was confined to a small room at the top of a staircase above the Hall of the Favourites, where for the next nine days his concubines could hear him weeping disconsolately. Ibrahim's plight won him the sympathy of the populace, which made those who had deposed the sultan alarmed that a counter-revolution would restore him to the throne. This led the imperial council to obtain a *fetva* authorizing the execution of Ibrahim, and on 17 August 1648 the chief executioner Kara Ali was sent to strangle him. Evliya Çelebi gives his version of what followed when Kara Ali entered Ibrahim's room:

Ibrahim asked, 'Master Ali, wherefore art thou come?' He replied, 'My emperor, to perform your funeral service.' To this, Ibrahim replied, 'We shall see.' Ali then fell upon him; and while they were struggling, one of Ali's assistants came in, and Ibrahim was finally strangled by a garter. Kara Ali received a reward of five hundred ducats, and was urged to remain no longer in Constantinople, but to proceed on a pilgrimage to Mecca.

Evliya goes on to describe the funeral and burial of Ibrahim, who was interred beside his uncle Mustafa I in the former baptistery of Haghia Sophia, two mad sultans laid side by side in the domed tomb:

The corpse of the emperor was washed before the Has Oda, and the last prayers were read under the cypresses before the Hall of the Divan, in the presence of all the vezirs, and of Sultan Mohammed himself, the Shaikh-ul-Islam acting as Imam. The vezirs wore black veils, and horses covered with black were led before the coffin, which was deposited in the mausoleum of Sultan Mustafa I, the uncle of Sultan Ibrahim ... In his time no beggars were seen, and treasures were lavished every where. Some hundred poets breathed out chronographs on his death, with the most heartfelt sorrow. He reposes in the courtyard of Aya Sofya along with Sultan Mustafa; and his tomb is much visited by women, because he was much addicted to them ...

Such was the end of Deli Ibrahim, the third mad sultan to pass away in a single decade.

Chapter 10

THE HUNTER CAGED

When Mehmet IV ascended the throne he was just over six and a half years old, the youngest sultan in the history of the Ottoman Empire. His mother Hadice Turhan, who was now *valide sultan*, would normally have been appointed to serve as her son's regent, as had happened thrice before in the first half of the seventeenth century. But Turhan was only twenty-three, the youngest ever to be *valide*, and because of her inexperience the imperial council appointed Kösem as regent, giving her the title of *büyük* (elder) *valide sultan*.

During the next three years Hadice Turhan gathered support to undermine Kösem, determined to assume her rightful place as *valide sultan* and rule as regent for her son. Turhan was supported by the chief black eunuch Süleyman Ağa, who was her go-between in gaining supporters among the leaders of the Sipahis and other powerful pashas.

The Sipahis rose up in revolt in Üsküdar, but they were put down by the Janissaries. Nevertheless the revolt soon carried over to the populace of Istanbul, who rioted and marched to Topkapı Sarayı. Kösem decided that in order to protect her position she would overthrow Mehmet IV and enthrone his younger brother Süleyman. Prince Süleyman, who was three months younger than the sultan, was the son of Ibrahim's *haseki* Saliha Dilaşub, whom Kösem believed to be more complaisant and 'not anxious to exercise the

Sipahi standard-bearer

authority of the *valide sultan's* station', according to Naima. Kösem was backed by Bektaş Ağa, commander of the Janissaries, to whom she communicated her plot. But the plot was thwarted by Süleyman Ağa and the grand vezir Siyavuş Pasha, who obtained a *fetva* ordering the execution of Kösem.

Süleyman Ağa took a group of twenty pages and led them to Kösem's apartment, where they were admitted by the black eunuchs on duty there. The only person they found inside the apartment was an old woman who served as Kösem's buffoon. The woman was armed with a pistol, which she pointed at them while they questioned her about the whereabouts of Kösem. The woman replied that she was the Old Queen and then fired at them before they disposed of her. They then went on into the bedroom, where a page named Deli (Crazy) Doğancı eventually found Kösem hiding in a clothes press.

She tried to bribe the pages, but they just took her money and brutally stripped her of her jewellery and other valuables. Süleyman Ağa then had Kösem dragged by her feet to Kuşhane Kapısı, the gateway leading from the harem into the Third Court, where he ordered his men to kill her. Kösem fought back and it took four men to subdue and strangle her, after which they left her for dead. But there was life in her yet, and as soon as the pages were out of sight she got to her feet and tried to escape through Kuşhane Kapısı. The executioners were called back, and this time they garrotted her until they were absolutely sure that she was dead. Then, as Paul Rycaut writes:

The Black Eunuchs immediately took up the Corpse, and in a reverent manner laid it stretched forth in the Royal Mosch; which about 400 of the Queens Slaves encompassing round about with howlings and lamentations, tearing the hair from their heads after their barbarous fashion, moved compassion in all the Court.

As soon as Kösem was dead Siyavuş Pasha ordered the sacred standard of the Prophet Mohammed to be taken from the Pavilion of the Holy Mantle and displayed above the main gate of Topkapı Sarayı, where the sight of it inspired a wave of religious fervour to sweep through the city, even among the rebellious Janissaries. Bektaş Ağa was abandoned by his followers, after which he and the other rebel leaders were hunted down and executed.

Kösem was buried without ceremony on the same day that she died, 2 September 1651. She was interred in the *türbe* beside the mosque of Sultan Ahmet I, laid to rest beside her husband and her son Murat IV.

Sultan Mehmet's mother, the *valide sultan* Hadice Turhan, now ruled in his stead as regent, exercising her power through a series of twelve grand vezirs who held office in turn over the next five years.

Turhan Sultan took her responsibilities as regent very seriously, and she tried to make up for her inexperience by learning everything there was to know about her job. When the question of funds for the navy came up she wrote to the grand vezir asking him to inform her about every detail involved: 'Bring me all the registers. I have learned that there are regulations governing everything down to the cloth for sails. I must know everything in precise detail.' Another letter to the grand vezir takes him to task for not looking after supplies in the Old Saray: 'There is not enough wood in the Old Palace to boil soup! What's the reason for this? Is it not a royal palace?' Turhan attended all of her son's audiences, and though she was concealed behind a curtain she spoke out whenever she had to advise Mehmet. At one meeting Mesut Efendi, the chief justice of Anatolia, voiced his opinion and Mehmet turned and asked his mother, 'Did you hear that?', to which she replied, 'He speaks the truth, what he says is right.'

The main problem that Turhan faced was shortage of funds, as is evident in the frantic letters that she exchanged with her grand vezirs. In one of her letters Turhan responds thus to a request from the grand vezir to meet the military payroll:

You have requested fifty purses by tomorrow. I am in tremendous debt. Still, let us suppose I borrow fifty purses and give that amount to you Sunday or Tuesday. What can you come up with? Have you been able to raise anything or not? Where should I find the money so that I might give it to you? You won't believe me, but I swear by God that I am in debt for more than three or four hundred purses. I myself am dumbfounded . . . what can I grab hold of?

Turhan managed to borrow one hundred purses from the pious foundations of Mecca and Medina, probably arranging the loan through the chief black eunuch, who was the imperial trustee of the holy cities.

Meanwhile the young sultan Mehmet IV had moved from the harem to the *selamlık* when he reached the age of puberty. During his youth he engaged in sports with the pages in the Palace School and early on developed a keen interest in hunting, which was to be his main activity for the rest of his reign.

The eleventh of the ephemeral grand vezirs appointed by Turhan was Boyuniğri (Crooked Nose) Mehmet Pasha, who was overthrown in a revolt by the Janissaries and Sipahis in 1656. The soldiers chose a spokesman who called upon the fourteen-year-old Sultan Mehmet to come out and address them himself, for he should be man enough to act as sultan on his own. But Mehmet did not come out to face the rebels, who finally dispersed without further bloodshed. Turhan in desperation appointed as grand vezir Köprülü Mehmet Pasha, an uneducated Albanian who was then seventy-one years old, but whose previous experience as a provincial governor indicated that he had outstanding administrative ability. Köprülü Mehmet served until his death in 1661, proving to be the most capable grand vezir since Sokollu Mehmet Pasha. He achieved his aims by severe justice, executing large numbers of rebels and transgressors of the sultan's laws.

Turhan's regency ended later in 1656 when her son Mehmet IV was considered to have come of age. But Mehmet took no greater part in the government thenceforth than he had before, for Köprülü Mehmet Pasha held all the power in his capable hands. Just before Köprülü died he gave some last words of advice to the young sultan, then in his twentieth year: 'Never heed the advice of a woman, never allow one of your subjects to become too rich, always keep the treasury well filled, always be on horseback, and keep the army constantly on the march.'

Mehmet Pasha was succeeded as grand vezir by his son Fazıl Ahmet Pasha, who proved to be every bit as capable as his father, relieving the young sultan of all state responsibilities. This left him free to spend all of his time in the chase, so that he came to be called Mehmet the Hunter. The sultan's love for hunting gave rise to a popular ditty comparing Mehmet's passion with that of his father Crazy Ibrahim: 'The father was cunt-mad/ the son is hunt-mad.'

Mehmet's hunting excursions often took him to Edirne, which he much preferred to Istanbul, and his visits to Edirne Sarayı became more frequent and his stays longer as time went on. Then in 1661 a terrible plague struck Istanbul, and to escape it Mehmet moved his entire court to Edirne, where he remained until the following

Street scenes in Ottoman Edirne

spring. There he spent all of his time hunting, as Rycaut notes, the sultan's extravagant expeditions exhausting the resources of the countryside around Edirne:

. . . never was Prince so great a Nimrod, so unwearied a Huntsman as this; never was he at quiet, but continually in the Fields on Horseback, riding sometimes at Midnight, to ride up to the Mountains, that he might more early discover the Sun in the Morning; by which extravagant course of life, he wearied out his Court and Attendants, who began to believe the amorous humour of his Father more supportable than the wandering Vagaries, and restless spirit of the Son. But not only were his Huntings tedious to his Court, but troublesome and expensive to the whole Country, which were all summoned in wheresoever he came, and sometimes thirty or forty thousand men appointed to beat the Woods for three or four days, carrying before them the compass of a whole days Journey about, inclosing all the Game and wild Beasts within that Circuit, which on the day of the Hunt, the G. Signior kills and destroys with Dogs, Guns, or any other way, with abundance of noise and confusion; which pastime, though lawful in itself, and commendable enough for so great a Prince, yet the frequent use of it, was a burden and oppression to his people, whilest in the winter they passed many cold nights in the woods, and being unused to that hardship, many of them paid for their Emperours Pastime with their own lives.

The plague having ended, the grand vezir prevailed upon Sultan Mehmet to return to Istanbul, where he finally arrived on 30 March 1662, nearly three months after his twentieth birthday. Evliya describes Mehmet's appearance at that time, every bit a sultan except in his disinclination to rule other than as a figurehead:

Though very weak when he mounted the throne, he acquired strength when, at the age of twenty, he took to field sports. He had broad shoulders, stout limbs, a tall figure, like his father Ibrahim; a powerful fist, like his uncle Murat, open forehead, grey eyes, a ruddy countenance, and an agreeable voice, and his carriage was princely, in short, that of an emperor . . . He had a small beard, large mustaches, and was much devoted to field sports.

Hadice Turhan had by this time retired from an active role in government. She now used her great wealth to have the architect Mustafa Ağa rebuild the imperial mosque on the Golden Horn that had been begun in 1597 by the *valide sultan* Safiye, mother of Mehmet III. The *külliye* that she commissioned included, besides the mosque, a hospital, *medrese*, mausoleum, public bath, two fountains and a huge market-hall known as the Egyptian Market, also called the Spice Bazaar. The complex came to be called Yeni Cami, the New Mosque, or, more formally, the New Mosque of the Valide Sultan. The new mosque was formally dedicated on 6 November 1663 by Turhan Sultan, with her son Mehmet IV and all of his court in attendance.

Fazıl Ahmet Pasha launched a campaign against the Habsburgs early in 1663, with Sultan Mehmet himself leading the vanguard of the army out of Istanbul. But Mehmet went only as far as Edirne, where he spent the summer hunting while the grand vezir led the army on campaign. That summer, according to Rycaut, the sultan fell in love with 'one Asan Aga, a sprightly youth of his Saraglio, a Polonian by Nation', taking 'an affection to him, so sudden and violent, as might be judged neither well founded, nor long durable. . .' The vezirs eventually persuaded Mehmet to give up Asan Ağa, whereupon 'the Sultan, the violence of whose love being with time moderated and abated . . . cast off his Favourite, creating him a Kapugibashee, or Chief Porter, with a hundred and fifty Aspers a day salary.'

Mehmet had by now set up his own harem, which he took with him in his peregrinations between Topkapı Sarayı and Edirne Sarayı. His favourite was Rabia Gülnüş Ümmetüllah, a Greek girl from Rethymnon in Crete, captured when she was a child at the beginning of the Turkish invasion of the island. While the court was in Edirne, Gülnüş bore Mehmet a son, the future Mustafa II, born on 5 June 1664. Mustafa was the first male in the imperial Osmanlı line to be born in twenty years, and his birth was the occasion of week-long celebrations in both Edirne and Istanbul. Mehmet's delight in his infant son led him to lavish affection on his *haseki* Gülnüş, as Rycaut writes:

In the mean time the Grand Signior, though he continued his Sports and Hunting, without regard to the violent heats of the Summer, yet he began to entertain something more of warm affection toward his Women, and to be reconciled to that Sex, in contemplation of his little Son, who beginning now to play and prattle, afforded him matter of entertainment in the Apartments of his Women; so that he affectionately doting on his Queen, gave order for increase of her Revenue and Attendance, and appointed the best artisans of Adrianople to make her a Crown studded with very precious stones to adorn her Head . . .

Mehmet's surviving younger brothers Selim, Ahmet and Süleyman had been incarcerated in the Cage at Topkapı Sarayı since their father Ibrahim's death. After the birth of his son, Mehmet wanted to invoke the Ottoman code of fratricide to do away with his brothers, but his mother Turhan took them under her protection even though they were not her own sons. She watched over the captive princes constantly, and when Mehmet summoned her to Edirne she took them with her for fear that they would be executed in her absence. Despite her precautions Mehmet managed to do away with Selim, the eldest of the three brothers, but the others survived.

Mehmet stayed on at Edirne Sarayı as long as he could, for his hatred of Istanbul and Topkapı Sarayı was so intense as to be an obsession, as Rycaut observes:

The Grand Signior continued all this time at Adrianople taken up with an extraordinary delight and pleasure in his Court there, with which his aversion to Constantinople so much increased, that he could not endure so much as the name of the place: and if accidentally in his Hunting (as is reported) he chanced to fall into the road which led thither, and remembring himself thereof, would immediately turn thence, as one that corrects himself of some desperate error, or avoids a path which tends to an inevitable destruction.

Mehmet decided to return from Edirne to Istanbul late in the summer of 1665, but before he reached the city a large part of the harem of Topkapı Sarayı was destroyed by fire. Repair work began immediately and the harem was ready for occupancy again within a few months. Meanwhile Mehmet had been living outside the walls of Istanbul in the palace of Davut Pasha, from where he occasionally rode into the city to check on the restoration of Topkapı Sarayı. But he chose not to spend even a single night in the imperial palace, because of the fearful memories of his childhood that were there evoked.

Mehmet spent the summer of 1673 at a small palace he had built north of Edirne, where he enjoyed some weeks in dalliance with a new favourite. Mehmet put his new *haseki* aside, at least temporarily, when on the last day of 1673 Gülnüş gave birth to another son, the future Sultan Ahmet III. The birth of Prince Ahmet and the subsequent celebrations are described in the diary of Dr Covel, who was chaplain to the English embassy in Pera in the years 1669–77:

It happen'd the Sultana [Gülnüş] was delivr'd of a second son this last Ramas [Ramazan], Decemb. 1673. The mirth was put off to the Biram, and then it was doubled; all were mad for 3 nights and three dayes, every shop open and drest up with laurell flowers, etc, many candle machines with pretty figures, puppet playes, dancing, etc.; the Janisary's chambers was the finest sight.

Dr Covel's diary entry for 17 July 1674 mentions Sultan Mehmet's passion for a beautiful prostitute who was in the employ of the infamous Sultana Sporca. Covel tells of how the captain of the grand vezir's guards also fell in love with the girl, whom he carried off and shared in a series of orgies. Sultana Sporca was beside herself and appealed to the sultan, who had the captain strangled and then took the girl into his harem.

Mehmet eventually fathered a total of eleven children, comprising four sons and seven daughters. His known concubines include five women besides Gülnüş, who always remained his favourite, though

*Selim II, enthroned, receives the greetings
of his pashas*

in 1675 he elevated a Polish concubine to the status of *haseki* after
she presented him with a son.

Rycaut notes that in the spring of 1675 Mehmet put aside all
other activities to celebrate a series of festivals, starting with
the circumcision of his son Mustafa, which lasted for eleven
days. A prominent feature of these festivals were the *nahils*, huge
decorations of various forms that were carried in procession, as
Rycaut writes:

*On this day the Grand Signior, with the young Prince his Son, went
to their Tents, which were pitched very sumptuously in the Plain
near the City, and indeed were very truly stately and magnificent;
all the great men, such as the Vizier, Mufti and others, having their
Pavilions erected; amongst which was raised a very stately Throne,
with a Canopy of Cloth of Gold, extended under the shady leaves
of two tall Elms, which, set off with many Lamps, in the Night
represented a very pleasant and glorious Scene ... Opposite to the
Tents were several poles fixed, between which at Night were hung
Lamps of several shapes, which being varied every Night made a
very pleasing and magnificent Object; by light of which in the
Evening were exercised several tricks of Activity, as Wrestling,
Dancing, and Singing, and sometimes were acted Turkish Comedies,
which consist only of Farces, and some ridiculous Dialogues, and
at last the divertisements of the night concluded with Fire-Works,
which were so many, that (as reported) 240 men were employed for
four months time in the making of them, and yet there are better
made in Christendome; only one seemed to exceed the rest, being
a sort of Rocket, which went up very high, without any tail of fire,
like the common ones, carrying only a small compacted Globe of
red fire like a Star, and making no noise in mounting, but raised to
its height breaks. These were the pastimes of the Night; in the day
all the several Arts and Trades, some one day and some another,
passed before the Tents, every one offering their Presents, as they
passed, representing by some kind of Pageant and Procession their
diversities of trade; this continued for fifteen days. On the 25th of
this instant May, was a solemn Cavalcade, in which marched the
Janisaries with all their chief Officers, Chiauses, and Mutafaracas,
etc. And of the Great Men, the Vizier, Mufti and Kul-ogli [Sarıkçı
Pasha], the first on the right hand and the second in the middle;
after them followed the young Prince who was to be circumcised,
extraordinary rich in the Furniture of his Horse, and the number
and largeness of the Diamonds, which were on his Tulbant and
Breast. In this Cavalcade were carried four small Nachils, and two
large ones, as high as the Mast of a Ship, which were carried by a*

hundred Slaves, and set before the Seraglio, which are in the form of triumphant Pyramids, adorned with Tinsils in thirteen Divisions . . .

On the 27th, being the day of Mahomet's Birth, the Grand Signior rode publickly to the Mosch of Sultan Selim, having no other attendance than the Retinue of his own Court, his Pages were very rich in Cloth of Gold, each carrying a Feather studded with a rich Jewel on his Head; after the Grand Signior rode the young Prince, who that Night was circumcised. During this Festival, a vast number of people was fed at the charge of the Grand Signior, and about two thousand circumcised, every one of which had a Quilt given him, with a small pay of three Aspers a day for his Life.

Dr Covel watched the procession to the mosque of Selim I, and in his account he gives a description of the sultan as he rode by:

He is a very swarthy man, his face shining, and pretty full eyes, black and sparkling; his nose something long, and beetled at the end, a full roundish high forehead, a severe brow, his beard black, very thin, and not very long . . . He hath a great deal of Majesty in his countenance, and terror, too, when he please to put it on. He hath been very lean and sickly (3 or 4 yeares since), but now he is exceedingly plump and hearty . . .

Another festival began two weeks after the circumcision, when Mehmet married off his daughter Hadice to Sarıkçı Pasha, one of his *musahibs*. Hadice was still too young for the marriage to be consummated, as Rycaut notes in describing the final days of the festivities, which lasted for two weeks:

These Presents being thus performed on the part of the Bridegroom to his Bride, the next Presents concerned the Grand Signior to his Daughter, which were in place of her Dowry according to the custom of the Eastern Countries: wherefore the 19th of this month the Presents were ushered with a most solemn Cavalcade of all the Grandees of the Court to the House of the Bridegroom, which were two Gardens made of Sugar, forty little Nachils, eighty six Mules

Mehmet IV, the Hunter, 1648–87

laden with Household-stuff, ten men with her Dressings, as Boots, Shoes, etc. embroidered with Pearl as the former; then were carried her Jewels set in Girdles, Bracelets, etc. promiscuously together, not in that rule as those which were sent her by her bridegroom. The Household-stuff was made up with coverts, yet however some parts were left open on the sides, to shew that the Cushions were embroidered with Pearl, and others were of Velvet embroidered with Gold. At last came twelve Coaches with Slaves and thirty six black Eunuchs. The 23d the Bride was conducted to her Bridegrooms Palace with a solemn Cavalcade, with two great Nachils of the same form and bigness as those carried at the Cavalcade of the Prince, with two smaller ones of Silver. The Bride was seated in a handsom Coach drawn with six Horses, and covered with Plates of Silver, and the sides adorned with long Streamers of Tinsel: before which went the Kuzlir Aga or chief black Eunuch of the Women: after followed four Coaches with six Horses apiece, and twenty one more with four horses, each carrying two Eunuchs: then at some distance

Procession to the Imperial Gate

off came the Hasakee or Queen-Mother to the Bride in a Coach all covered with Plates of Silver, and attended with ten other Coaches more: the night following the Bride was conducted to the Nuptial Chamber in ceremony only, she being not yet ripe for consummation of Marriage: all of which Solemnity was attended at the Bridegrooms Court, with the same Sports and Fire-works which were made at the Tents, with an addition of dancing on the Ropes, and sliding down a Rope fastened to the top of the Steeple of the Mosch of Sultan Selim, which had like to have proved fatal to one who came down with a Boy at his back; for when he was about twenty yards from the ground, the Rope broke, but falling on a tree first and then on a man, he was taken up with little hurt. The most remarkable of all these Shows, was a man that walked up a Rope as high as the second Balcony of the Menareh or Steeple of Sultan Selim, which is as high as commonly our Spire-Steeples are in England: And another hanging on a Rope with his hands, with his body extended, turned himself twelve times round with his hands: at all which Sights the Grand Signior was a constant Spectator. In this manner these Solemnities ended, the Mosayp or Favourite rich in the esteem of his Prince, and in high honour with all, had yet some allay to attemper and moderate his joy; for the Princess not yet fit for consummation, in case she dyed before that time, all her Jewels and Goods must return to the Grand Signior, notwithstanding which he would be obliged to pay her Dowry, which was said to be the Sum of two years Revenue of Grand Cairo; but let that be what it will, he will be insolvent, being, as reported, three hundred Purses already in debt.

Mehmet continued to abide mostly at Edirne Sarayı until 1676, when he suddenly announced his intention to set up his court again at Topkapı Sarayı. But when Mehmet approached Istanbul he stayed first at the palace of Davut Pasha outside the walls, from where he made visits to several palaces along the Bosphorus. All the while he obsessively avoided Topkapı Sarayı, his old aversion to the harem preventing him from spending even a single night in the dreaded labyrinth of his youthful nightmares.

The *valide sultan* Hadice Turhan died in 1682, aged fifty-five, having outlived her husband Ibrahim by thirty-four years. Sultan Mehmet led the mourners in carrying her remains to the great *türbe* she had erected behind Yeni Cami, her imperial mosque complex beside the Golden Horn. The French traveller Grelot, writing of Turhan Sultan just two years before her death, says that she was one of the 'greatest and most brilliant (spirituelle) ladies who ever entered the Saray', and that it was fitting that 'she should leave to posterity a jewel of Ottoman architecture to serve as an eternal monument to her generous enterprises.'

The following year the grand vezir Merzifonlu Kara Mustafa Pasha persuaded the sultan to mount a powerful expedition against Vienna, saying that when the Austrian capital fell to the Turks 'all the Christians would obey the Ottomans.' The Ottoman attempt to capture Vienna failed disastrously, and after a two-month siege

*Yeni Cami, the New Mosque of the Valide Sultan, founded
by Hadice Sultan*

in the summer of 1683 the defeated Turkish army fled in disorder,
with Mustafa Pasha leading the way. The grand vezir led the remnants of his army back to Belgrade, where he was beheaded by the
sultan.

The Ottoman defeat encouraged the Christian powers of Europe
to form a Holy League for another crusade against the Turks.
Emissaries from Austria, Poland and Venice met in March 1684,
with the support of Pope Innocent XI, and the following year they
invaded the Ottoman dominions on several fronts, beginning a war
that would last for thirty years. A series of Ottoman reverses led to
fears that Istanbul itself would come under attack. This caused the
ulema and the populace of the city to demand the overthrow of
the sultan, who seemed oblivious to all in his endless hunting
expeditions.

The *mufti* Mehmet Efendi warned the sultan that if he did not give up hunting and concentrate on state affairs his throne would be in jeopardy. Mehmet heeded this warning and gave up the chase for a month, but the unhappiness and sleepless nights that this brought on led him to resume his hunting. Then, early in November 1687, the troops in Istanbul revolted and were joined by many of the populace in taking control of the city. The rebels thereupon assembled in Haghia Sophia and demanded that the sultan be overthrown and replaced by his brother, Prince Süleyman, who was much admired for his piety.

At that moment word came that Sultan Mehmet had sent some of his chamberlains to kill his brothers, the princes Süleyman and Ahmet, so they could not replace him on the throne. But the *bostancı-başı*, the head of the palace guards, was informed of this and put a strong guard around the Cage in Topkapı Sarayı to protect the two princes. The mob in Haghia Sophia then renewed their demand for the overthrow of Sultan Mehmet. They would have had him executed too were it not for the calming influence of Köprülü Mustafa Pasha, who persuaded them to send delegates to the sultan with a demand that he abdicate his throne in favour of his brother Süleyman.

The sultan was at first reluctant to admit that he was finished, but the delegates told him plainly that if he did not abdicate of his own accord the rebels would depose him by force. Mehmet then finally gave in, saying 'since I see the divine indignation, raised by the sins of the Musulmans, discharged on my head, go and tell my brother, that God's decree is declared by the mouth of the people, and he is appointed governor of the Ottoman Empire.'

Mehmet IV was deposed on 8 November 1687, after which he was led away to the Cage, where his brothers Süleyman and Ahmet had been imprisoned throughout his reign, except for occasional excursions to Edirne. Mehmet spent the remaining five years of his life imprisoned in the Kafes, never again to enjoy the pleasures of the hunt that had been the joy of his life since his early youth. The royal chase was over, the hunter was caged.

Chapter 11

A CAGE FOR PRINCES

When Mehmet IV was deposed, after a reign of thirty-nine years, his eldest son Mustafa was twenty-three years old, and in earlier centuries would have inherited the throne as the eldest son of the departed sultan. But after some discussion he was passed over in favour of Mehmet's brother Süleyman, in keeping with the principle of seniority that had now been in use for seventy years. Thereupon Mustafa and his younger brother Ahmet were imprisoned in the Cage along with their father, while their uncle emerged from the same prison to take the throne as Süleyman II.

Süleyman's younger brother Ahmet remained in the Cage. Never before had it enclosed so many royal captives, housing one deposed sultan and three princes. But by now their imprisonment was more humane than it had been in the past, particularly when the captives were brought to Edirne Sarayı, where the Cage was less of a prison than it was in Topkapı Sarayı.

Süleyman II had been a prisoner in the Cage for thirty-nine years, during which time he had learned calligraphy, spending his days copying out Kurans and praying. When the *bostancıbaşı* came to release him from the Cage Süleyman thought that he was going to be executed by his brother, and his first words were, according to Cantemir, 'Why, in the name of the immortal God, do you endeavour to disturb my tranquility? Suffer me, I entreat you, to pass in peace, in my cell, the few days I have to live, and let my brother rule the

Othman Empire; for he was born to rule, but I to the study of eternal life.' To which the *bostancıbaşı* responded, according to Cantemir: ' "You must give way, most resplendent Emperor, to the entreaties and wishes of the Musulman people": and with these words forces him, as it were, out of the chamber, and leads him to the throne.'

Süleyman was midway through his forty-sixth year when he came to the throne, having known no life other than the Cage, except for occasional trips that he and his brother Ahmet had made with the late Hadice Turhan. Süleyman had not been allowed to have concubines while he was in the Cage, and in fact he showed no interest in women after his release, being of a contemplative spirit and exceedingly religious. Thus for the first time in the history of the Ottoman Empire there was a sultan without his own harem. Süleyman's mother Saliha Dilaşub became *valide sultan* on his accession, but when she died two years later the feminine hierarchy in the harem was without a head. The former *haseki*, Rabia Gülnüş Ümmetüllah, mother of the captive princes Mustafa and Ahmet, had been relegated to the Old Palace on the Third Hill, and so the harem of Topkapı Sarayı was virtually uninhabited, except for some women slaves and the black eunuchs who guarded them.

Süleyman's first official act as sultan was the reappointment of Siyavuş Pasha as grand vezir. Siyavuş was immediately confronted by the commanders of the Janissaries, who demanded the payment for their troops that was customary on the accession of a new sultan. The grand vezir was unable to pay the *bakşis*, since he had just inspected the imperial treasury and found it to be empty. The Janissaries, urged on by the *ulema*, the leaders of the religious hierarchy, then marched on the palace of the grand vezir. Siyavuş and his officers fought to the last man against the Janissaries, who cut the grand vezir's body into pieces and threw his remains out of the palace windows. Cantemir describes the events that followed:

After this, excited by a rage unheard of among the Turks, they break into the women's apartment, and, cutting the noses, hands and feet of the Vizir's wife and sister, drag them naked through the streets, and commit other execrable crimes upon the slaves and female-servants. The Vizir's family being destroyed, they rove, like ravenous wolves, through the city, and kill and plunder all they meet, as if partners with the Vizir in his guilt. A dreadful face of things appears, and the whole city would have been ruined, if the Ulema, first authors of the tumult, had not composed it: for they perseiving the danger, immediately assemble at the imperial palace, and there display Mahomet's Sancaki Sherif *[the sacred standard of the Prophet], and, by the cryers, proclaim that all Musulmans, who would not be esteemed infidels, should meet under that standard. The citizens and inhabitants of Constantinople first hasten thither; and insist then the Janizaries, that they might not appear rebels, and regardless of the standard of their prophet, lay down their arms, and submit to it, crying out, they had armed, not against the Sultan, but his perfidious enemy, the Vizir, whom they had punished; and therefore they were now ready to do whatever the Sultan should think proper, since they had given him power of life and death over them.*

The Janissaries revolted again the following year, running amok through the city once more. Süleyman took charge himself to call a meeting of the notables of the city on 1 March 1688, persuading them to form their own defence force. The sultan took personal command of this force, which included retired Janissaries who had become merchants and artisans, and soon they put down the insurrection, slaughtering all the rebels who did not flee from the city.

Despite this, the populace had by now become disillusioned with the new sultan, who was proving to be as incompetent as his predecessor. This growing discontent frightened Süleyman, who decided to move his court from Istanbul to Edirne, hoping to find a haven there. But when he gave orders for the move he was told by his equerry that there were not enough animals in the palace stables to transport the whole court, and his *defterdar*, or treasurer, said that there was no money to buy any more horses. Cantemir writes:

*The sultan, escorted by Janissaries, in procession from
the Imperial Gate of Topkapı Sarayı*

*Soliman commands the gold and silver vessels and jewels to be sold
in the public market, and with the money his necessities to be
supplied. Thus with difficulties he departs from Constantinople
upon hired horses and chariots, and by this means prevents the
sedition just ready to break out.*

Süleyman passed away in Edirne on 22 June 1691, succumbing
to what Cantemir refers to as 'an inveterate dropsy'. The deceased

sultan's body was packed in ice and carried to Istanbul, where he was buried at the Süleymaniye in the *türbe* of his renowned namesake Süleyman I. Cantemir concludes his chapter on the reign of Süleyman II with a judgement on the character of the departed sultan, whose only memorable virtue was apparently his sanctity:

Soliman was ... of a gross body, low stature, a pale and bloated face, with eyes like those of an ox, a black oblong beard, with a mixture of grey hairs, of a heavy understanding, and easily moved by the whispers of his chamberlains ... But none among the Turkish Sultans was more eminent for sanctity, devotion, and observation of the law.

Süleyman was succeeded by his younger brother, who was raised to the throne as Ahmet II, the third son of Ibrahim to become sultan. The new sultan was girded with the sword of Osman at Edirne Sarayı rather than at the mosque of Eyüp in Istanbul.

Ahmet was forty-eight years old when he became sultan and had been a virtual prisoner in the Cage since the age of five. His mother Hadice Muazzez had died four years before, and so there was no *valide sultan* during his reign. Ahmet had not been allowed to have concubines during his confinement in the Cage, but as soon as he became sultan he chose at least two women for his harem, Rabia and Sayeste, and probably others as well, though their names are not known.

Rabia, the sultan's *haseki*, gave birth on 10 July 1692 to two boys, Ibrahim and Selim, the first twins to be born in the Osmanlı dynasty. Cantemir writes of their birth and the ensuing celebration, known as the Donanma:

... in the year 1104 [1692] the Sultan, at Constantinople, has twin sons born to him, namely Selim and Ibrahim. As this had never happened to any Sultan before, the Turks, considering it as a presage for their future success, devote eight whole days throughout the Empire to rejoicings, every day and night celebrating the Donanma, and other sports usual upon such occasions.

Prince Selim died on 15 May 1693, while his brother Ibrahim lived until 1714. Sultan Ahmet also fathered three daughters by other women in his harem, but they all seem to have died in infancy.

Meanwhile the deposed Sultan Mehmet IV died in the Cage of Edirne Sarayı on 6 January 1693, the cause of his death being given by various chroniclers as gout, depression or poison. He was four days past his fifty-first birthday when he died. His body was brought back from Edirne to Istanbul for burial, and he was laid to rest in the *türbe* of his mother Hadice Turhan behind Yeni Cami.

Ahmet II himself passed away in Edirne Sarayı on 6 February 1695, the cause of his death given variously as dropsy, depression or apoplexy. He died nineteen days before his fifty-second birthday, having ruled a little over three and a half years. His body was brought back to Istanbul for burial at the Süleymaniye in the *türbe* of Süleyman the Magnificent, where he was laid to rest beside his brother Süleyman II. Cantemir concludes his chapter on the reign of Ahmet II with his usual characterization of the departed sultan:

In his temper and disposition, he entirely resembled his brother Soliman, but of a little more lively, though not acute genius. He listened to the calumnies of his domestic officers, and upon their instigation, for slight causes often changed the most important affairs. He affected to appear a lover of justice, though by reason of his stupidity, he could not perfectly discharge the function of a judge, and believed every thing that his friends, bribed by the contending parties, represented to him.

He had large black eyes, a pale complexion, a round beard, inclining to red, with a mixture of black, a strait and long nose, a middle stature, a prominent belly, occasioned by the dropsy rather than fat. With respect to devotion and Mahomet's law, he is said to have been a little inferior to his brother Soliman.

The heir apparent was Prince Mustafa, the eldest son of Mehmet IV, but the grand vezir Şam Tarabolus Ali Pasha tried to supplant him with Prince Ibrahim, the infant son of Ahmet II. Nezir Ağa,

left: *Süleyman II (1687–91)*; middle: *Ahmet II (1691–5)*;
right: *Mustafa II (1695–1703)*

the chief treasurer, stole a march on the grand vezir by releasing
Mustafa from the Cage and having him acclaimed as sultan.

The new sultan ascended the throne as Mustafa II, the girding
ceremony again being conducted at Edirne Sarayı. Mustafa was
nearly thirty-one when he became sultan, having spent the previous
seven years confined in the Cage. Prior to that he had lived mostly
in Edirne Sarayı, where in the liberal atmosphere of his father's
court he and his brother Ahmet had been much more exposed to
the outer world than had the princes who were raised in Topkapı
Sarayı. His mother, Rabia Gülnüş Ümmetüllah, had been confined
to the Old Palace in Istanbul since the deposition of her husband
Mehmet IV, and Mustafa now sent for her to join him at Edirne
Sarayı, where she took her place as *valide sultan*.

The new sultan began his reign with the noblest of intentions,
issuing a *hatti şerif*, or imperial rescript, in which he announced his
intention of ridding the government of its corrupt practices and of

renouncing the pleasures of the harem to lead his army in person against the infidels who threatened the empire. As he declared:

Henceforth voluptuousness, idle pastime, and sloth are banished from this court ... I therefore have resolved, with the help of the lord, to take a signal revenge upon the unbelievers, that brood of hell; and I will myself begin the holy war against them.

After all preparations were complete, Mustafa commanded the grand vezir Şam Tarabolus Ali Pasha to muster the army in Edirne. When the sultan inspected the artillery he found that the carriages of the large cannon had not been properly made, for which he blamed the grand vezir and had him put to death. But Cantemir says that the real reason for Ali Pasha's execution was that 'he had endeavoured to raise young Ibrahim to the throne, to the exclusion of Mustafa.'

Mustafa then appointed Elmas Mehmet Pasha as grand vezir. But the real power behind the throne was Mustafa's long-time tutor, Feyzullah Efendi, whom he appointed as *şeyhülislam*.

Mustafa set off on his first campaign in June of 1695, and after capturing two fortresses he defeated the Habsburgs in a particularly bloody battle in which the Turks lost many more men than their enemy. He then returned in triumph to Edirne, where he was acclaimed as Gazi, a title in which he took great pride for the rest of his days.

Among the captives brought back to Edirne was a beautiful young German woman named Anna Sophia von Wippach. Anna was taken captive along with her infant son Heinrich, and after being brought to Edirne she was given to Sultan Mustafa as his concubine. Neither Anna nor her son was ever heard from again after she entered the sultan's harem, though they may have assumed new identities with Turkish names.

The names of six other concubines of Mustafa are known, the most notable being those who subsequently became *valide sultans* when their sons in turn succeeded to the throne. Mustafa's first son, the future Mahmut I, was born on 2 September 1696 to Saliha, a slave girl of unknown origin. His second son, the future Osman III, was born on 2 January 1699 to Şehsuvar, a concubine of Russian parentage. Hafise, Mustafa's last favourite, bore him five sons, including a set of twins, all of whom died in infancy, and she also had a daughter, the only one of her children to survive. Mustafa fathered a total of twenty children, ten boys and ten girls, all born within a span of seven years, fourteen of them dying in infancy. Mahmut and Osman lived to become sultan in turn, while all of the surviving girls were married off to pashas, Princess Emine being wed four times in succession before she died at the age of thirty-two, having outlived all of her husbands.

Meanwhile, Mustafa's younger brother Ahmet continued to live in the Cage at Topkapı Sarayı, though he seems to have been confined in Edirne Sarayı whenever the sultan moved to Edirne or went off on campaign. Confined along with Ahmet was his young cousin Ibrahim, son of Ahmet II. Cantemir notes that Sultan Mustafa was particularly fond of Prince Ibrahim and always took the boy with him on his journeys between Istanbul and Edirne.

Early in the summer of 1697 Mustafa led a huge army from Belgrade on another campaign against the Habsburgs. But this time he had the ill fortune to encounter an army led by Prince Eugene of Savoy, the greatest general of his day, who routed the Ottomans in a battle near Temesvar. Some 30,000 Turkish soldiers were killed, including the grand vezir Elmas Mehmet Pasha, and the sultan escaped only by fleeing from the battlefield in disguise. The peace treaties after this war acknowledged the Ottoman loss of vast territories in the Balkans, representing the end of the 'Turkish menace' that had terrified Christian Europe for two and a half centuries.

Sultan Mustafa took refuge in Edirne Sarayı, where he hunted in the surrounding countryside as he had done as a youth with his father, remote from the increasing discontent of the army and people with his disastrous rule.

Late in the summer of 1703 a revolt broke out in Istanbul among the *cebecis*, or armourers, who were soon joined by the Janissaries and many of the poorer townspeople. When news of the insurrection reached Mustafa in Edirne, he sent his secretary to Istanbul to deal with the dissidents. But the rebels beat the secretary brutally and sent him away, after which some fifty thousand of them assembled in the Hippodrome and prepared to march on Edirne. When Mustafa learned of this he sent an army under the grand vezir Rahmi Mehmet Pasha to put down the rebels. When the two forces met, midway between Istanbul and Edirne, the rebels persuaded the soldiers to make common cause with them, whereupon the grand vezir fled for his life and went into hiding in Istanbul. Meanwhile the rebels, joined by the army, marched on to Edirne, where they demanded that the sultan deliver up to them a number of his ministers and advisors, most notably Feyzullah Efendi. Mustafa had no choice but to give in to their demands, and soon afterwards the rebels tortured Feyzullah to death and then flung his body into the river, as Cantemir writes, 'as if he had been an infidel, and unworthy of burial'.

Mustafa then confirmed the leaders chosen by the rebels, appointing Dorocan Ahmet Pasha as grand vezir to replace Rahmi Mehmet Pasha, whom he promised to give up to the rebels as soon as he was found. But this did not satisfy the rebels, who now decided to depose Mustafa in favour of his imprisoned brother Ahmet. When Mustafa learned of this he was undecided as to what he should do, abdicate or kill his brother, as his ministers advised. But Mustafa could not bring himself to order the execution of his brother, and so he decided to abdicate and 'commit himself to the divine Providence', as Cantemir writes. Prince Ahmet was at that time confined in the Cage at Edirne Sarayı. Cantemir writes of how the sultan went to his brother to tell him that he had now succeeded to the throne, after which Mustafa exchanged places in the Cage with Ahmet:

He [Mustafa] goes therefore to his brother, and, embracing him with great affection, informs him that he was universally desired to fill the throne, and first salutes him Sultan. At his departure, he speaks to him as follows: 'Remember, brother, that while I was on

*the throne, you enjoyed the utmost liberty; I desire you will allow
me the same. Moreover, think that you justly indeed ascend this
throne, as having been possessed by your father and brother; but
that the instruments of your advancement are treacherous rebels,
whom, if you suffer to escape with impunity, they will quickly treat
you as they do me at present.'*

Mustafa was deposed in Edirne on 22 September 1703, and on
that same day his brother succeeded him as Ahmet III. Mustafa
was taken to Istanbul and confined in the Cage at Topkapı Sarayı,
where he died on 29 December of that same year. His death was
attributed to dropsy, but there were rumours that he had been
poisoned. The day after his death Mustafa was buried beside his
father Mehmet IV in the *türbe* of Yeni Cami.

Two of Mustafa's sons survived him, the future sultans Mahmut
I and Osman III, both of whom were consigned to the Cage in
Topkapı Sarayı by their uncle Ahmet III. Cantemir, curiously, seems
to have been unaware that these princes were still alive, for in
concluding his chapter on the reign of Mustafa II he remarks that
the deposed sultan had no sons still living when he passed away:

*He was happier in the first years of his Empire than in the latter.
He had greater advantages from nature than both his predecessors;
for he was of a mature judgment, great application and sobriety;
neither prodigal nor avaritious in collecting and distributing the
publick monies; just, a good archer and horseman, and very devout
in his religion . . . He was of a moderate size, his face round, and
beautified with red and white; his eyes blue, and his eye-brows thin
and yellow. In the spring he used to have spots break out in his face,
which disappeared again in the winter. He left no son alive, though
he had been father of several. He was particularly fond of Ibrahim,
son of his uncle Ahmed, whom he always carried with him, and
was said to design for his successor, in case he died without issue.*

Ibrahim was also confined to the Cage, where he died on 4 May
1714. Cantemir notes Ibrahim's passing in a footnote at the end of

his chapter on the reign of Mustafa II: 'He was a hopeful; and good-natured Prince. After I left Constantinople, I heard that he died there.'

Mustafa was survived by three of his wives: Saliha, mother of Mahmut I; Şehsuvar, mother of Osman III; and Hafise, the departed sultan's last favourite. Saliha and Şehsuvar were relegated to the Old Palace after Mustafa's death, while Hafise was married off to Ebubekir Efendi, the aged secretary of state, one of the rare instances in which the wife of a departed sultan was allowed to wed anyone after her master died. Hafise bitterly opposed the marriage, as she told Lady Mary Wortley Montagu, wife of the English ambassador Edward Wortley Montagu, who arrived in Istanbul in 1717. Lady Mary writes of Hafise in a letter to a friend in England dated 10 March 1718:

I went to see the Sultana Hafise, favourite of the last Emperor Mustafa, who, you know (or perhaps you don't know) was deposed by his brother, the reigning Sultan, and died a few weeks later, after being poisoned, as it was generally believed. The lady was immediately after his death saluted with an absolute order to leave the Seraglio and choose herself a husband from among the great men at the Porte . . . She threw herself at the Sultan's feet and begged him to poniard her rather than to use his brother's widow with that contempt. She represented to him in agonies of sorrow that she was privileged from this misfortune by having brought five princes into the Ottoman family, but all the boys being dead and only one girl surviving, this excuse was not received and she was compelled to make the choice. She chose Ebubekir Efendi, then secretary of state, and above fourscore years old, to convince the world that she firmly intended to keep the vow she had made of never suffering a second husband to approach her bed, and since she must honour some subject so far as to be called his wife she would choose him as a mark of her gratitude, since it was he who had presented her at the age of ten years old to meet her lost lord. But she has never permitted him to pay her one visit, though it is now fifteen years since she has

*been in his house, where she passes her time in uninterrupted
mourning with a constancy very little known in Christendom,
especially in a widow of twenty-one, for she is now but thirty-
six.*

Lady Mary goes on to tell of how Hafise talked about life in the
harem of Mustafa II, for whom she still mourned:

*The Sultana seemed in very good humor, and talked to me with the
utmost civility. I did not omit this opportunity of learning all that
I possibly could of the Seraglio, which is so entirely unknown
among us. She assured me that the story of the Sultan's throwing a
handkerchief is altogether fabulous, and the manner upon that
occasion no other but that he sends the Kuzlair Aga to signify to
the lady the honour he intends her. She is immediately complimented
upon it by the others, and led to the bath where she is perfumed
and dressed in the most magnificent and becoming manner. The
Emperor precedes his visit by a royal present and then comes into
her apartment. Neither is there any such thing as her creeping in at
the bed's feet. She said that the first he made choice of was always
after the first in rank, and not the mother of the eldest son, as other
writers would make us believe. Sometimes the Sultan diverts himself
in the company of all his ladies, who stand in a circle round him,
and she confessed that they were ready to die with jealousy and
envy of the happy she that he had distinguished by any appearance
of preference . . .*

*She never mentioned the Sultan without tears in her eyes, yet she
seemed very fond of the discourse. 'My past happiness,' said she,
'appears a dream to me, yet I cannot forget that I was beloved by
the greatest and most lovely of mankind. I was chosen from all the
rest to make all his campaigns with him. I would not survive him
if I was not passionately fond of the Princess, my daughter, yet all
my tenderness for her was hardly enough to make me preserve my
life when I lost him. I passed a whole twelvemonth without seeing
the light. Time has softened my despair, yet I now pass some days
every week in tears devoted to the memory of my Sultan.' There*

was no affectation in her words. It was easy to see she was in a deep melancholy, though her good humor made her willing to divert me.

Hafise lived on into the middle of the eighteenth century, and when she finally passed away she was laid to rest in the *türbe* of Yeni Cami, next to her beloved husband Mustafa II.

Chapter 12

TULIP TIME

Ahmet III was nearly thirty when he succeeded to the throne. He had spent the previous sixteen years nominally imprisoned in the Cage, both in Topkapı Sarayı and Edirne Sarayı, where his brother Mustafa II apparently allowed him a great deal of freedom. Mustafa and Ahmet had spent their early years in Edirne, where their father Mehmet IV and their Cretan mother Rabia Gülnüş Ümmetüllah had allowed them to join the royal hunts and feasts and other activities of the court, so that they had much more exposure to the outside world than had been the case for royal princes before their time.

Ahmet was girded with the sword of his ancestor Osman Gazi in Edirne Sarayı. He was the last sultan to ascend the throne in Edirne, for during his time the court was moved back to Istanbul and all of his successors went through the ancient ceremony of being girded at the mosque of Eyüp above the Golden Horn.

Ahmet moved his court from Edirne back to Istanbul three weeks after his accession. He found life in Topkapı Sarayı far more restrictive than in Edirne Sarayı, and in a letter to the grand vezir he complained about the rigid rules imposed upon him by the elaborate ceremonials of the Ottoman court: 'If I go up to one of the chambers, forty Privy Chamber pages are lined up; if I put on my trousers, I do not feel the least comfort, so the swordbearer has to dismiss them, keeping only three or four men so that I may be at ease in the small chamber.'

Ahmet would normally have been deprived of women during his years in the Cage, although palace records indicate that he sired a son in 1697, the child dying within two years. Cantemir notes that while Ahmet was still in the Cage, during the reign of his brother Mustafa II, he fell madly in love with a beautiful Circassian girl who worked for his mother, the *valide sultan* Gülnüş. Ahmet was not allowed to take her as his concubine while he was confined in the Cage, which grieved him greatly, and so his mother had the girl married off to the son of her physician Nuh Efendi. But the *valide* told her doctor that the girl must remain inviolate until such time as her son succeeded to the throne, when he would take her into his harem. Then, when Ahmet became sultan his mother said that it would be in violation of imperial custom to bring a married woman into the harem. Ahmet could only agree, so he forced Nuh Efendi's son to divorce the girl, after which he married her off to Baltacı Mehmet, his equerry, who had no objection to his wife being the sultan's mistress. As Cantemir writes of Sultan Ahmet:

He gave his mistress in marriage to this Baltaji Mehemed aga, whom he had already created master of the horse: but not withstanding this, he very frequently went privately to her; and what was very unusual, and never known before, had her often brought with great pomp into the Seraglio . . .

Cantemir goes on to tell of how Ahmet promoted Baltacı Mehmet several times, twice making him grand vezir, according to Cantemir, 'upon account of the Sultan's love for his wife'.

Meanwhile Sultan Ahmet had set up his harem in Topkapı Sarayı, where his mother Gülnüş continued to head the female hierarchy as *valide sultan*. The population of the harem, which had declined during the seventeenth century, increased dramatically during Ahmet's reign. The names of fourteen of his concubines are known, more than any other sultan in the Osmanlı line up to that time. He fathered fifty-two children, twenty-two of them boys and thirty girls, of whom thirty-four died in infancy. His children included three sets of twins, comprising one pair of boys, one of girls, and a

Ahmet III (1703–30), the Tulip King, with one of his sons

boy and girl. Two of his sons eventually succeeded to the throne, the future sultans Mustafa III, born to his concubine Mihrişah on 28 January 1717, and Abdül Hamit I, born on 20 March 1725 to Rabia Şermi. Nine of his daughters were married off to pashas, including several grand vezirs.

A number of structures from the reign of Ahmet III have survived in the palace. The most notable of these is the enchanting little chamber in the harem known as Yemiş Odası, the Fruit Room, because of the painted panels of fruit with which it is decorated. Ahmet had been trained in his youth as a calligrapher, and several of his works decorate the chambers of Topkapı Sarayı. One is over the main doorway of the Pavilion of the Holy Mantle; on the left the inscription reads, 'The king of the world, the illustrious ruler', while on the right it says 'Sultan Ahmet, who follows the Holy Law'.

Ahmet also built the magnificent street-fountain that still bears his name outside the Imperial Gate of Topkapı Sarayı. Ahmet's principal foundation is the imperial mosque in Üsküdar known as Yeni Valide Camii, which he erected in the years 1708–10. This was dedicated to his mother the *valide sultan* Gülnüş, who was buried in an ornate open *türbe* there when she died on 2 November 1715.

During the first thirteen years of his reign Ahmet had a succession of twelve grand vezirs. Then he finally settled on Nevşehirli Ibrahim Pasha, who was appointed grand vezir on 26 August 1717, holding the office for the remainder of Ahmet's reign. Six months prior to his appointment Ibrahim had been married to the sultan's second daughter, Fatma, who was only thirteen at the time, while her husband was fifty-one. The marriage of the little princess and the grand vezir was noted by Lady Mary Wortley Montagu in a letter to Lady Bristol from Adrianople (Edirne) dated 1 April 1717:

The Grand Signior's eldest daughter was married some few days before I came, and upon that Occasion the Turkish ladies display all their magnificence. The bride was conducted to her husband's house in very great Splendour. She is widow of the late Vizier [Kömürcü Ali Pasha] who was killed at Peterwaradin, though that ought rather to be called a contract than a marriage, not having ever lived with him . . . He had the permission of visiting her in the Seraglio and, being one of the handsomest men in the Empire, had very much engaged her affections. When she saw this second Husband, who is at least fifty, she could not forbear bursting into tears. He is a man of merit and the declared favourite of the Sultan, which they call Mosaip, but that is not enough to make him pleasing in the eyes of a girl of thirteen.

Lady Mary then goes on to describe Sultan Ahmet as he appeared on his procession to the mosque for the Friday prayer:

I went yesterday with the French Ambassadress to see the Grand Signior in his passage to the mosque. He was preceded by a numerous

Yeniçeri Ağası, Ağa of the Janissaries

*guard of Janissaries with vast white feathers on their heads, Spahis
and Bostangees, these are the foot and Horse Guard; and the royal
gardeners, which are a very considerable body of men, dressed in
different habits of fine, lively colours that at a distance they appeared
like a parterre of tulips; after them the Aga of the Janissaries in a
robe of purple velvet lined with silver tissue, his horse led by two
slaves richly dressed; next to him the Kuzlair Aga (your ladyship
knows this is the chief guardian of the Seraglio ladies) in a deep
yellow cloth (which suited very well to his black face) lined with
sables; and last His Sublimity himself in green lined with the fur of
a black Muscovite fox, which is supposed worth 1,000 Sterling,
mounted on a fine horse with furniture embroidered with jewels.
Six more horses richly furnished were led after him, and two of his
principal courtiers bore, one his gold and the other his silver coffee
pot, on a staff. Another carried a silver stool on his head for him*

to sit on. It would be too tedious to tell your ladyship the various dresses and turbans (by which their rank is distinguished) but they were all extreme rich and gay to the number of some thousands, that there cannot be seen a more beautiful procession. The Sultan appeared to us a handsome man of about forty [actually forty-three], with a very graceful air but something severe in his countenance, his eyes very full and black. He happened to stop under the window where we stood and (I suppose being told who we were) looked upon us very attentively that we had full leisure to consider him, and the French Ambassadress agreed with me as to his good mien.

Lady Mary, in a letter to the Abbé Conti dated 17 May 1717, writes of her husband's audience at Edirne Sarayı with Ahmet III, who sat enthroned with his son Süleyman near by:

I tell you nothing of the order of Mr. Wortley's entry and his audience. Those things are always the same and have been so often described, I won't trouble you with the repetition. The young Prince [Süleyman], about eleven year old [actually nearly seven], sits near his father when he gives audience. He is a handsome boy, but probably will not immediately succeed the Sultan, there being two sons of Sultan Mustapha (his eldest brother) remaining, the eldest about twenty years old, on whom the hopes of the people are fixed. This reign has been bloody and avaricious. I am apt to believe they are very impatient to see the end of it.

Wortley's predecessor, Robert Sutton, had described Sultan Ahmet in a despatch as 'exceedingly covetous, haughty and ambitious . . . hasty, violent and cruel, but variable and unsteady'.

Prince Süleyman never succeeded to the throne, for he passed away in 1732, the fifteenth of Ahmet's twenty-two sons to predecease their father, most of them dying in childhood. The two sons of Mustafa II referred to by Lady Mary were the future sultans Mahmut I and Osman III, who at the time were confined in the Cage at Topkapı Sarayı.

Ibrahim Pasha, a master of diplomacy, finally brought peace

and stability to the empire. He also managed to pacify the unruly populace of Istanbul by his frequent largesse. The *bailo* Giovanni Emo, in a report written in 1721, remarks on Ibrahim's skills in dealing with both the sultan and the public: 'From the once ferocious attitude of the Sultan he has the art and industry necessary to defend himself. He is also most attentive to cater to the humour of the populace by permitting all that was formerly forbidden, and by scattering benefices with liberality.'

Emo, in another report written in 1721, remarks on the sultan's return from a month's stay in the grand vezir's palace of Neşabat on the Bosphorus. As Emo writes, 'It is not usual to find an Example of a Sultan's being away from the royal Palaces for so long a time.' Ibrahim amused the sultan with fireworks, illuminated floral spectacles, and mock naval battles on the Bosphorus. After this extended stay Ibrahim felt that the palace was no longer his own, so he gave it to Ahmet and had another one built for himself, the palace of Şerafabad at the mouth of the Bosphorus in Üsküdar. By that time Ibrahim had built two more palaces on the Bosphorus, one at Çırağan on the European shore, and the other at Kandilli on the Asian shore, in the valley known as the Sweet Waters of Asia. He also founded a *külliye* near Şehzade Camii comprising a *medrese*, library, *türbe* and *sebil*, or fountain-house.

Ibrahim Pasha sought to broaden the empire's contacts with Western Europe, sending ambassadors to Paris, Vienna, Moscow and Poland. The first Turkish ambassador to Western Europe was Yirmisekiz Çelebi Mehmet Efendi, who was instructed by Ibrahim Pasha 'to visit the fortresses, factories and works of French civilization generally and report on those that might be applicable' in the Ottoman Empire.

Mehmet Efendi returned from Paris with sketches of Fontainebleau, whereupon Ibrahim Pasha commissioned him to build a similar palace for Ahmet III at Kâğıthane, on the upper reaches of the Golden Horn, the valley that came to be known to Europeans as the Sweet Waters of Europe. Ibrahim Pasha called this pleasure dome Sa'adabad, 'The Palace of Eternal Happiness'. The dedication of the palace was celebrated by the court poet Nedim, Ibrahim's 'boon companion', who in the first stanza of his poem bids his love to join him in a journey to Sa'adabad:

Let us give a little comfort to this heart that's wearied so,
Let us visit Sa'adabad, my swaying Cypress, let us go!
Look, there is a swift caique all ready at the pier below,
Let us visit Sa'adabad, my swaying Cypress, let us go! . . .

Emo reported that Ahmet planted flower gardens and thousands of trees in the grounds of Sa'adabad, which were patterned on those of Versailles. One of the two streams that made up the Sweet Waters of Europe was constrained by marble embankments to form a canal three-quarters of a mile in length, flowing through pools and over cascades, its banks lined with villas and pavilions built by more than two hundred of the sultan's courtiers. Each of these buildings was painted a different colour and decorated with symbols of the owner's office, with, for example, a small galley above the gateway of the supervisor of the shipyard, a wooden cannon painted bronze for the chief of artillery, and birds carved on the doorway of the chief falconer. For the dedication ceremonies a thousand bottles of champagne and nine hundred bottles of Burgundy were ordered from France. As Nedim wrote at the time, 'Let us laugh, let us play/ Let us enjoy the delights of the world to the full.'

The *bailo* Emo, writing in February 1723, noted that Sultan Ahmet was celebrating the birth of his fifth son. This would have been Prince Numan, who was actually Ahmet's seventeenth son, twelve other boys having died in infancy before his birth. Ibrahim's wife, the Princess Fatma, was about to become a mother too, and so Ahmet prolonged the festival until she gave birth, bearing a boy, who was called Mehmet. During the summer of that same year Ahmet built another palace for one of his daughters of marriageable age; it is difficult to say which one, since three of his daughters were wed in 1724, one of the bridegrooms being a nephew of Ibrahim Pasha. When Ibrahim was showing Ahmet the rings which the bridegrooms were going to buy for their brides-to-be, the sultan

Revellers along the Sweet Waters of Europe

told him that he had a better selection, which he offered to sell to the grand vezir. This led Emo to remark that 'One hopes that this was the first time the Ruler of so great an Empire has modestly represented a simple Jewellery Merchant.'

Another example of Ahmet's love of gold was noted by the *bailo* Daniele Dolfin. He reports that one of Ahmet's sons presented him a jewelled belt, which he accepted with great pleasure. A few days later the sultan had the belt appraised, and when he learned how expensive it was he had it returned to the jeweller and took the cash instead.

At around the same time Ahmet celebrated the simultaneous circumcision of four of his sons. A thousand other young boys were circumcised at the sultan's expense along with the princes, and tents were erected in the outer gardens of the palace to house the youths and the doctors who performed the operations. After the four

*Ahmet III throwing coins to his pages and sons in
celebration of the circumcision of the princes*

princes were circumcised, there was a ceremony to exhibit what
the nineteenth-century Austrian historian Joseph von Hammer-
Purgstall describes delicately as 'the irrefutable evidences of the
competency of the surgeon, indications which the grand vezir, then
the *mufti* and the viziers covered with heaps of gold'. After all the
circumcisions were done, the princes paraded with the other boys
in a cavalcade accompanied by all of the guilds of the city.

Sultan Ahmet erected the palace of Emnabad on the Bosphorus for
his daughter Fatma, wife of Ibrahim Pasha. The palace is described
by Lady Mary in a letter to the Abbé Conti, dated 19 May 1718,
where she refers to the Bosphorus as 'the Canal', adding a comment
on the contrast between the Western and Eastern attitudes toward
life:

It is situated on one of the most delightful parts of the Canal, with a fine wood on the side of a Hill behind it. The extent of it is prodigious; the guardian assured me there is eight hundred rooms in it. I will not answer for that number since I did not count them, but 'tis certain the number is very large and the whole adorn'd with a profusion of marble, gilding, and the most exquisite painting of fruit and flowers . . . I shall only add that the chamber destined for the Sultan, when he visits his daughter, is wainscoted with mother of pearl fasten'd with emeralds like nails; there are others of mother of pearl and olive wood inlaid, and several of Japan china. The galleries (which are numerous and very large) are adorned with jars of flowers and porcelain dishes of fruit of all sorts, so well done in plaster and coloured in so lively a manner that it has an enchanting effect. The garden is suitable to the house, where arbours, fountains, and walks are thrown together in an agreeable confusion. There is no ornament wanting except that of statues.

Thus you see, sir, these people are not so unpolish'd as we represent them. Tis true their magnificence is of a different taste from ours, and perhaps of a better. I am almost of opinion they have a right notion of life; while they consume it in music, gardens, wine, and delicate eating, while we are tormenting our brains with some scheme of politics or studying some science to which we can never attain, or if we do, cannot persuade people to set that value upon it we do our selves . . . I allow you to laugh at me for the sensual declaration that I would rather be a rich Effendi with all his ignorance, than Sir Isaac Newton with all his knowledge.

Early on in Ahmet's reign he instituted an annual extravaganza to celebrate the blossoming of the tulip, known in Turkish as *lale*. The Ottoman court developed such a passion for this flower – a veritable tulipomania – that the reign of Ahmet III is known as *Lale Devri*, the Tulip Period, and the sultan himself came to be called the Tulip King. Ahmet and Ibrahim Pasha presided over a series of fêtes that climaxed each year with the blossoming of the tulip, celebrated in the three days surrounding the first full moon in April. The principal festival was held in the gardens of the fourth court of Topkapı Sarayı, where rows of shelves were built to hold vases of tulips alternating with tiny lamps of coloured glass and globes containing liquids of various hues. The topmost shelves and the branches of the overhanging trees held caged canaries and nightingales and other singing birds, while the walks in the garden were embowered with floral displays and flanked by kiosks. The sultan sat enthroned in a pavilion erected in the centre of the gallery, where on separate evenings he entertained in turn his courtiers and the women of his harem, while the palace musicians, singers and dancers provided entertainment.

Ahmet created a special post, known as the Master of Flowers, whose rose-crested card bore this imperial declaration:

We command that all gardeners recognize for their chief the bearer of this diploma: that they be in his presence all eyes like the narcissus, all ears like the rose; that they have not ten tongues like the lily; that they transform not the pointed pistil of the tongue into the thorn of the pomegranate, dyeing it in the blood of inconvenient words. Let them be modest, and let them keep, like the rosebud, their lips closed. Let them not speak before their time, like the blue hyacinth, which scatters its perfume before men ask for it. Finally, let them humbly incline themselves before him like the violet, and let them not show themselves recalcitrant.

During the winter months Ahmet and his courtiers enjoyed themselves in parties known as *helva* fêtes, named for the sweet known in the West as Turkish delight, which they were served while being entertained by musical recitals, dancing, poetry readings and performances of *karagöz*, the Turkish shadow puppets. As the court poet Çelebi Zade wrote in one of his couplets: 'Spring has garden lighting/Winter has *helva* feasts.'

The French ambassador Louis de Villeneuve reported to Paris that he managed to see Ibrahim Pasha only once during a period of eight months; whenever he requested an interview he was told that the grand vezir would see him 'after the *fetes*', which unfortunately

The sultan in his pazar caique, *or imperial barge*

'lasted always'. Villeneuve writes of the Tulip King's progress from one of his palaces to another in the celebration of these festivals, his report catching on the wing the exotic splendours of the age:

Sometimes the court appears floating on the waters of the Bosphorus or the Golden Horn, in elegant caiques, covered with silken tents; sometimes it moves forward in a long cavalcade toward one or another of the pleasure palaces. These processions are made especially attractive by the beauty of the horses and the luxury of their caparisons; they progress, with golden or silver harnesses and plumed foreheads, their coverings resplendent with precious stones.

The conspicuous luxury of the imperial court was paid for by exorbitant taxes, which caused such widespread discontent among the sultan's subjects that they eventually rose up in revolt against him. The revolt began on 28 September 1730 under the leadership of an Albanian ex-Janissary named Patrona Halil, who made his living as a dealer in second-hand clothes. Patrona and two of his close companions, Muslu the fruit-vendor and Ali the coffee-seller, led about thirty of his followers into the market quarter in Beyazit and called on the populace to help them in implementing the *şeriat*, the sacred law of Islam, which was being violated by the sultan and the grand vezir in their hedonistic way of life. The mob followed Patrona on a rampage through the city, opening the prisons and freeing the slaves of five galleys, while they sacked many of the shops in town and looted the houses of the wealthy, killing anyone who stood in their way. Some of the villas and gardens at Sa'adabad were destroyed, and the poet Nedim was killed fleeing from the mob. Within two days the rebels gained control of the arsenal and cut off supplies of food and water to Topkapı Sarayı, whereupon they demanded that the sultan surrender to them the grand vezir and other ministers. Ahmet was so terrified he had Ibrahim Pasha strangled, along with the deputy grand vezir and the captain pasha, after which he gave up the dead bodies to the rebels. But the mob was furious that Ibrahim and the others had not been surrendered alive so that they could tear them to pieces, and they demanded that the sultan abdicate. As Emo wrote in his report on the revolt, 'The Sultan believed perhaps that there had been sufficient sacrifice for his safety, but the thirst of a people in revolt is never satisfied with a little blood.'

Ahmet had no choice, and on 1 October 1730 he abdicated in favour of his nephew Mahmut, who had been confined to the Cage since the death of his father Mustafa II. Ahmet then took his nephew's place in the Cage, along with the new sultan's brother Osman and his own six surviving sons, Süleyman, Mehmet, Mustafa, Beyazit, Abdül Hamit and Seyfeddin.

Emo writes that Mahmut made a favourable impression when he appeared at a grated window of the palace to satisfy the mob, and also when the ağa of the Janissaries spoke to him. He also won over the army when he promptly paid the customary *bakşis* of twenty-five piasters to each of the soldiers. Five days after his accession Mahmut rode to and from Eyüp to be girded with the sword of Osman Gazi, and Emo notes that the new sultan left 'in everyone an agreeable idea of his royal appearance and propitious predictions for the future'. Emo does not mention that Mahmut was a hunchback, in Turkish *kanbur*, the name by which he was known to his subjects, a deformity which is evident in his imperial portrait.

Mahmut was thirty-four when he succeeded to the throne, having spent the previous twenty-seven years in the Cage. As soon as he came to the throne his mother Saliha was installed in the harem of Topkapı Sarayı as *valide sultan*, having been relegated to the Eski Saray after the death of her husband, Mustafa II. Mahmut then set up his harem, which eventually included at least six favourites, though he never fathered any children.

Mahmut's position was very precarious in the first weeks after his accession, for the Janissaries and the other rebels under Patrona Halil still controlled the city. Mahmut's popularity increased when he distributed money to the old and indigent. Shops that had been closed because of the general looting were reopened, and the rebels began dispersing.

During the nineteen months after coming to the throne Mustafa appointed a succession of four grand vezirs, none of whom could exert their power over Patrona Halil. Patrona sought no office for himself, and at first he continued to wear the ragged costume of a second-hand-clothing merchant. Later, when he was prevailed upon to don a proper uniform, he still wore his rags beneath with pride. But his mood soon began to change, and his original modesty turned to arrogance and insolence, as he behaved like an independent warlord with his private army of 12,000 Albanians. He demanded that he be appointed as captain pasha and tried to commandeer a palace for his mistress.

Mahmut decided to rid himself of Patrona, and to that end he plotted with his trusted commanders, most notably Canım Hoca Pasha. Mahmut invited Patrona to Topkapı Sarayı on the pretext of appointing him as a pasha of three tails, the highest rank in the Ottoman army. Canım Hoca had hidden four hundred well-armed soldiers in the palace, and when Patrona entered with his lieutenants

Mahmut I (1730–54)

and a guard of twenty-six Albanians they were ambushed and slaughtered to a man. Mahmut and his supporters then began a reign of terror in which they executed some seven thousand Janissaries who had taken part in Patrona's revolt, Emo reporting that 'the Bosphorus was continually covered with Cadavers, agitated at the Pleasure of Winds and Waves.'

Mahmut proved to be a weak and irresolute ruler, dependent on the advice of his mother, the *valide sultan* Saliha, and the chief black eunuch Hacı Beşir Ağa. Hacı Beşir now emerged as the power behind the throne, using the knowledge of statecraft that he had acquired by being at the centre of affairs during the reigns of three sultans.

Another revolt broke out in Istanbul on the morning of 26 March 1731 under the leadership of an Albanian named Kara Ali. Mahmut held a council of war in the palace and unfurled the sacred standard of the Prophet outside the Imperial Gate. The grand vezir then led out a force of Janissaries that quickly dispersed the rebels, killing three or four hundred of them, and by noon the insurrection was over.

Soon afterwards the Princess Fatma, daughter of Ahmet III and widow of Ibrahim Pasha, was implicated in a plot to restore her father to the throne. The plot was aborted and Fatma was confined to the Eski Saray, where she died on 3 January 1733. Ahmet III himself died in the Cage on 11 July 1735, after which he was buried in the *türbe* of Yeni Cami.

These disturbances led Mahmut to take severe repressive measures, and Emo's reports note that more than ten thousand people were executed within ten days. Mahmut closed all of the coffee-houses in town, since these were places where politics were discussed, and an ominous quiet descended upon Istanbul, leading Emo to remark that 'Sad it is to see the aspect of this city.'

A treaty ending a war between Turkey and Iran in 1746 was followed by the longest period of peace in Ottoman history, lasting for twenty-two years. This allowed Sultan Mahmut to revive for a time the tulip fêtes that had ceased with the fall of Ahmet III, and the gardens of the fourth court of Topkapı Sarayı were once again decorated as they had been during the reign of the Tulip King. Jean-Claude Flachat, a French merchant who lived in Istanbul during the years 1740–55, writes of one of these fêtes, his somewhat fanciful description probably based on what he was told by Hacı Beşir Ağa, the chief black eunuch:

The Sultans kiosk, or pavilion, is the centre. It is there the presents sent by the Court grandees are displayed. They are pointed out to his Highness, the source of origin being explained in each case. It is a good opportunity to show one's anxiety to please . . .

When all is ready the Grand Seigneur causes kalvet [the state of complete privacy, either alone or with the harem] to be announced. All the gates of the Serail leading to the garden are closed. The

Bostanchis *stand on guard outside, and the black eunuchs inside.
All the Sultanas come there from the Karem after the Sultan. The
Keslar Aga, at the head of the other eunuchs, officiates. The women
rush out on all sides, like a swarm of bees settling on the flowers
and stopping continually at the honey they find. There are numbers
of them of every kind and sort. The Keslar Aga has assured me
several times that the gaiety of these occasions seems to bring out
any skill they claim to possess, or arts which they display in anything
they do to amuse. These little games that the poets invented for
Cupid and the nymphs may give some slight idea. Each tries to
distinguish herself; they are all a mass of charms; each has the same
object to accomplish. One has never seen elsewhere to what lengths
the resources of the intellect can go with young women who want
to seduce a man they love through vanity, and especially by natural
inclination. The grace of the dance, the melody of the voice, the
harmony of the music, the elegance of the dresses, the wit of the
conversation, the ecstasies, the effeminacy, and love – the most
voluptuous, I may add, that the cleverest coquetry has invented –
all unite in this delightful spot under the eyes of the Sultan.*

*The Kiahia Caden [Kaya Kadın, the chief stewardess of the harem]
finally presents to him the girl that most takes his fancy. No pains
have been spared to ensure her success. She hastens to exhibit every
pleasing talent she possesses. The handkerchief that he throws to
her signifies his wish to be alone with her.*

*The curtain which covers the sofa on which he is sitting is made
to fall. The Keslar Aga remains to pull it aside again at the first
signal, and the other women, who have scattered here and there,
all occupied – some with dancing, others with singing, these with
playing on their instruments, and those with partaking of refreshments – all come to the kiosque in a moment to pay their respects
to the Sultan and congratulate the new favourite. The* fete *continues
some time longer, and terminates by the distribution which the
Keslar Aga makes of jewels, stuffs, and trinkets, following the wishes
of his master. The presents are proportional to the pleasure received.*
But Mahmut always saw to it that they were of sufficient value

Kaya Kadın (Chief Stewardess of the Harem)

for the girls to return to the Karem with an air of gratitude and contentment.

Flachat was able to make an extensive tour of Topkapı Sarayı in the company of Hacı Beşir Ağa, who brought him in with the workmen who were installing some new mirrors in the harem, presents from Louis XV to Mahmut I. Among the places he describes are the dormitory of the sultan's favourites and the harem baths:

One next passes into the gallery where are situated the apartments of twelve Sultanas. They are large and richly furnished. The windows have iron grilles, and look into the courtyard. They have on the garden side . . . little jutting-out gazebos, where they sit and see the country and all that happens in the gardens without being seen. In the middle of the northern façade they have built a fore-part, which serves as an assembly room, as you might call it. All the women go there to pay their addresses to his Highness, and try and please him

*with a thousand amusements which follow on one after the other,
and to which the inexhaustible fertility of the genius of these women
always imparts the air of novelty.*

*From there one goes to the large bath. It consists of three rooms,
all of which are paved with marble. The middle one is the most
ornamental; its dome is supported by marble pillars and cut glass
is let in to give it light. The rooms communicate one with the other
by glass doors so that all that goes on can be seen. Each basin has
two taps, one supplying hot and the other cold water. The basins
are neither of the same shape nor used for the same purposes. They
have an eye for utility and beauty alike. The women of lesser rank
and the black eunuchs have baths apart, very neat and comfortable.*

Flachat tells an amusing story about Mahmut I in connection
with the women's bath in the harem, a tale that he seems to have
heard from Hacı Beşir Ağa. It seems that Mahmut arranged for all
of his concubines to be given new chemises, and these were handed
out to them when they arrived together at their bath in the harem,
where the sultan was observing them secretly from behind a screened
window. Mahmut had ordered his tailors to remove all of the stitches
from the new chemises, which were instead held together by glue,
and so when they were exposed to the heat and moisture of the bath
they fell apart, leaving the girls naked. The sultan gave away his
concealed presence by his laughter on seeing this, with some of his
concubines joining in the merriment, but others were very angry,
or so the story goes.

The most fascinating part of Flachat's account is his description
of the Cage, the apartments within the Inner Palace where the
captive princes were kept. Here he mentions Osman III, younger
brother and successor of Mahmut I, who apparently modified the
structure of the Cage to make it more open and less oppressive:

*On leaving the grand Karem one goes down a corridor quite dark.
It crosses the detached building which the eunuchs inhabit and leads
directly to the prison of the Princes, the Sultan's sons who can aspire
to the throne. This prison is like a strong citadel. A high wall is*

built all around it. Osman [III] caused the wall to be lowered and to have the windows opened. It is entered by two doors carefully guarded by Eunuchs both within and without, each having a double iron railing. The place has a dismal appearance. There is a pretty enough garden well watered. The Princes have fine apartments and baths in the detached buildings which surround the court. The Eunuchs detailed to their service all live on the ground floor, and there is a large number of them. They spare no pains to mitigate their hard lot, and to make their prison at least endurable. For some long time the severity with which they were treated has been lessened. Women are given them, although it is a fact that they no longer bear children, or else great care is taken to obviate their becoming pregnant. They have all kinds of masters, and they even encourage them to perfect themselves in all handiworks that are applicable to their rank. In a word, they leave nothing to wish for save freedom. They are, however, not limited to the apartments of the Grand Serail alone; the Sultan often conducts them to other Imperial houses, and especially to Besictache [Beşiktaş], where they are shut up in the same way. These trips, always agreeable, make a welcome change for them.

Beşiktaş, on the European shore of the Bosphorus, was the site of the palace of Çırağan, built in 1719 by Nevşehirli Ibrahim Pasha. This was one of a number of seaside residences used by Mahmut, who was noted by the foreign envoys as always being *en route* from one of his palaces to another, perpetuating the sybaritic way of life of his predecessor, the Tulip King.

Mahmut spent the last six years of his reign building an imperial mosque complex on the Third Hill, but he did not live to complete it. His health had been failing in the autumn of 1754, and he felt unable to ride to the mosque of Haghia Sophia for the noon prayer on Fridays, but public criticism of his absence forced him to resume this practice. When returning from the service on 14 December of that year he rode as far as the first court of Topkapı Sarayı, when he suffered a stroke and fell from his horse, apparently dying instantly.

Mahmut was fifty-eight when he died, having ruled for just over twenty-four years. He was interred in the *türbe* of Yeni Cami the following day, the third generation of the imperial Osmanlı dynasty to be buried there, beginning with his grandfather Mehmet IV. Soon afterwards a strange story spread through the city that Mahmut had been buried alive, and despite all testimony to the contrary from those who had seen him die the legend became part of the folklore of Istanbul, repeated by those who passed the *türbe* of Yeni Cami and its growing collection of imperial catafalques.

The Tulip Period had ended and the palace of Sa'adabad was beginning to fall into ruins, its celebrants now mouldering in the tomb. The party was over, but it would be remembered whenever celebrants quoted Nedim's poem, 'Let us laugh, let us play/ Let us enjoy the delights of the world to the full.'

Chapter 13

MURDER IN
THE MUSIC ROOM

On the day that Mahmut I died he was succeeded by his half-brother
Osman III, the son of Mustafa II and Şehsuvar, who thus became
valide sultan. Osman was almost fifty-six when he came to the
throne, having spent more than fifty-one years in the Cage. Like his
late brother Mahmut I, Osman never fathered any children. The
names of two of his concubines are recorded, Leyit and Zerki, both
of whom probably came to Osman's harem after his accession.
Osman seems to have had little regard for his concubines, for
he seldom visited them. According to palace tradition, he wore
hobnailed shoes so that the sound of his approach could be heard
by the women of his harem, who then scattered in fear to avoid
him.

At the time of Osman's accession four of his cousins were still in
the Cage: Mehmet, Mustafa, Beyazit and Abdül Hamit. Since Osman
had no children, the oldest of his cousins, Mehmet, was heir to the
throne. Mehmet was extremely popular, and this may have been
what led Osman to eliminate the crown prince, who was executed
in the Cage on 2 January 1756, his thirty-ninth birthday. He was
apparently poisoned, which led his surviving brothers to take precautions that they did not meet the same fate. The execution of
Prince Mehmet was the last instance of such an execution other
than those of deposed sultans, a total of seventy-eight princes having
been slaughtered over a span of four and a half centuries.

Osman III (1754–7)

Osman changed his grand vezirs frequently, averaging two a year. Each time he dismissed one he took the opportunity to seize the grand vezir's belongings, adding to his own considerable private fortune. While his grand vezirs administered the empire Osman busied himself with repressive measures to keep the populace under control, closing coffee-houses, forbidding women to leave their houses more than four days a week, and regulating the dress of his non-Muslim subjects. Osman often made excursions in disguise into the city to see if his regulations were being obeyed. Whenever he did so he took the opportunity to visit the markets of Istanbul to buy delicacies for his table, for his main interest in life was eating good food, and he had an insatiable appetite.

During the first year of his reign Osman completed work on the imperial *külliye* that his brother Mahmut had founded on the Third Hill. He called it Nuruosmaniye Camii, the Mosque of the Sacred Light (Nur) of Osman. Designed by a Greek architect named Simeon, this was the first monumental Ottoman building to exemplify the new baroque style introduced from Europe during the Tulip Period.

Osman died of a stroke on 29 October 1757, after which he was laid to rest in the *türbe* of Yeni Cami, the fifth sultan to be buried there, along with his grandmother Hadice Turhan. He was succeeded by the eldest of his surviving cousins, who came to the throne as Mustafa III.

Mustafa, a son of Ahmet III, was thirty-nine at the time of his accession, having spent the previous twenty-seven years in the Cage, where his younger brothers Beyazit and Abdül Hamit remained as prisoners. His mother Mihrişah died before he came to the throne, and so there was no *valide sultan* during his reign.

Mustafa had at least six concubines, and together they bore him eleven children, comprising two boys and nine girls. Only one of the boys survived childhood, and just three of the girls. The boy who survived was Mustafa's first son, the future Selim III, born on 24 December 1761 to Mihrişah, a slave girl of Georgian origin. Selim was the first royal prince to be born since the reign of Ahmet III, and the entire city joined in the celebration.

Sir James Porter writes of an extraordinary incident that took place soon after Mustafa's accession, when a shortage of grain led the women of Istanbul to storm the imperial granary:

No opposition could stop them; and while the public officers were perplexed what course to take, they broke open locks, bars, and bolts, burst into the magazines, took with them such quantities as they could carry off, and went away unmolested. None of these female rioters were ever punished, as far as we know, and if you spoke to a grave Turk about it, he answered with a sneer, it was only a meeting of turbulent women.

During the first four years of his reign Mustafa III built two imperial mosques: Ayazma Camii in Üsküdar and Laleli Cami on the Fourth Hill. Ayazma Camii was dedicated to the memory of Mustafa's mother Mihrişah. Laleli Cami, the Tulip Mosque, was the work of

Mehmet Tahir Ağa, the greatest of the Turkish baroque architects.

A terrible earthquake in 1766 destroyed or damaged many important buildings in Istanbul, most notably Fatih Camii, the Mosque of the Conqueror, which was totally ruined. Sultan Mustafa immediately set out to erect a new mosque on the same site, though with a very different architectural plan, and this was completed in 1771.

Despite the declining fortunes of the Ottoman Empire, which was threatened by the aggressive policy of Catherine the Great, the sultan and his court continued to enjoy themselves at evening parties in the palace gardens. These fêtes are described by Baron de Tott, an Hungarian officer in the Ottoman service:

The garden of the Harem . . . is used as a theatre for these nocturnal fetes; vases of all kinds, filled with real or artificial flowers, are brought here temporarily in order to increase the riot of colour and illuminated by an infinite number of lanterns and candles set in glass tubes, the light from which is reflected in mirrors placed there for that purpose. Boutiques stocked with a variety of merchandise, specially built for the fete, are occupied by women of the Harem who, wearing appropriate costumes, represent the merchants who ought rightly to be in charge. Sultanas, sisters, nieces or cousins are invited to these fetes by the Grand Seigneur, and they join with His Highness in buying from these boutiques jewels and fabrics which they then present to each other; they also extend their generosity to the wives of the Grand-Seigneur who are admitted with him or who occupy the boutiques. Dancing, music and a sport rather resembling jousting extend the entertainment far into the night, and fill with a temporary gaiety an interior that would appear to be essentially designed for sadness and ennui.

Mustafa died of heart failure on 21 January 1774, a week before his fifty-seventh birthday. The following day he was buried in the *türbe* of Laleli Cami, the beautiful mosque he had built on the Fourth Hill. Prince Beyazit had died in the Cage in 1771, and so when Mustafa passed away the only son of Ahmet III still alive was Abdül Hamit, who thus succeeded his brother as sultan. His place in the Cage was taken by his nephew Selim, the only surviving son of Mustafa III.

When Abdül Hamit came to the throne he was almost forty-nine, having spent the previous forty-three years in the Cage. During his time in the Cage he seems to have fathered at least one child, a daughter named Dürrüşehvar, whose mother's name is not recorded. The names of ten of his concubines are known. Altogether he fathered twenty-six children, comprising thirteen boys and thirteen girls, of whom only two sons and three daughters survived their childhood. Both of his surviving sons in time succeeded to the throne. These were the future sultans Mustafa IV, born on 8 August 1779 to Ayşe Seniyeperver, and Mahmut II, born on 20 August 1785 to Nakşidil. An apocryphal story has it that Nakşidil was originally Marie Martha Aimée Dubuc de Rivéry of Martinique, cousin of the Empress Joséphine of France. Aimée is supposed to have been captured by pirates and sold to the slave market in Istanbul, from where she was purchased for the harem of Abdül Hamit, but there is no factual basis for this tale.

During the latter years of his reign Abdül Hamit became immersed in the pleasures of his harem and less interested in affairs of state. He seemed totally besotted by his new favourite, Ruşah, as evidenced by one of his abjectly submissive love letters to her, now preserved in the Topkapı Sarayı museum:

My Ruşah, Hamit is yours to dispose of. The Lord Creator of the Universe is the Creator of all things and would never torment a man for a single fault. My mistress, I am your bound slave, beat me or kill me if you wish. I surrender my self utterly to you. Please come tonight, I beg of you. I swear you are going to be the cause of my illness and maybe even my death. I rub my face and eyes under the soles of your feet and beg of you. I swear to God I can no longer control myself.

Ruşah was apparently too much for Abdül Hamit, who suffered a stroke on the evening of 6 April 1789 and died the following morning. Abdül Hamit was sixty-four years old at the time of his death, the longest-lived sultan since Süleyman the Magnificent. That same day Abdül Hamit was succeeded by his nephew, who was raised to the throne as Selim III. The following day Selim arranged for the funeral of his uncle, leading the procession to the *türbe* that Abdül Hamit had erected on the Second Hill near the Golden Horn.

Selim had already acquired the reputation of being able and energetic, and so his accession was greeted with enthusiasm. He began his reign with an intense flurry of activity, issuing orders to his vezirs and publishing decrees to regulate the conduct of his subjects, for he was afraid that the empire was in mortal danger and was determined to reform it along Western lines. As he said at the time, 'I am ready to content myself with dry bread for the state is breaking up.' The unprecedented vigour with which the new sultan began his reign was reported by the French ambassador Choiseul-Gouffier in a letter to a friend: 'In fifteen days the enthusiasm which he had inspired has turned into general consternation. All trembles in this capital.'

When Selim was released from the Cage his place was taken by Abdül Hamit's two surviving sons, Mustafa, who was then nearly ten years old, and Mahmut, who was nearly four. Selim made their confinement as comfortable as possible and supervised their education, just as Abdül Hamit had treated him during his own time in the Cage.

Selim III was twenty-seven when he succeeded to the throne, having spent the previous fifteen years in the Cage. He had at least eight concubines in his harem, but he never fathered any children.

Selim's mother Mihrişah, who had been relegated to the Old Saray on the death of her husband Mustafa III, now returned to Topkapı Sarayı to take her place as *valide sultan*. Selim built her a large and luxurious apartment, after which he erected a contiguous suite of rooms for himself. Mihrişah later built a large *külliye* in Eyüp, including a baroque *türbe*, where she was buried in 1805.

Selim was very close to his three sisters, Şah, Beyhan and Hadice, all three of whom were married to pashas. Şah Sultan, the oldest, had been engaged in turn to two grand vezirs while still in her extreme youth, but both of the pashas had been executed before

Selim III (1789–1807)

they could marry her. She was finally married to Kara Mustafa Pasha, who on their wedding night fell a victim to the ungovernable temper of the princess, according to a story told by Charles Mac-Farlane in *Turkey and its Destiny* (1850):

When Shah Sultana, sister to Selim III, was married to Kara Mustafa Pasha, her Highness established the superiority of her rank over her husband in a summary manner; and this upon their wedding night. The impatient Pasha, not aware of the fiery and capricious character of his imperial bride, vainly waited until within an hour of dawn for the wonted summons to the nuptial chamber. At length, fearing that the muezzin would announce morning prayer before he could enter his wife's apartment, and that he should consequently be accused of neglect, he set aside his twentieth pipe, and boldly proceeded to the harem. Here he opened the Sultana's door, said his prayer, and approached the foot of the couch. Better had he disturbed a sleeping lioness. As he was in the act of stooping to kiss the hem of the coverlet, the recumbent Sultana cast him prostrate with a blow of her feet. Then, springing from her couch, she flew at his face, and in spite of his supplications of 'My Sultana! my soul! my lamb! corner of my liver! Aman! aman!' (mercy!) she lacerated his cheeks and nose so piteously, that blood streamed on the floor. Then, clapping her hands for her female attendants, she bade them drive the insolent intruder from her presence, and retired to her bed to compose herself.

Not satisfied with this explosion of choler, the irritated princess proceeded next morning to the Seraglio, and throwing herself upon her knees, at her Imperial brother's feet, demanded the immediate disgrace of the 'infringer of etiquette,' and her divorce from 'the insulter of her dignity.' Sultan Selim listened attentively and, when she had finished speaking, highly applauded her spirit and promised to admonish and chastise the husband. He then dismissed his sister, with an earnest recommendation to pardon the offender, and burst into a fit of laughter.

Selim's court was a centre for the introduction of European culture into Turkish society, particularly from France, the oldest ally of the Ottoman Empire. Dallaway, in *Constantinople, Ancient and Modern*, mentions this:

His countenance is handsome and impressive, and his figure good; he is affable, and possesses much speculative genius . . . and has every inclination to reconcile his subjects to the superior expediency of European maxims, both in politics and war . . . I have heard it asserted that the young men in the seraglio are now instructed in the French language by his command; and his partiality to French wine is no secret among the well-informed.

Selim gave permission for a French dancing-master and a number of musicians to enter some outer building of the harem, where, supervised by several black eunuchs, they gave lessons to the concubines who were selected to perform in one of the entertainments for the sultan and his other women. Selim himself may have played for the women, for he had been trained as a musician and was an accomplished composer and performer on the *ney*, the Turkish flute. Other entertainments included plays, usually farces, dances, *karagöz*, the Turkish shadow-puppets, and recitations by a *masalçi*, or story-teller. One of the dances known to have been performed here by the harem girls was called *tavşan*, or hare, in which they danced and hopped about like bunnies. Another was the traditional Turkish belly-dance, such as one that led Lady Mary Wortley Montagu to say of the performers that 'I am very positive the oldest and most rigid prude on earth could not have looked upon them without thinking of something not to be spoken of.'

By Selim's time most of the women in the harem of Topkapı Sarayı would have been brought to Istanbul by the slave trade from the Caucasus. Female slaves were sold in Istanbul at the Avret Pazarı, the Women's Market, located in the ancient Forum of Arcadius on the Seventh Hill. The *valide sultan* Mihrişah, mother of Selim III, was purchased there for the harem of Mustafa III. Dallaway, in his *Constantinople, Ancient and Modern*, describes the Avret Pazarı as it was in his day:

The females of the seraglio are chiefly Georgian and Circassian slaves, selected from all that are either privately bought, or exposed to sale in the Avret Bazar, and, for many reasons, are admitted at an early age. We may readily conclude that an assemblage of native beauty so exquisite, does not exist in any other place.

The Avret Bazar consists of an inclosed court, with a cloister and small apartments surrounding it. It is supplied by female slaves brought from Egypt, Abyssinia, Georgia and Circassia, who are exposed to sale every Friday morning. Those from the first mentioned countries are generally purchased for domestic services, which, in a menial capacity, no Turkish woman will condescend to perform;

The Nuruosmaniye Mosque, from the Slave Market

their persons or countenances are rarely beautiful, and their price seldom exceeds forty pounds English. The exquisite beauty of the others is enhanced by every art of dress and oriental accomplishments, and they are usually sold for several thousand piastres. Many are reserved for the seraglio, where though they are considered as most fortunate.

Dallaway goes on to describe the training and way of life of the girls purchased in the slave market for the harem of Topkapı Sarayı:

The education of these girls is very scrupulously attended to; they are taught to dance with more luxuriance than grace, to sing and play upon the tambourin, a species of guitar; and some of them excel in embroidery. This arrangement is conducted solely by the elder women, though from the taste for European fashions, which Sultan Selim openly avows, some Greek women have been lately introduced to teach them the harp and piano-forte, which they had learned for that purpose ... The superiors spend their time in a series of sedentary amusements. Dress, the most sumptuous that can be imagined, changed frequently in the course of the day, the most magnificent apartments and furniture; visits of ceremony with each other, and the incessant homage of their subordinate companions, fill their minds with a sort of supine happiness, which indeed is all that Turkish women aspire to, or are qualified to experience.

Sometimes, as an indulgence, they are permitted to go to kiosques near the sea, of which circumstance the officers of police are informed, that no vessel should approach too near the seraglio point. Every summer the sultan visits his palaces in rotation for a short time with his harem, where every pass and avenue, within three or five miles distance, is guarded by fierce bostandjis, *lest the approach of any male being should contaminate them.*

They depend entirely on their female slaves for amusements, which have any thing like gaiety for their object, and recline on their sofas for hours, while dancing, comedy, and buffoonery, as indelicate as our puppet show, are exhibited before them. Greek and Frank ladies occasionally visit them, whose husbands are connected with the Porte as merchants and interpreters, under pretence of showing them curiosities from Europe. From such opportunities all the accurate information of the palace must be collected, and to such I am, at present, indebted.

Selim often gave parties in the gardens of Topkapı Sarayı. The journal of his private secretary, Ahmed Vasif Efendi, records that on 5 June 1791 the sultan watched a wrestling match there as well as a circus performance involving three lions, a leopard and a number of dogs and cocks, after which Selim retired to the Yalı Köşk, or Shore Pavilion, to eat and to perform his prayers. Another entry in his secretary's journal notes that on 15 April 1797 Selim gave a 'tulip *fete*' in the palace gardens, the last known instance of such a party.

Selim was far more active physically than his sedentary predecessors, and he often played *cirit* with the palace pages in the lower gardens of the palace. Prince Mahmut joined him in these games when he was old enough, and the two of them played on opposing teams, which were named for two of the corps of gardeners who worked there, the *bahmıacıs*, who looked after the okra, and the *lahanacıs*, who tended the cabbages. Palace records note that Selim played with the cabbage-men and Mahmut with the okra team.

Selim's preference for things European led him to restore parts of the palace and its surrounding gardens in the Western manner. The gardens were redesigned by the Austrian Jacob Ensle, brother of the imperial gardener at Schönbrunn, who was brought to Istanbul by Selim in 1792 and remained for ten years. Ensle laid out new gardens around the so-called 'Summer Harem', an open complex of kiosks and pavilions on the Marmara side of Saray Point. Ensle had a lodge in the palace gardens and often invited guests to visit him there, and if the court was away he would take his guests on a tour of the Summer Harem and other parts of Topkapı Sarayı. One of his guests was Edward Daniel Clarke, who, describing his first visit, tells of how two of Ensle's friends caught a glimpse of the *valide sultan* and the four wives of the sultan:

Presently followed the Sultan Mother, with the four principal Sultanas, who were in high glee, romping and laughing with each other. A small scullery window of the gardener's lodge looked directly towards the gate through which these ladies were to pass, and was separated from it only by a few yards. Here, through two small gimlet holes, bored for the purpose, they beheld very distinctly the features of the women, whom they described as possessing extraordinary beauty. Three of the four were Georgians, having dark complexions and very long dark hair, but the fourth was remarkably fair; and her hair, also of singular length and thickness, was of a flaxen colour ... Long spangled robes, open in front, with pantaloons embroidered in gold and silver, and covered by a profusion of pearls and precious stones, displayed their persons to great advantage; but were so heavy, as actually to encumber their motion, and almost to impede their walking. Their hair hung in loose and very thick tresses; falling quite down to the waist, and covering their shoulders behind. Those tresses were quite powdered with diamonds, not displayed according to any studied arrangement, but as if carelessly scattered, among their flowing locks. On the top of their heads, and rather leaning to one side, they wore, each of them, a small patch or diadem. Their faces, necks, and even their breasts were quite exposed; not one of them having any veil.

Clarke and a friend made a second and much more lengthy visit to Topkapı Sarayı during the holy month of Ramadan, when, as Ensle assured him, '. . . the guards, being up all night, would be stupified during the day with sleep and intoxication.' Clarke's exploration of the Inner Palace brought him into the heart of the harem. There he entered rooms from which the sultanas had only recently departed, apparently for a lengthy stay at one of the imperial palaces on the Bosphorus, their belongings still scattered about, as he notes:

I was pleased with observing a few things they had carelessly left upon the sofas, and which characterized their mode of life. Among these was an English writing-box, of black varnished wood, with a sliding cover, and drawers; the drawers contained coloured writing paper, reed pens, perfumed wax, and little bags made of embroidered satin, in which their billets-doux are sent, by negro slaves, who are both mutes and eunuchs. That liqueurs are drunk in these secluded chambers is evident; for we found labels for bottles, neatly cut out with scissars, bearing Turkish inscriptions, with the words, 'Rosoglio,' 'Golden Water,' and 'Water of Life.'

Clarke goes on to write of the 'Summer Harem', which he describes as being 'a small quadrangle, exactly resembling that of Queen's College, Cambridge . . . the principal side of the court containing an open cloister, supported by small white marble columns.' From this court he passed through a dormitory 'prepared for the reception of a hundred slaves: [this] reached the whole extent of a very long corridor'. There a stairway led him to another dormitory for slaves on two tiers and to a series of small apartments for slaves of higher rank. This brought him to what he calls 'the Great Chamber of Audience, in which the Sultan Mother receives visits of ceremony, from the Sultanas, and other distinguished ladies of the Charem'. The chamber that he describes here was the salon of the *valide sultan's* apartment, which Selim III had recently built in the harem for his mother Mihrişah:

Nothing can be imagined better suited to theatrical representation than this chamber ... It is exactly such an apartment as the best painters of scenic decoration would have selected, to afford a striking idea of the pomp, the seclusion, and the magnificence of the Ottoman court ... It was surrounded with enormous mirrors, the costly donations of Infidel Kings, as they are styled by the present possessors. These mirrors the women of the Seraglio sometimes break in their frolics. At the upper end is the throne, a sort of cage, in which the Sultana [valide] sits, surrounded by latticed blinds; for even here her person is held too secret to be exposed to the common observation of slaves and females of the Charem. A lofty flight of broad steps, covered with crimson cloth, leads to this cage, as to a throne ... To the right and left of the throne, and upon a level with it, are the sleeping apartments of the Sultan Mother, and her principal females in waiting. The external windows of the throne [room] are all latticed: on one side they look towards the sea, and on the other into the quadrangle of the Charem; the chamber itself occupying the whole breadth of the building, on the side of the rectangle into which it looks. The area below the latticed throne ... is set apart for attendants, for the dancers, for actors, music, refreshments, and whatsoever is brought into the Charem for the amusement of the court ...

Clarke next entered what he called the 'Assembly Room of the Sultan, when he is in the Charem'. This is the great hall of the Privy Chamber, which Clarke describes with surprising brevity:

The Sultan sometimes visits this chamber during the winter, to hear music, and to amuse himself with his favourites. It is surrounded by mirrors. The other ornaments display that strange mixture of magnificence and wretchedness, which characterize all the state-chambers of Turkish grandees.

He then passed the baths of the *valide sultan* and the four principal wives of the sultan, after which he came to what he called the Chamber of Repose, the suite of rooms on the east side of the Third Court that now houses the Treasury of the Topkapı Sarayı museum.

The next stop on Clarke's tour was a 'large apartment' in the harem overlooking the lower gardens, a chamber known as the *mabeyn*, which served as an anteroom between the harem and the *selamlık*:

We now proceeded to that part of the Charem which looks into the Seraglio gardens, and entered a large apartment, called Chalved Yiertzy, *or, as the French would express it,* Salle de promenade. *Here the other ladies of the Charem entertain themselves, by hearing and seeing comedies, farcical representations, dances, and music. We found it in the state of an old lumber room. Large dusty pier-glasses, in heavy gilded frames, neglected and broken, stood, like the Vicar of Wakefield's family picture, leaning against the wall, the whole length of one side of the room. Old furniture; shabby bureaus of the worst English work, made of oak, walnut, or mahogany; inlaid broken cabinets, scattered fragments of chandeliers; scraps of paper, silk rags, and empty confectionary boxes; were the only objects in this part of the palace.*

Clarke and his companion went on through another part of the harem that was even more dilapidated than the *mabeyn*. They then ascended from the lower gardens to the Fourth Court, toward a kiosk that Clarke calls the Chamber of the Garden of Hyacinths, now vanished:

This promised to be interesting, as we were told the Sultan passed almost all his private hours in that apartment; and the view of it might make us acquainted with occupations and amusements, which

*Selim III, enthroned in front of the Gate of Felicity,
receives the greetings of his court. Painting by Constantine
of Kapıdağ, c. 1800*

*characterize the man, divested of the outward parade of the sultan.
We presently turned from the paved ascent, towards the right, and
entered a small garden, laid out into very neat oblong borders, edged
with porcelain, or Dutch tiles. Here no plant is suffered to grow,
except the Hyacinth; whence the name of this garden, and the
chamber it contains. We examined this apartment, by looking
through a window. Nothing can be more magnificent. Three sides
of it were surrounded by a divan, the cushions and pillows of which
were of black embroidered satin. Opposite the windows of the
chamber was a fire-place, after the ordinary European fashion; and
on each side of this, a door covered with hangings of crimson cloth.
Between each of these doors and the fireplace appeared a glass-case,
containing the Sultan's private library; every volume being in manu-*

script, and upon shelves, one above the other, and the title of each book written on the edges of its leaves. From the ceiling of the room, which was of burnished gold, opposite each of the doors, and also opposite to the fireplace, hung three gilt cages, containing small figures of artificial birds: these sung by mechanism. In the centre of the room stood an enormous gilt brazier, supported, in an ewer, by four massive claws, like vessels seen under sideboards in England. Opposite to the entrance, on one side of the apartment, was a raised bench, crossing a door, on which were placed an embroidered napkin, a vase, and bason, for washing the beard and hands ... In a nook close to the door was also a pair of yellow boots; and on the bench, by the ewer, a pair of slippers of the same materials. These were placed at the entrance of every apartment frequented by the Sultan ... Groups of arms, such as pistols, sabres, and poignards, were disposed, with very singular taste and effect, on the different compartments of the walls; the handles and scabbards of which were covered with diamonds of very large size: these, as they glittered around, gave a most gorgeous effect to the splendour of this sumptuous chamber.

We had scarce ended our survey of this costly scene, when, to our great dismay, a Bostanghy made his appearance within the apartment; but, fortunately for us, his head was turned from the window, and we immediately sunk below it, creeping on our hands and knees, until we got clear of the Garden of Hyacinths. Thence, ascending to the upper walks, we passed an aviary of nightingales.

The neglected state of some of the harem rooms was due to the fact that the sultans were now spending less time in Topkapı Sarayı, preferring the greater privacy of their seaside palaces along the Bosphorus.

Meanwhile, Selim continued his attempts to reform the empire, particularly the armed forces, developing an infantry force known as the Nizamı Cedit, or New Order. This aroused bitter opposition among the Janissaries and Sipahis, who saw Selim's new army as a threat to their continued existence.

On 28 May 1807 the Janissary auxiliaries in Istanbul known as the *yamaks* revolted under the leadership of Kabakcı Mustafa Ağa and were joined by the religious students in the *medreses*. Early the following morning the rebels obtained a *fetva* from the *şeyhülislam* Ataullah Efendi justifying the removal of Selim, after which they marched to Topkapı Sarayı shouting their support for 'Sultan Mustafa'. At that moment the sultan's secretary Ahmet Bey was killed by the mob, who sent his severed head in to Selim, which so terrified him that he immediately agreed to abdicate if his life was spared. Selim then summoned his cousin Mustafa from the Cage, offering to give over his throne to him, although the prince was so mentally handicapped that it was unlikely that he had the capacity to rule. Mustafa, after making a show of reluctance, finally agreed, whereupon Selim took his place in the Cage, joining Prince Mahmut.

The new sultan succeeded as Mustafa IV on 29 May 1807, enthroned outside the Gate of Felicity, with the rebel mob thronging the courtyard to cheer him and wish him long life.

Mustafa, a son of Abdül Hamit I, was nearly twenty-eight when he came to the throne, having spent the previous eighteen years of his life in the Cage. His mother Ayşe Seniyeperver moved from the Old Palace to Topkapı Sarayı to take up her place as *valide sultan*. The new sultan had four concubines in his harem, his favourite being Peykidil. These women bore him a son and a daughter, both of whom died in infancy.

Once Selim was in the Cage and Mustafa on the throne, power fell into the hands of Ataullah Efendi and Köse Musa Pasha, the deputy grand vezir, who moved quickly to eliminate all of their opponents from the old regime. The most notable of these was the grand vezir Ibrahim Hilmi Pasha, who was assassinated and replaced by Çelebi Mustafa Pasha. The opposition to the new regime was led by Bayraktar Mustafa Pasha, who led all of his loyal troops to Ruschuk on the Danube.

Meanwhile, Köse Musa Pasha and Ataullah Efendi began to struggle with one another for supremacy. This left the balance of power to Kabakcı Mustafa Ağa and his *yamaks*, who began a reign

Mustafa IV (1807–8)

of terror in Istanbul. The Ruschuk committee then put in motion their plan to depose Mustafa, keeping it secret so that the sultan would not kill Selim. Bayraktar moved his army to Edirne and then to Istanbul, where he arrived outside the walls on 18 July 1808. Eight days of devious manœuvring followed, as the Ruschuk committee tried to free Selim from the palace so that they could restore him and depose Mustafa. The grand vezir Çelebi Mustafa learned of their plot early on the morning of 27 July and warned the sultan, but Mustafa did not take the message seriously and did nothing about it. Çelebi Mustafa then decided that he would execute Prince Selim, and when Bayraktar learned of this through an informer he decided that he would march his army into Istanbul the following morning. Bayraktar sent a detachment to the Sublime Porte to seize the grand vezir, while he himself led the rest of his men to Topkapı

Sarayı, where they made their way into the second court. He then sent the *şeyhülislam* into the Inner Palace to persuade Mustafa to abdicate and free Selim, but the sultan refused, locking the Gate of Felicity. Then, while Bayraktar was mustering his forces to break into the Inner Palace, Mustafa sent the chief black eunuch and his men to kill both Selim and Mahmut, which would leave him as the only living male in the imperial Osmanlı line.

At that moment Selim was in the music room of the harem, having been allowed to leave the Cage to spend some time there playing one of his compositions on the *ney*. A number of the harem women were there listening to him, when the chief black eunuch and his men burst in and attacked him. Selim fought them off until they finally overcame his resistance and killed him, after which his body was thrown out into the second court. Bayraktar was momentarily overcome with grief at the sight of Selim's body, but then he recovered himself and broke into the Inner Palace and arrested Mustafa, after which he sent his men in search of Prince Mahmut.

Meanwhile, Mahmut had barely escaped from the chief black eunuch and his men, the prince's servant woman Cevri Kalfa having thrown hot ashes into their eyes when they entered his room, thus allowing him to make his way up on to the roof of the harem. He then made his way down into an empty room and remained in hiding there. MacFarlane describes the climax of this dramatic chase:

At length, after a long and most anxious search through the interior of the serraglio, Mahmood . . . was discovered in a dark, neglected corner, and drawn from beneath a heap of carpets and mats, almost half dead and trembling; and it required time to convince him that those who came to place him on the throne were not the emissaries of his brother, despatched to kill him. It is generally asserted that Mustapha had determined to strangle his brother as well as his cousin, and that Mahmood owed his safety to an old female slave, who concealed him at the first violent approach of the bairactar. The events of the tragedy were precipitate – he was not discovered by the kislar-agha, when the search was ordered, and in a few minutes the insur-

gents were masters of the palace, and of the person of Mustapha.

When Mahmood appeared before Mustapha-Bairactar, whom grief, alarm, and sentiments of deadly revenge, had driven to a state of frenzy, he was hailed by the chiefs and all present as their lawful sultan, the worthy successor of the great and good Selim. The bairactar prostrated himself, and kissed the earth at his feet; nor did he rise from that posture of humiliation until Mahmood ordered him to do so, and proclaimed him his liberator and grand vizir.

Bayraktar obtained a *fetva* from the *şeyhülislam* deposing Mustafa, who was thereupon imprisoned once again in the Cage. Later that same day, 28 July 1808, his brother was raised to the throne as Mahmut II.

The following day Selim was buried in the *türbe* of his father Mustafa III at Laleli Cami. He is remembered today for his poetry and music as well as for his efforts at reform. One of Selim's poems, which he wrote under the pseudonym of Ilhami, 'the inspired', is a couplet in the Persian style, often quoted when Turks speak of him and his time:

O Ilhami, do not be indolent and do not trust in the things of this world.
The world stops for no one and its wheel turns without ceasing.

Some of Selim's compositions are still heard on Radio Istanbul, including the tune he may have been playing at the hour of his death, when he was murdered in the music room of the House of Felicity.

Chapter 14

THE AUSPICIOUS EVENT

Mahmut II was just short of twenty-three when he succeeded to the throne of his brother Mustafa IV, who took his place in the Cage. Mahmut himself had spent nineteen years in the Cage before his accession, having been confined since the age of four, although he had enjoyed far more freedom than the caged princes of earlier times.

Mahmut's first official act as sultan was to appoint Bayraktar Mustafa Pasha as grand vezir. Bayraktar then ordered his men to eliminate all of those who had been responsible for Selim's overthrow and death. Bayraktar would have killed the deposed Mustafa IV as well, but Mahmut spared the life of his brother and kept him imprisoned in the Cage. The bloodbath that followed is described by Charles MacFarlane:

On the day that Mahmood ascended the throne, thirty-three heads were exposed at the gate of the seraglio, among which, the hideous deformity of the chief of the black eunuchs shone conspicuously on a silver dish, allotted to him on account of the dignity of his office. The officers of the Yamacks ... were strangled and thrown into the Bosphorus; and such of the women of the serraglio who had manifested joy at Selim's death, were sewn up in sacks and drowned at the tower of Kiz-Koulessi, opposite the serraglio point.

Bayraktar Mustafa Pasha then set out to carry through the reforms that Selim III had begun, and to which Mahmut II was also committed. He began by mustering the survivors of the Nizamı Cedit, adding to them a large number of conscripts as well as troops contributed by the Anatolian war-lords, thus forming a new army called the Segbanı Cedit.

Bayraktar also attempted to reform the Janissaries as well as the *ulema*, but this only added to the growing resentment against his autocratic behaviour. The grand vezir's arrogance made him numerous enemies, and when he transferred some of his army to Ruschuk they took the opportunity to move against him.

The uprising began on 14 November 1808, when the first public appearance of the troops of the Segbanı Cedit led the Janissaries to revolt, instigated by the rumour that Bayraktar intended to abolish their corps altogether. The rebels stormed Topkapı Sarayı, but they were repulsed by the garrison, reinforced by troops from the new army, the *segban*. Early the next morning the rebels broke into the grand vezir's headquarters at the Porte, forcing Bayraktar and his men to take refuge in a powder magazine. Shortly afterwards the powder exploded, killing Bayraktar and all his men, along with several hundred Janissaries. A full-scale civil war then ensued, as the Janissaries gained the support of the city's artisans and unemployed labourers, cutting off the water supply of Topkapı Sarayı and putting the palace under siege. The Ottoman fleet remained loyal to the sultan, and when the captains saw that Topkapı Sarayı was being besieged their warships in the Golden Horn began firing on the rebels there as well as bombarding the main Janissary barracks in Beyazit. Meanwhile the *ulema* had instigated the fanatical students of the *medreses* to join the revolt, and they started fires that ravaged the entire area from the First Hill to the Third, which together with the bombardment and the fighting between the rebels and the troops loyal to the sultan killed thousands of civilians as well as combatants, turning Istanbul into a blazing hell.

When the loyal troops withdrew within the walls of Topkapı Sarayı the rebels stormed the palace again, calling for the restoration of Mustafa. This finally convinced Mahmut to order the execution of his brother, who was strangled on 16 November 1808. Mustafa

Janissary in full uniform

was twenty-nine when he died, having spent more than eighteen years of his life in the Cage. His death finally ended the revolt, as the rebels, after impaling the corpse of Bayraktar Mustafa Pasha in the Hippodrome, finally agreed to a ceasefire the following day. That same day Mustafa was interred without ceremony in the *türbe* of his father Abdül Hamit, the houses around the tomb still smouldering from the fire that had destroyed a large part of the city.

The ceasefire agreement called for the disbanding of the Segbanı Cedit, providing that their troops who had been garrisoning Topkapı Sarayı be given safe conduct to return to their homes. But when the loyal troops left the palace they were slaughtered by the mob, who also killed a number of the notables who had supported Mahmut's reforms.

Thus Mahmut managed to save his throne, as well as his life, but he now realized that before trying to create a new army he would first have to rid himself of the old one. He would have to bide his time, but he was determined to destroy the Janissaries, whatever the cost.

Meanwhile Mahmut manœuvred as best he could in the turbulent cross-currents that troubled the early years of his reign, ruthlessly eliminating those who stood in his way. The only surviving part of the Segbanı Cedit was the Artillery Corps, which Mahmut eventually built up into a loyal and effective force of some 15,000 men.

Robert Adair, British ambassador to the Porte, was granted an audience with Mahmut on 4 July 1810, bringing along with him two English travellers who had recently arrived in Istanbul. These were Lord Byron and his companion John Cam Hobhouse, Lord Broughton, who describes the sultan thus in his journal:

Sultan Mahmoud was placed in the middle of the throne, with his feet upon the ground . . . He was dressed in a robe of yellow satin, with a broader border of the darkest sable; his dagger, and an ornament on his breast, were covered with diamonds: the front of his white and blue turban shone with a treble sprig of diamonds, which served as a buckle to a high straight plume of bird-of-paradise feathers. He for the most part kept a hand on each knee, and neither moved his body nor his head, but rolled his eyes from side to side, without fixing them for an instant upon the Ambassador or any other person. Occasionally he stroked or turned up his beard, displaying a milk-white hand glittering with diamond rings. His eye-brows, eyes, and beard, being of a glossy jet black, did not appear natural, but added to that indescribable majesty that would be difficult for any but an Oriental sovereign to assume: his face was pale, and regularly formed, except that his nose (contrary to the usual form of that feature in the Oriental princes) was slightly turned up and pointed; his whole physiognomy was mild and bene-volent, but expressive and full of dignity. He appeared of a short and small stature, and about thirty years old, which is somewhat more than his actual age. [He was not quite twenty-five.]

Mahmut was now the only surviving male in the imperial Osmanlı line, and if the dynasty were to continue it was imperative that he should sire an heir to the throne. His concubine Fatma was pregnant, and there was great anticipation as her time approached, but then on 4 February 1809 she gave birth to a girl, the first child born in Topkapı Sarayı in twenty years. The baby died on 5 August of that year, and on the following day another one of Mahmut's concubines gave birth to a daughter, who passed away the following year. Altogether Mahmut's eighteen concubines of record bore him nineteen boys and seventeen girls, of whom only two sons and four daughters survived into their adult years. The two surviving sons were the future sultans Abdül Mecit I and Abdül Aziz, the first of whom was born on 23 April 1823 to Bezmialem, and the second on 9 February 1830 to Pertevniyal. According to MacFarlane, Mahmut was a very affectionate father, at least with regard to his sons Abdül Mecit and Abdül Aziz:

His affections as a father (and the feeling seems general among the Turks) is confined to his sons, on whom, I have been informed by those who have access to his palaces, he passionately dotes. He is often seen to join them in their sports, and to excite them, by his example, to deeds of address, and to manly exercises; and a scene was once described to me, in which, on his hands and knees, he was enacting the part of a horse . . .

Since the beginning of his reign Mahmut had been trying to rebuild his military forces, particularly the Janissaries. The Janissary officers had eventually agreed to cooperate in the programme, but many of them had been secretly plotting an insurrection against the sultan. Mahmut was aware of the plot, and his agents had been assassinating some of the rebel leaders among the Janissaries.

The revolt began on the evening of 14 June 1826, when the Janissaries mustered outside their main barracks on the Et Meydanı in Beyazit and overturned their *kazans*, the huge bronze cauldrons in which they were served their daily portion of *pilaf*, this being the traditional sign of their discontent. The following day they were joined by thousands of artisans as well as unemployed labourers and drifters. The revolt began in earnest that evening when the Janissaries mustered again in the Et Meydanı, after which they and their supporters sacked the palace of the grand vezir, Selim Benderli Pasha, who was at his palace on the Bosphorus.

Meanwhile, Mahmut was at his kiosk in Beşiktaş meeting his commanders, and when he heard that the revolt had begun he deployed his forces, sending his infantry and artillerymen to surround the Et Meydanı. He himself returned to Topkapı Sarayı and took the sacred standard of the Prophet Mohammed from its shrine, after which he walked in procession with his ministers and the *ulema* to the mosque of Sultan Ahmet, where the *mufti* issued a *fetva* sanctioning the dissolution and destruction of the Janissaries.

Mahmut then sent an ultimatum to the rebels, offering to pardon them if they laid down their arms immediately. When they rejected his offer scornfully, as he knew they would, he ordered his forces to attack them mercilessly. His artillerymen advanced along all the narrow streets that led to the Janissary headquarters on the Et Meydanı, where all of the rebels were crowded together in the square. The Janissaries, seeing that they were trapped, charged down one of the streets toward the advancing artillerymen, who had brought along two artillery pieces loaded with grapeshot. When the sultan's troops wavered an officer named Karacehennem (Black Hell) Ibrahim rushed to one of the guns and fired it by discharging his pistol over the priming, the grapeshot wreaking havoc among the Janissaries. A shot from the second gun routed the Janissaries and sent them fleeing back to the Et Meydanı, where the sultan's troops annihilated them.

Mahmut then gave orders for the Janissaries to be hunted down and exterminated, and even those who had retired from the corps were taken from their homes and executed. Some of them took refuge in the Belgrade Forest north of the city, but Mahmut had the woods burned down to drive them out, after which the survivors were shot down like wild animals. As the British ambassador Stratford Canning noted in a letter on 22 June of that year, describing what he himself saw when he visited Topkapı Sarayı at the time: 'The only entrance to the Seraglio, the shore under the Sultan's windows, and the sea itself are crowded with dead bodies – many of them torn and in part devoured by the dogs.'

Meanwhile, the imperial council, meeting early on Friday 16 June 1826, issued a decree formally abolishing the Janissary Corps. The decree was immediately approved by Mahmut, and at the noon prayer that day it was announced to the faithful in all the mosques of Istanbul. The Janissaries were no more, and the day of their fall was thereafter known as Vakayı Hayriye, the Auspicious Event.

Four years earlier Mahmut had commissioned a mosque to be erected near the new cannon foundry he had built at Tophane, on the European shore of the lower Bosphorus. The mosque, which was designed in the baroque style by Kirkor Balian, the first of a family of Armenian architects who would erect many buildings for the sultans in the next three decades, was finished in 1826, soon after the Auspicious Event. Thus Mahmut called it Nusretiye Camii, the Mosque of Victory, to commemorate his triumph over the Janissaries. Mahmut usually went to his new mosque whenever he was staying at his palace in Beşiktaş, but when he was residing in Topkapı Sarayı he rode to one of the imperial mosques in Istanbul. MacFarlane watched a number of these processions, one of which he writes of in *Constantinople in 1828*, giving a detailed description of Mahmut's personal appearance:

At the point of day, at the moment when the munedjim, or astrologer, announced that the sun appeared on the horizon, the procession began to issue from the serraglio gate . . . the sultan appeared about midway in the long cavalcade, with some of his ministers and courtiers preceding him, and some following him. He rode a magnificent Arabian, whose housings and trappings were richly embroidered, and studded with gold and jewels; he wore a high white turban, with a straight plume fastened in front with a large diamond aigrette; his pelise was scarlet, lined with sable. He neither turned his eyes to the right nor to the left, but looked straight before him, as if

The new palace on the Bosphorus at Beşiktaş

his eyes were fixed on vacancy. From the glimpses I had of his countenance, I thought it wore an expression of melancholy or ill-humour; but it was difficult to see him through the high waving feathers of the chamberlains and pages that marched around him on foot. He certainly looked better and more manly in his plain cavalry costume, as I have often seen him; and I fancy he might feel disgusted with the oriental luxury and finery, the feathers, silks and shawls, and other effeminate trappings that surrounded him; but which, it must be said, produced a rich and splendid effect to the eye . . . His lofty and orientally arched eye-brows, his large coal-black eyes (which are habitually however rather heavy than otherwise), his thick black beard and mustachioes, which completely veil the expression of the lower features, the lordly carriage of his head, are all calculated to strike, and coincide perfectly, with our picturesque idea of an eastern despot . . . His stature is not tall, but a fine breadth of shoulders, an open chest, and well set arms denote robustness and great bodily strength . . .

According to MacFarlane, Mahmut had a good sense of humour, albeit coarse, and he heard many stories about the sultan's earthy witticisms:

We should scarcely expect facetiousness and a love of coarse humour and drollery to exist in a mind like Mahmut's, yet a hundred well-attested stories tend to prove they really do. All the Turkish witticisms I ever heard were so gross, that they could scarcely bear repetition in an English ale-house; and I regret to say, that the sallies attributed to the sultan, are marked with the general character . . .

MacFarlane reports on the sultan's growing addiction to alcohol, which became more and more evident to his discontented subjects:

Some of the discontented Osmanlis (who then evidently formed a considerable body at the capital, as well as in Asia Minor, where I had recently listened to their complaints) said he must be mad, while certain rayahs [non-Muslim minorities] whispered he is only drunk. The latter opinion, that the sultan drank wine, and occasionally to excess, I may mention, in passing, was pretty generally established at Constantinople. These assertions it is of course difficult to prove or disprove, but they are countenanced to a certain degree, by an irregularity of purpose, and by the emanation of violent measures, conceived in the night, and sometimes, though not always, abrogated in the morning; and confirmed (if my informant told the truth) by the fragments of certain long-necked bottles, which are never seen to contain any thing but good French wines, that were now and then espied thrown in heaps in the garden of a small lonely kiosk on the hills of Asia, close behind the beautiful village of Kanderli [Kandilli], to which the sultan was wont to resort nearly every evening during the summer of 1828. The usual associate in these convivial moments was said to be his selictar or sword-bearer.

Meanwhile, the Ottoman Empire had suffered a series of defeats at the hands of the Russians, losing large parts of its territory, in addition to Greece emerging as an independent nation in 1833 and Egypt becoming virtually autonomous under Mehmet Ali Pasha. According to Helmuth von Moltke, the future Prussian field marshal, then in Ottoman service, Mahmut shed bitter tears when he signed the humiliating peace treaties that gave Greece freedom and Egypt autonomy, and for weeks afterwards he shut himself off in one of his palaces on the Bosphorus, almost crushed in spirit. As von Moltke wrote of Mahmut:

He had failed in the object for which he had striven all his life. Rivers of blood had been shed, the old institutions and sacred traditions of the country had been destroyed, the faith and pride of his people had been undermined for the sake of reform, and that reform was condemned by the event.

During the remaining years of Mahmut's reign he tried to carry out his Westernizing reforms, personally supervising the work of rebuilding the empire's armed forces. The reforms also brought Western ways to Istanbul, particularly in the sultan's court. Mahmut dressed like a European monarch rather than an oriental potentate, appearing on state occasions and cultural events outside the palace clad in trousers and the black frock-coat known as the Stambouline, wearing the red Moroccan fez rather than the robes and turban of his predecessors. In 1829 he issued a decree forbidding the wearing of the old-fashioned costumes except by the clergy, and thenceforth the fez became the accepted head-dress. Stratford Canning remarked on the change in dress:

Every person who has been absent and has now returned, notices the change, which has been most extraordinary. Very few years more and not a turban will exist . . . employees of every description now wear the red cap, Cossack trousers, black boots, and a plain red or blue coat buttoned under the chin. No gold embroidery, no jewels, no pelisses.

The clothing reform infuriated religious conservatives. One day, when Mahmut was riding through the streets of Istanbul in his carriage, a dervish shouted at him, 'Infidel sultan, God will demand an accounting for your blasphemy! You are destroying Islam!' Nevertheless Mahmut continued with his reforms, among which was a guarantee of equality in Ottoman civil law for all of his people regardless of their religion: as he insisted, 'I distinguish between my subjects Muslims in the mosque, Christians in the church, Jews in the synagogue, but there is no difference among them in any other way.'

European symphonies and operas had been brought to Istanbul by Giuseppe Donizetti, whom Mahmut had hired as his musical director in 1828, making him a pasha. Donizetti Pasha, elder brother of the famous Gaetano Donizetti, trained the imperial band in music *alafranga*, i.e., in the manner of the 'Franks', or Europeans, and wrote the Ottoman national anthem; later he built the first opera house in Istanbul, bringing foreign musical groups to perform there. The first theatre in the city was founded in 1840 with the financial support of the Ottoman government together with the foreign embassies; this was erected in Pera by a Genoese named Giustiani, whose successor, the Italian Bosco, put on his own magic shows as well as bringing in European plays and operas. Several other theatres soon opened, all of them catering principally to foreigners and the non-Muslim minorities, though the sultan often attended première performances.

By this time Mahmut had virtually abandoned Topkapı Sarayı in favour of his new palace at Beşiktaş on the European shore of the Bosphorus, which had been rebuilt for him in the European style by his Armenian architect Kirkor Balian. Julia Pardoe describes the palace in *The Beauties of the Bosphorus* (1839), where she would seem to have overestimated the number of Mahmut's residences:

... *every pretty bay in the Bosphorus has its kiosque; and the number of his residences in the vicinity of the capital amounts to fifty-seven. The palace of Beshik-Tash is the last and most extensive of the whole, but decidedly the least picturesque and elegant. Its Armenian architect was not, however, selected without due consideration on the part of the Sultan, who was won to decide on the present plan by the assurance that it was thoroughly European; a fact which could not be disputed, were the glittering and well-proportioned columns that support the open peristyle swept away, when this huge pile, which has cost upwards of a million sterling, would present precisely the appearance of a manufactory.*

By 1838 only six of Mahmut's thirty-six children were alive: his sons Abdül Mecit and Abdül Aziz, and his daughters Saliha, Mihrimah, Atiye and Adile. The extremely high rate of infant mortality in the imperial Osmanlı line led to rumours among the Europeans of Pera that the old Ottoman practice of infanticide was still being carried out in the harem, along with abortions performed by incompetent midwives. Charles White claims that infanticide was being practised in the Ottoman family to eliminate unwanted heirs to the throne, particularly in the Cage:

Whenever younger sons or brothers have been permitted to live, they have been immured within the Seraglio, in that part of the third court called 'the Cage'. There, at a certain age, they are provided with small harems, but care was provided to select sterile slaves. If, however, in spite of this precaution, symptoms of maternity appeared, the offspring, or sometimes even the mother, was destroyed. This barbarous practice, still in force, was adopted to prevent the birth of collateral competitors for the succession, which always passes to the eldest male, whether brother or cousin . . .

Mahmut married off his daughter Mihrimah in the spring of 1836 to Mehmet Said Pasha, admiral of the Ottoman navy. The festivities are described by von Moltke, who notes that the bride had never seen the groom until the day of the wedding:

The wedding festivities and feasts began on 28 April and ended on 5 May, when the bride went to the palace of her husband.
The day before yesterday the sultan gave a magnificent banquet

*The Ottoman Court celebrating a festival during the
Tulip Period, painting by Jean-Baptiste Vanmour, c. 1720*

*for the ambassadors in honour of the marriage of his second daughter
Mihrimah. Everyone assembled in a mansion with windows on
every side and a panoramic view of Constantinople, Pera and the
sea. Under the windows tightrope walkers, acrobats on horseback,
and Iranian pantomime artists performed for innumerable spectators. The women, wearing voluminous ferajes [cloaks] and yash-
maks [veiled headdresses] were seated in rows on a high slope.
Before the sun set they took us to a large old Turkish pavilion where
a table was set for a hundred people. The bronze trays, silver cutlery
and porcelain were truly magnificent. Over two hundred candles
illuminated this gathering of the diplomatic corps, the sultan's
son-in-law, viziers, and high-ranking officers of the empire.*

*Yesterday the princess's trousseau was taken to her new residence.
Guarded by cavalrymen and preceded by several pashas, the pro-*

cession consisted of forty mules loaded with bales of precious cloth, twenty coaches loaded with shawls, carpets, silk garments and other items, and behind these came one hundred and sixty porters bearing large silver trays on their heads. On the first of these trays was a splendid Koran with a gold binding set with pearls, followed by large silver chairs, braziers, boxes of jewellery, gold bird cages and the Lord knows what else ...

Today the princess was to be given to the husband she had not yet seen. The cavalry led the procession, followed by all the palace officials, all the pashas, the mufti, and my friend the Minister of War. Behind these came the sultan's two sons in an open carriage, and finally a magnificent coach, entirely closed, carrying the bride. The coach and six horses were the gift of the Czar of Russia. This was followed by about forty coaches in which the odalisques were seated.

Early in the summer of 1839 the Ottoman army was annihilated in Syria by the forces of Ibrahim Pasha, son of Mehmet Ali Pasha of Egypt. The news reached Mahmut just before he died on 1 July 1839, succumbing to the combined effects of tuberculosis and cirrhosis of the liver. That same day he was succeeded by his son Abdül Mecit. Charles White notes that Mahmut's addiction to fortified wine hastened his end:

During the last ten years of his life his passion for indulgence gradually increased, until within the last two years, when, finding all ordinary mediums of excitement ineffectual, he had recourse to pure alcohol. (The imperial wine-merchant was a Belgian, Mr. Le Moine, established at Galata. He stated that he was compelled to falsify all wines by adding brandies. The strongest unadulterated wines were found too insipid.) If we are to give credit to the assertions of well informed persons, the delirium tremens, which prematurely terminated the great reformer's career, on the 1st of July, 1839, must be mainly attributed to this fatal indulgence.

Mahmut was buried in a huge *türbe* that was erected for him on the Second Hill beside Divan Yolu, the main avenue of Istanbul.

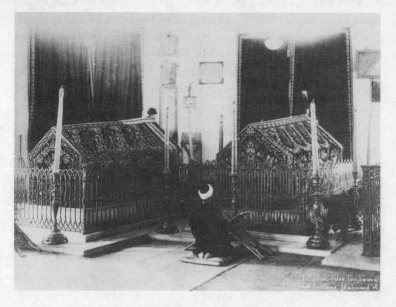

Tomb of Mahmut II (1808–39);
catafalques of Mahmut II (right) and Abdül Aziz (left).
Photograph by Abdullah Frères, c. 1880

The mausoleum, designed in the baroque style by Karabet Balian, was not completed until the year after Mahmut's death.

MacFarlane, writing a decade after the sultan's death, tells how the sight of this *türbe* reminded him of the Mahmut that he had known:

One evening, as the sun was setting, I stopped, not without interest and emotion, before the spacious white marble Tourbe which contains all that is left of Sultan Mahmoud. The last of the many times I saw the energetic potentate was close by this very spot, when he was full of life and health, and looked like one almost certain to attain his three score years and ten. His robust vigorous frame, his magnificent breadth of chest, his most striking countenance, proud, haughty and handsome, and his large jet black very peculiar eyes (I never saw eyes like them), which looked you through and through, and which were never quiet, all rose before me. He was quiet enough now! Disappointment and excess, Ibrahim Pasha and brandy, had sent him prematurely to his grave; and here he lay in a wooden sarcophagus covered with rich Cashmere shawls, and his red fez and blue tassle at the head . . .

Stratford Canning's summing-up of Mahmut's accomplishments and failures ended with this appraisal of his complex character: 'It may be said with truth that whatever merit he possessed was his own, and that much of what was wrong in his character and conduct resulted from circumstances beyond his control. Peace be to his memory!'

Chapter 15

ON THE SHORES OF
THE BOSPHORUS

Abdül Mecit was sixteen years old when he became sultan, succeeding his father Mahmut II. He was the first son to succeed his father to the throne in two centuries, and thus was never in the Cage, where his eleven predecessors had in succession been confined. As soon as Abdül Mecit came to the throne his brother Abdül Aziz, who was then nine years old, would normally have been confined to the Cage, but instead he was allowed to remain in the harem with his mother Pertevniyal until he reached the age of puberty. Charles White notes that the other wives and children of the deceased sultan were also treated with great kindness by Abdül Mecit:

Upon the death of Mahmoud, his young unmarried family were removed by their elder brother, Sultan Abdoul Medjit, to his palace, and were there carefully and tenderly educated. At the same time the four surviving kadinns of Mahmoud were established in palaces on the Bosphorus, two near Beglerbey and two near Tcheraghan, where they enjoy full liberty.

Abdül Mecit's mother Bezmialem, who was then only thirty-one, now became *valide sultan*, the first to hold that title since Nakşidil, mother of Mahmut II, who had died twenty-two years before. The other women in the departed sultan's harem would ordinarily have been relegated to the Eski Saray, but Abdül Mecit abandoned that practice and moved them to some of the smaller palaces along the Bosphorus.

According to Charles White, the first thing that Bezmialem did when she became *valide* was to persuade her son to destroy his late father's stock of wine and other alcoholic beverages in the hope that the new sultan would not become addicted to drink:

On the demise of Mahmood, his cellar contained many hundred bottles of the choicest wines and most powerful spirits. The Valida Sultan, eager to inspire her son with detestation for the beverage that led to his father's death, induced the young Sultan to order every bottle to be broken and cast into the Bosphorus, and with them all the decanters and glasses that served as accessories. Abdoul Medjid Khan has shown himself a full participator in his mother's sentiments. Up to the present time, he has abstained from wine and smoking, and is known, as regards diet, to be extremely temperate and abstemious.

Abdül Mecit was committed to continuing the Tanzimat, or reform movement, that had been started by his father Mahmut II, a programme principally implemented by Reşid Pasha. These reforms were embodied in a *hatti şerif*, proclaimed on 3 November 1839 at a pavilion in the lower gardens of Topkapı Sarayı known as Gülhane, the Rose House. The Gülhane Decree stated that Abdül Mecit intended to rule as an enlightened monarch, promising that he would protect the lives and property of all his subjects – Muslims, Christians and Jews alike – and that he would create a government in which there would be equitable taxation, regular legislative councils and a fair system of conscription to obtain manpower for a modern army and navy. But as Charles White wrote less than two years later: 'Recent events have shown that Abdoul Medjid's worthy intentions have given way to the pernicious advice of evil counsellors, aided by foreign intrigue.'

Abdül Mecit was not the man his father had been, neither in his physical appearance nor in his character. As MacFarlane remarked:

A greater contrast between a son and a father is scarcely to be conceived than in the person and character of Sultan Abdul Medjid, who is frail, narrow-chested, dull-eyed, sickly-looking, with an expression of countenance that is gentle and amiable, but not very intellectual, and with features that are not at all handsome.

The archaeologist Austen Henry Layard, who later served as British ambassador to the Porte, writes of Abdül Mecit in his autobiography:

He differed in every respect from his bold and resolute father, Mahmoud. He was a kind-hearted, well-intentioned man, desirous of promoting the prosperity and welfare of his subjects, but weak and constitutionally feeble. His face agreed with his character. He was small in stature, thin and pale, and sat with downcast eyes; but the expression of his countenance, although melancholic, was kindly and benevolent, and when lighted up with a smile, which it frequently was when the conversation took a turn which pleased him, was very attractive and sympathetic. Like several of his predecessors, and like his successors, he has the taint of madness which has existed in the family since Sultan Ibrahim, who was known as 'the madman.' It showed itself particularly in a kind of exaggerated horror of anything which he imagined to be unclean. If a plate or glass were brought to him which appeared to his excited imagination not to have been scrupulously cleansed, he would order it to be thrown out of the window at once; and an attendant upon whose garment he could detect a speck of dirt was at once banished from his presence. He was constantly haunted by the dread of impurity.

Foreign observers were unaware that Abdül Mecit was suffering from tuberculosis, which would eventually kill him. There were rumours that the sultan was addicted to drink and that he was an epileptic, as MacFarlane notes, which leads him into a diatribe against the 'Oriental' way of palace life that had so obviously weakened the young sultan:

There was a prevalent report that Abdul Medjid had addicted himself to the vice which had killed his father; but I was assured by some who knew the truth, if they chose to tell it, that he drank

Abdül Mecit I (1839–61)

neither wine nor spirits. As to the other cause of debility and premature decay, I never heard a doubt expressed about that. Some said that he was subject to epileptic fits; and his whole appearance certainly went to confirm rather than to shake this assertion. Still, however, his countenance was most gentle and prepossessing. I pitied him as I thought of the accursed system of Oriental life into which he had been initiated as a mere boy, and of which there was not the slightest hope that he ever would or could free himself. Before he was twenty years old, the puny stripling was the father of eight children, born to him by different women in the imperial harem, in the course of little more than three years.

MacFarlane goes on to mention the sultan's younger brother, Abdül Aziz, who had been confined at first to the harem and then to the Cage ever since the accession of Abdül Mecit:

Of his younger brother Abdul Haziz [Aziz], who will be his successor, nothing was ever seen or heard. He was a mere state prisoner, closely shut up in a harem, like the princes of the blood in the old times, or before reform and Reschid Pasha were things known or spoken of. At first there were a few flourishes in the newspapers about this 'excellent and enlightened' young prince, and of the affection which existed between him and his imperial brother; and the visits which the Sultan paid to his state prison were pompously inserted in the Court intelligence; but this has ceased long ago, and the name of the captive was now no longer mentioned. He might have been dead and buried, and yet not more completely forgotten . . .

Abdül Mecit sired eleven more children during the years 1843–8, comprising five sons and six daughters. The birth of each of the royal children was marked by cannonades, as MacFarlane reports, noting that most of the infants died soon after their birth:

While we were in the country, or between the month of August, 1847, and June, 1848, the Sultan had four children, whose births were announced to the world by tremendous and long-repeated discharges of artillery. The weakness and unhealthiness of the imperial harem is notorious; three of these infants died before they were a month old . . . I have noted in my diary, on Saturday the 22nd of April, 1848:– 'Very early in the morning we were started out of our sleep by a tremendous firing of salutes. The Sultan has another son. Only last week he had another daughter! These salutes for the male child will be repeated five times a-day for seven days; for a female child they keep up the salutes only three days.'

Altogether Abdül Mecit fathered eighteen sons and twenty-five daughters, including two sets of twins, with twenty-five of his children dying in infancy. Among his sons were the future sultans Murat V, Abdül Hamit II, Mehmet V Reşat and Mehmet VI Vahidettin, the last four rulers of the Ottoman Empire. Murat was born on 21 September 1840 to Şevkefza, a Circassian girl whom Abdül Mecit had married on 1 August 1839, elevating her to the rank of *haseki* after she bore his son. Abdül Hamit was born on 22 September 1842 to Tirimüjgan, another Circassian girl, whom he had married on

10 November 1841. Ordinarily Tirimüjgan would have been elevated to the status of *haseki* on giving birth to a son, but several months earlier, while in the sultan's bed, she had coughed up some blood, leading him to suspect that she had tuberculosis. Thus Abdül Mecit never again took Tirimüjgan to his bed, and after the birth of Abdül Hamit she took her son with her to her own apartment in the harem, where they were never favoured by a visit from the sultan. Tirimüjgan died of tuberculosis on 26 April 1853, and the Greek doctor Zographos describes how Abdül Hamit crept back into his mother's room after her death and pulled aside the sheet that covered her, so as to look upon her face for the last time. Abdül Mecit then assigned the care of the young prince to Perestu, a barren concubine whom he had kept on from the harem of his deceased father Mahmut II, and she looked after Abdül Hamit like a mother for the rest of her days.

Mehmet Reşat was born on 3 November 1844 to Gülcemal, a girl of unknown origin whom Abdül Mecit had married on 27 March 1853. Mehmet Vahidettin was born on 2 February 1861 to Gülüştü, a Circassian girl whom the sultan had taken into his harem the previous year. Abdül Mecit never went through a formal ceremony of marriage with Gülüştü, who died in May 1861. Her infant son was given into the care of another of the sultan's concubines, whose name is unknown.

The sultan's programme of reforms was opposed by a group of conservatives led by Riza Pasha. Riza Pasha's power stemmed from his relationship with the *valide sultan* Bezmialem, who exerted considerable influence over her son Abdül Mecit, according to MacFarlane:

I have hinted more than once that the Sultana Valide or mother of Sultan Abdul Medjid had a powerful influence in the court and government. So great was her sway over her affectionate, gentle, and weak-minded son, that she could at any time defeat whatever project was displeasing to her or her friends, and change ministers and high functionaries as she chose. This woman was originally a purchased Circassian slave. Her harem education could scarcely have developed her intellect or raised her moral character. Yet the

Valide had her good qualities, she was charitable and very generous; and her munificence was most advantageously displayed in the recent creation and endowment of a splendid hospital for the poor over in Constantinople. Many other outward acts betokened goodness of heart, if not soundness of judgment. It had been found in innumerable cases that she thought and acted with Riza Pasha, making his cause her cause; and that no party combination was strong enough to stand against the influence she exercised over her son. That the rival of Reschid Pasha, the active Riza Pasha, a remarkably handsome man, was her paramour, and had been ever since the death of Sultan Mahmoud, might be a scandal, but if so, it was certainly a scandal in which everybody seemed to believe. Reschid Pasha's friends or admirers were constantly quoting this liaison as the source of difficulty and embarrassment to his government. The liberty allowed to the Sultana Valide was more than sufficient for affording her the opportunities of carrying on such an intrigue. She went and came as she chose; she had her separate establishment, her separate revenues and administrator; few women, whether Turkish or unrestrained Christians, were so much abroad as she was; still proud of her faded beauty, she took little trouble to cover her face – I believe there was hardly a ghiaour [infidel] dwelling in Galata or Pera but knew her face and person . . . Her neutralized black gentlemen in embroidered frock-coats were more frequently seen about Constantinople and in the Christian suburbs than almost any other class of officials.

Again according to MacFarlane, Abdül Mecit spent most of his time in his palace on the Bosphorus at Beşiktaş, where his preferred entertainment was Western music:

Except for the Friday visit to the mosques, the Sultan, during our long stay at Constantinople, very rarely left his palace at Beshiktash . . . Everybody knows that his harem was absolutely crowded with women, and that by far the greater part of his time was spent in it . . . For music he had a perfect passion and a very good taste. His own Turkish band, trained by German and Italian masters, executed the best of modern compositions. The rude barbaric music of the Turks was seldom heard in the palace, or even indeed in the regimental bands. Whatever noted player visited Constantinople – whether pianist, flutist, or fiddler – he was sure to be invited to the palace to play for one or more evenings to the Sultan, and equally sure to get a good sum of money, and a gold, diamond-set snuff-box. The most refined, or I should not be far wrong in saying the only refined amusements of the serraglio, began and ended in music. The most sensual of all the fine arts was the most spiritual of Abdul Medjit's pastimes. From these musical soirées his women were of course rigidly excluded. If the kadinns and odalisks heard the sweet strains, it must have been at a distance, and through screens and wooden partitions.

Charles White writes about the harem of Abdül Mecit and their way of life in the imperial palace at Beşiktaş, where the sultan seems to have had his hands full with his multitudinous wives and concubines:

The Kadinns are now exclusively Circassians, although, in former times, the imperial harem contained women of all countries and creeds. They are without exception slaves, presented to the Sultan by his mother, aunts, sisters, and favourites, or purchased by his own commissioners. These Kadinns enjoy equal rights and privileges. Their establishments are distinct, but in all respects similar. They have separate suites of apartments, baths, and offices, and to each is allotted an equal number of Aghas and female slaves acting as ladies of honour, readers, dressers, and attendants. Their pin or slipper money amounts to about twenty-five thousand piastres per month; all other expenses are defrayed by the Sultan's treasurer.

Minute attention is paid to all points of etiquette, and the utmost partiality is observed in the distribution of presents or other marks of favour, in order to obviate jealousies. For, although the Sultan is never approached by these ladies without the humblest demonstrations of deference, even, as it is admitted, to their entering the imperial couch at the foot, his Majesty is nevertheless subject to

Dolmabahçe Sarayı, in the Illustrated London News *of 1856*

frequent explosions of ill-humour, during the intervals of which the little artifices of tears, poutings, tender reproaches, and hysterics are not spared. Although slaves, for they are never manumitted, unless they become de jure *free, as Validas, their claims upon the Sultan's attentions are the same as those of married women, in the few private families in which there is more than one legal wife . . .*

Around 1846 Abdül Mecit commissioned Karabet Balian and his son Nikoğos to erect a new palace at Beşiktaş, whereupon the old palace on the site was condemned to be demolished. The new imperial residence came to be known as Dolmabahçe Sarayı, the Palace of the Filled-in Garden, since it was erected on ground that had been filled in on the shallows of the Bosphorus at the time of the Conquest.

While Dolmabahçe Sarayı was being built Abdül Mecit resided principally at the nearby palace of Çırağan, which would itself be rebuilt in the following decade. During that time the sultan commissioned Nikoğos Balian to build two small summer palaces for him, one of them on the hills above the European shore of the Bosphorus, and the other across the straits on one of the two streams known as the Sweet Waters of Asia. The European summer residence was known as Ihlamur Kasrı, the Palace of the Linden Trees, and the Asian was called Küçüksu Kasrı, the Palace of the Little Stream. Around the same time the sultan built a new pavilion in the Fourth Court of Topkapı Sarayı, the Mecidiye Köşk, which he used as a *pied-à-terre* whenever he visited the old palace.

One of the few descriptions of life in the old Çırağan Sarayı is that of Leyla Hanım, daughter of the sultan's physician, who first entered the palace in 1853 when she was a small child. In her memoirs she tells an anecdote about the palace, where one evening Abdül Mecit was a surprise guest in the room of one of his favourites. As the sultan approached the room he heard the sound of music, and he remarked, 'Well, it seems that we are having some music, so much the better!' He then entered the room and announced his presence:

'Would you kindly admit to your gracious company he who has chanced to arrive so unexpectedly and guided only by his good fortune towards this most agreeable encounter?' The young favourite had invited one of her companions, and both of them were playing some music and dancing quite intimately. The unexpected appearance of the Sultan caused them a joyous surprise which was quickly followed by a certain unease. In these days it was considered improper for ladies of station to succumb to the pleasure of the dance. The Sultan, seeing that the ladies were disconcerted, hastened to put them at their ease.

'I have not come to interrupt your pleasure: please permit me to stay here in a corner so that I may watch and listen to you. I beg you to continue your pastimes and not deprive me of the pleasure of participating in your divertisements.'

The ice was broken. The doors were closed again and there followed a very gay and most agreeable evening in complete privacy. The Sultan was enchanted and presented the ladies, as a remembrance of this encounter, some magnificent jewels which he had brought by a haznedar; *he also made presents to the* kalfas *and withdrew while begging them to let him know when they intended to have a similar meeting in the future.*

Abdül Mecit periodically changed his residence with the seasons, moving from one of his palaces along the Bosphorus or Golden Horn to another, going to Topkapı Sarayı only on ceremonial occasions. White describes these seasonal peregrinations:

The period when the Sultan changes his residence is always a moment of recreation and diversity to the whole harem. Unless some extraordinary occurrence should intervene, these migrations take place nearly at the same period every year. Until lately, the court quitted the winter palace of Beshiktash about the first of May, old style. It then removed for a month to the small palace of Khiat Khana, during which time the public was forbidden to approach within three-quarters of a mile, as the ladies were accustomed to stroll and divert themselves in the surrounding meadows . . . Lately, this palace has been found inconvenient and unhealthy; and, in consequence, the Sultan has removed direct from Beshiktash to the splendid palace of Tcheraghan, or to that of Beglerbey, immediately opposite. The return to Beshiktash takes place about a fortnight before the autumnal equinox, although the month of October is the most temperate and agreeable of the whole year. These changes do not take place without referring to the Munejim Bashy [the chief astrologer], who fixes the most propitious hour. Indeed, few events of importance occur without his being consulted.

Lady Hornby, wife of Sir Edward Hornby, Lord Commissioner to the Ottoman Government, describes life in the British Embassy in Pera during the Crimean War in her memoir, including an account of a ball given in 1855 by Lord and Lady Stratford at which Abdül Mecit was the guest of honour:

Lord Stratford and his Staff, of course, met him at the carriage door, and as he alighted, a communication by means of a galvanic wire was made to the fleet, who saluted him with prolonged salvos of cannon. Lady Stratford and her daughters received him at the head of the staircase . . . Every one of course made way, and Abdul Medjid quietly walked up the ballroom with Lord and Lady Stratford, their daughters, and a gorgeous array of Pashas in the rear. He paused with evident delight and pleasure at the really beautiful scene before him, bowing on both sides, and smiling as he went. A velvet and gold chair, raised a few steps, had been placed for him at one side of the room; but, on being conducted to it, he seemed much too pleased to sit down, and continued standing, looking about him with the undisguised pleasure and simplicity of a child. He was dressed in a plain dark-blue frock-coat, the cuffs and collar crimson, and covered with brilliants. The hilt of his sword was covered entirely also in brilliants. Of course he wore the everlasting fez. There is something extremely interesting in his appearance. He looks languid and careworn, but, when spoken to, his fine dark eyes brighten up and he smiles the most frank and winning of smiles.

The end of the Crimean War was celebrated at a banquet in Dolmabahçe Sarayı on 13 July 1856, an occasion that also marked the dedication of the new palace. Thenceforth Dolmabahçe became the principal imperial residence, while Topkapı Sarayı was used only for certain state occasions. A fire at Topkapı Sarayı the previous winter had destroyed the Summer Harem, which was never thereafter rebuilt. The old palace of Topkapı Sarayı was thenceforth used to house the women of departed sultans and their servants, just as the Eski Saray in Beyazit had done in former times.

Abdül Mecit also added a large building within the palace grounds to house the theatre, which officially opened on 12 January 1859 with the sultan and his court in attendance along with the foreign diplomatic corps and their wives. The programme included two acts of the opera *Scaraccia*, by Luigi Ricci, followed by a performance by Padovani of one of his own compositions on the violin, and then finally the ballet *Chasse de Diane*. The theatre was also used for art exhibitions, including the works of foreign artists, which the sultan examined with particular interest.

Banquet in Dolmabahçe Sarayı on 13 July 1856 to celebrate
the end of the Crimean War and the opening of the palace,
Illustrated London News, *1856*

Abdül Mecit impoverished the empire with his extravagances.
Cevdet Pasha, in a report written a quarter of a century later, noted
that the bill paid by Abdül Mecit to the Armenian firm of Küçükoğlu,
who provided the French furniture for the sultan's new palaces and
the jewellery and European dresses for the women of his harem,
was equal to the amount expended on the entire Ottoman army in
Thrace for that year. Melek Hanım, wife of the grand vezir Kıbrıslı
Mehmet Emin Pasha, writes in her memoirs of the extravagance
and scandalous behaviour of the sultan's women, who, from her
account, would seem to have broken free of his control:

The Sultan's love for his wives – and very numerous they were –
was ruining the country. They contrived at once to gratify their

caprices, whatever might be their object. They availed themselves of it to obtain from him the most costly presents. Covered with diamonds, and attended by numerous slaves, they drove out in carriages, each of which, with its equipments, costs about 900,000 piastres (£8,000). Their apartments were constantly replenished with new furniture. In the space of two years the seraglio was furnished about four times over.

Far from recompensing their master for his kindness by their fidelity, they were seen driving about, almost entirely unveiled, and conversing with the young men in the liveliest manner. At night, sitting at their windows, they accosted the passersby, and introduced them into the palace. Those who were without paramours formed the exception. Frequently the favours of one of the Sultan's wives, or odalisques, were attended with bounties and presents big enough to make the fortune of him who received it. In fact, these women were utterly regardless of the costliness of what they bestowed; it was a regular case of pillage . . . The Valideh-Sultan, the mother of the sovereign, was the most powerful of all, and far surpassed all of the other ladies of the palace by her libertinism and thirst for power. Judge what consequences such a system must produce throughout the whole of the administration.

Melek Hanım goes on to tell the shocking story of the sultan's favourite wife Besme, whom he had first noticed when she was a slave of Mısırlı Hanım, widow of Ibrahim Pasha of Egypt. Besme refused to enter the sultan's harem until he agreed to marry her, which he did in 1851. Abdül Mecit then entrusted Besme with the care of the youngest of his three sons, the seven-year-old Mehmet Reşat, whose mother had recently died. But Besme mistreated the young prince, while at the same time she carried on illicit love-affairs with a number of menservants on the palace staff, at least according to the story told by Melek Hanım, who says that Abdül Mecit eventually learned of his wife's affairs and sent her off into exile on 'a pleasure-galley which he had presented to her'.

Abdül Mecit's mother and married sisters were no longer confined

Sultan in the harem with two of his Circassian concubines,
with a black eunuch in the background

to the harem, nor, according to MacFarlane, were the women of his
pashas and other ministers. MacFarlane's description of their way of
life shows that the women of the Ottoman aristocracy were enjoying
themselves in endless excursions around the town and along the shores
of the Bosphorus and the Golden Horn, activities that would have
been inconceivable in earlier times. He writes, disapprovingly:

Nothing that I could hear from any reliable source was proper to
raise my estimate of the character, or intellects, or tastes, of any of

*the great Turkish ladies. It would be a great mistake to treat them
merely as the inmates of the harem, or as recluses, or caged birds.
If the Sultan's own women were caged, none others were. His
married sisters, as well as his mother, were constantly abroad. The
women of the Pashas and other great employés were more out of doors
(in the daytime) than our fashionable and most stirring ladies during
the London season: they were to be seen every day, when the weather
was fine, on the Bosphorus, in the Golden Horn, in the bazaars, on
the great square near the Seraskier's tower, and in the streets; they
were incessantly going and coming, shopping and paying visits; they
were greater gadabouts than the belles of Paris in the old and gay time.
If their graceless, cumbersome, out-of-door dresses spoiled or utterly
concealed their figures, and if their loose, shapeless, yellow-morocco
boots, and their awkward slippers, hid their feet and spoiled their
gait, the younger and handsomer of them took good care that their
yashmacs should not conceal their faces. The gauze worn by these
dames of highest fashion was as transparent as the famed textile of
old Cos, and it was drawn across only the chin and forehead. The
bosom was exposed, as I have already mentioned. From some of the
handsomest and greatest one not unfrequently heard language which
a nymph or matron of Billingsgate would not use.*

Abdül Mecit spent enormous sums on the weddings of his daughters, three of whom – Refia, Cemile and Münire – were married
within a two-week period in June 1858. The sultan built a new
palace on the Bosphorus for each of the three princesses as one of
his wedding gifts. Thus the shores of the Bosphorus came to be
lined with palaces, with *pazar caiques* rowing the imperial family
and their court from one pleasure dome to another in an endless
series of weddings and other celebrations.

The extravagance of Abdül Mecit and his court forced the government to take out a series of foreign loans at very high interest rates,
and the empire was soon saddled with debts far beyond its ability
to pay. Abdül Mecit made futile attempts at economizing, such as
chaining the wheels of the carriages used by the women of his harem

*Palace of Hadice Sultan, daughter of Abdül Mecit,
on the Bosphorus at Ortaköy*

to stop them from going on shopping sprees in Pera, but to no avail. He seemed to be depressed at his inability to halt the decline of his empire, according to Melek Hanım, who tells how his ministers influenced the sultan to leave concerns of state to them:

In utter despair, he saw that his efforts would be powerless to retard the fall of the power of the Osmanlis. His ministers, far from endeavouring to revive his hopes, persuaded him to forget, in sensual delights, the sombre thoughts that assailed him. 'You are our Sultan,' they would say; 'to you belong repose and pleasures; the bustle and fatigue of public affairs are our portion.' While speaking thus they made it a rule to offer their master as frequently as possible the most sumptuous repasts, at which they induced him to drink copiously; in this manner they habituated him to the immoderate use of wine and other strong drink, and led him to abandon to themselves the reins of government. They also endeavoured to distract him from public affairs, by favouring his natural taste for luxury and dissipation.

Abdül Mecit's health had been failing for years, for he had long been suffering from tuberculosis that had not been properly treated. On 11 April 1861 he rode from Dolmabahçe to Topkapı Sarayı, where for two hours he sat before the Gate of Salutations receiving greetings from all the notables of his empire, weak and ill though he was. After the ceremony he collapsed in the harem of Topkapı Sarayı and remained unconscious for some time before he recovered sufficiently to return to Dolmabahçe, which he managed to do only with great difficulty. His physicians examined him and found that he had contracted pneumonia, which soon drained what little strength he had. As his end neared Abdül Mecit tried to arrange for the succession of his eldest son, Murat, who was then in his twenty-first year. But the grand vezir Kıbrıslı Mehmet Emin Pasha succeeded in maintaining the law of succession that had been in use since the early seventeenth century. Thus the throne went to the eldest male in the Osmanlı line, in this case the sultan's half-brother Abdül Aziz, who in anticipation of this had been given the title of *veliaht*, or crown prince. When Abdül Mecit was informed of this he called for his brother and with his last breath gave him his blessing as his successor. According to Dr Zographos, who was tending him at the time, the sultan spoke thus to Abdül Aziz: 'You can see, brother, there is no hope for me. I am finished. Now everything is yours. The people around us never allowed us to come together. We have never known true brotherhood. God bless you!'

Abdül Aziz was overcome with grief, leaving his brother's room in tears. A short while afterwards, in the early evening of 25 June 1861, Abdül Mecit passed away. The word of his death quickly spread to the harem, where his women filled the palace with their wailing. The doctors informed the grand vezir, who immediately went to wake the crown prince and tell him the news. But Abdül Aziz had already been awakened by the wailing and knew what it meant; shaking with sobs he looked at Mehmet Emin Pasha and asked, 'Is my brother really dead? When did he die?'

The final illness of Abdül Mecit had been kept secret by the grand vezir Mehmet Emin Pasha, who withheld the news of the sultan's death until Abdül Aziz had been girded with the sword of Osman Gazi and officially proclaimed as successor.

Abdül Mecit was two months past his thirty-eighth birthday when he died, having reigned for nearly twenty-two years. Later that day he was buried in the *türbe* that he had built behind the mosque of Sultan Selim I on the Fifth Hill. He had chosen that site for his mausoleum because of his admiration for his great warrior ancestor, Selim the Grim, for in his youth he had dreams of being a great sultan. But his dreams were never realized, for reasons that were apparent to Stratford Canning, writing fondly of Abdül Mecit in his memoirs:

. . . the graciousness of his manner and the intelligent, though gentle and even melancholy, expression of his countenance warrant a hope, perhaps a sanguine one, that with riper years and a more experienced judgement he may prove a real blessing and source of strength to his country . . . He possessed a kindly disposition, a sound understanding, a clear sense of duty, proper feelings of dignity without pride, and a degree of humanity seldom, if ever, exhibited by the best of his ancestors. The full development of these qualities found a check in the want of vigour which dated from his birth and which his early accession to the throne and consequent indulgence in youthful passions served to increase. The bent of his mind inclined him to reform conducted on mild and liberal principles. He had not energy enough to initiate measures of that kind, but he was glad to sanction and promote their operation.

Abdül Mecit had ruined the empire by his extravagances, particularly by the building of Dolmabahçe and his other seaside pleasure domes. But though the empire has vanished the palaces remain, and with them the fading memory of a sybaritic way of life that once graced the shores of the Bosphorus.

Chapter 16

THE YEAR OF THE
THREE SULTANS

Abdül Aziz was thirty-one when he became sultan, having spent the previous twenty-two years nominally confined to the Cage. His mother Pertevniyal was installed as *valide sultan*, a title that had been vacant since the death of Abdül Mecit's mother Bezmialem in 1853.

Abdül Mecit was survived by four sons. Murat, the eldest, who was then approaching twenty-one, had been given the title of *veliaht*. Abdül Hamit, the second eldest, was nearly nineteen; Mehmet Reşat was midway through his seventeenth year; while Mehmet Vahidettin was only three and a half months old. The three eldest princes were confined to the Cage when their father died, though their uncle Abdül Aziz allowed them considerable freedom. Vahidettin remained in the care of his stepmother in the harem until he reached the age of puberty, after which he too was confined in the Cage.

Abdül Aziz had fathered a son named Yusuf Izzeddin in 1857, four years before he succeeded to the throne. Yusuf's birth was kept secret at the time, and his existence was revealed only when his father became sultan, whereupon he was given the title of *veliaht*. Yusuf's mother, Dürrünev, then became *birinci kadın* and *haseki*, and Abdül Aziz promised her that he would never take another wife. This was in keeping with his intention of ending the extravagances of his predecessor's harem, which he began to put into effect by sending all of Abdül Mecit's wives and concubines to Topkapı Sarayı, now known as the Old Palace.

But then one of his sisters presented Abdül Aziz with a new concubine, whom he could not refuse without giving offence. Soon afterwards, according to Melek Hanım, 'being struck with the charms of another slave, he made her also his odalisque.' And thus, despite his good intentions, Abdül Aziz eventually took a total of seven women into his harem who acquired the title of *haseki*, besides which he acquired numerous concubines. He fathered a total of eleven children, comprising six sons and five daughters. One of his sons and three of his daughters died in infancy, a lower rate of infant mortality than in the past, probably reflecting the better medical care and healthier conditions in Dolmabahçe than in the crowded labyrinth of Topkapı Sarayı.

The cramped conditions in the harem at that time are evident in a letter written by the Princess Behice, a daughter of Abdül Mecit, who complains to her housekeeper that a younger princess is being moved into apartments next to hers:

My dear kalfa, I have just heard from someone that she is moving into the apartments next to ours. No, the world is based on rank and I want those for myself. I cannot have my junior occupying such fine rooms. If his majesty hears about it he will not say anything. You must tell the valide sultan about this.

Why should she go there, while I stay in the other rooms. It is impossible and I demand my rights. If nothing is done about it I cannot go to the palace at all, and that is that. I will not let her have that apartment with a bath …

Abdül Aziz was very different than his half-brother Abdül Mecit, both in his physical appearance and in his personality. The new sultan was a veritable bear of a man, weighing some 250 pounds and powerfully built, a physique that served him well in his favourite activity, wrestling. His subjects knew him as Güreşçi, or the Wrestler, a complete contrast with his puny predecessor. Although he was interested in European architecture and painting, he cared little for the other cultural activities favoured by Abdül Mecit, preferring to spend his time wrestling with his intimate friends and pages. Nor was he committed to the reform programme of his late brother, whose only quality he shared was his extravagance, despite his original intention to the contrary.

At the beginning of his reign Abdül Aziz commissioned Sarkis Balian to build him new palaces at Beylerbey and Çırağan, the first of which was completed in 1865 and the second in 1872. Meanwhile Abdül Aziz had built a new summer palace at Kâğıthane, on the Sweet Waters of Europe, a hunting lodge at Maslak, in the hills above the European shore of the upper Bosphorus, and two villas on the shores of the Marmara outside the city. Besides these he also erected an imperial mosque in Istanbul at Aksaray, the ancient Forum Bovis; this was completed in 1871 and dedicated to his mother Pertevniyal, the *valide sultan*. Abdül Aziz took an interest in the design and decoration of these buildings, as the Turkish historian Enver Ziya Karal writes in his account of the sultan's upbringing and cultural interests:

Abdül Aziz had spent his childhood in the palace, in the company of women and eunuchs. Although not forced to spend his years as crown prince in confinement, he had been kept under very close supervision. No great importance had been given to his education, and he lived very much according to his own inclinations.

He had no interest in scientific education. The environment in which he spent his childhood and youth had offered no incentive in this direction. While prince he had received tuition from Hasan Efendi, a medrese *graduate who had remained completely untouched by contemporary currents of thought. He taught Abdül Aziz only language and traditional knowledge, which was, of course, quite inadequate for a Sultan. He had natural aptitude for the fine arts. He appreciated the pictorial arts and actually produced some pencil sketches himself, mostly of the sea, ships and trees. Of the distinguished artists of the time he very much liked Aivazowsky, some of whose paintings he purchased. He also had an interest in music. He played the* ney, *no doubt because of his sympathy for the Mevlevi sect. He disliked Western music but was interested in European architecture; he himself examined the plans for the palaces built during his reign, made various amendments to suit his own taste, and closely supervised the actual construction.*

Karal goes on to write of the sultan's capricious behaviour and coarse sense of humour:

The refined taste that led him into an interest in the fine arts was transformed into a coarse, ill-tempered impetuosity when it came to his sports and pastimes ... one of his favourite sports was wrestling. He had famous wrestlers contend in his presence, and rumour has it that he sometimes wrestled himself. He also enjoyed camel-wrestling and ram and cock-fights. He would hang the medals intended for generals and statesmen around the necks of the victorious animals and have beautifully decorated hutches built for them. He also liked clowns and impersonators. He also used to make the impersonators imitate statesmen he disliked, and he would sometimes smear the greasy remnants of the food over the clown's clothes and then set the dogs on him. He also liked playing practical jokes on members of his entourage ... But he would always win back the hearts of his victims afterwards by presenting them with rich gifts.

Abdül Aziz went to Paris in 1867 at the invitation of the Emperor Louis Napoleon to see the Great Universal Exhibition, the first Ottoman sultan to leave the bounds of his empire for any purpose other than going to war. The sultan took along with him his son Yusuf Izzeddin and his two elder nephews, Murat and Abdül Hamit. The sultan and his entourage stayed at the Elysée Palace, where the Emperor Napoleon received them as if they were oriental potentates in the *Arabian Nights*. According to the press, the sultan and his party consumed two roasted lambs and fifty hard-boiled eggs for breakfast every morning, with chorus girls from the *Folies Bergère* brought in to entertain them in the evening. During a reception at

left: *Prince Mahmut Celaleddin (1862–88), son of Sultan
Abdül Aziz and Edabil; photograph by Abdullah Frères, 1873*
right: *Prince Yusuf Izzeddin (1857–1916), son of Sultan
Abdül Aziz and Dürrünev, committed suicide in 1916;
photograph by Abdullah Frères, 1873*

the Tuileries, the Empress Eugénie chatted with the three princes
and gave Yusuf Izzeddin a box of chocolates, the latter incident
eliciting a rare smile from the sultan, who otherwise seemed glum
and apathetic throughout the festivities. Abdül Hamit maintained
his reserve and scarcely touched his wine glass during supper parties
at Maxim's, where beautiful girls from the Variétés were provided
for their entertainment, but Murat developed a taste for champagne
and brandy that he brought back with him to Istanbul, undermining
both his mental and his physical health. Abdül Aziz took an intense

dislike to Louis Napoleon, who had the temerity to suggest that they might be related through their grandmothers, referring to the myth that the *valide* Nakşidil, mother of Mahmut II, was Aimée Dubuc de Rivéry, cousin of the Empress Joséphine.

The Sultan and his party sailed from Boulogne on the Emperor's yacht and crossed to Dover, where the Prince of Wales came aboard to welcome them. They were transported to London in a high-speed train that took only a little over two hours, greeted in the flower-bedecked station by a cheering throng. Then they were escorted to Buckingham Palace by the Household Cavalry, after which they were invited to lunch in the Guildhall, with the sultan riding there on a white charger, his uniform bristling with medals, a diamond aigrette sparkling on his fez. Abdül Aziz, speaking through an interpreter, gave a speech that was enthusiastically cheered by the City merchants, some of whom had invested in the recently floated Ottoman Loan shares, issued by a cartel of international financiers to consolidate the huge Turkish debt.

Queen Victoria had been reluctant to come out of retirement to meet Abdül Aziz, and, after Lord Derby had finally persuaded her to do so, she wrote in her diary that at least 'the Sultan was not likely to come again.' The day after their arrival in London, the queen invited the sultan and the princes to lunch at Windsor Castle. The high point of their visit was a naval review at Spithead, where they joined the queen aboard the royal yacht. It was a bright but windy day, with occasional squalls of rain, and the yacht rolled and tossed about as the great iron-clads of the fleet passed in review and then fired at one another in mock battle, making a tremendous impression on the sultan and his party. Abdül Aziz saw only parts of the review, since the rough weather made him seasick and frequently forced him to go below to his cabin, while Queen Victoria sat it out unperturbed on the salon deck. As she noted in her diary: 'It must have been a curious sight, the Sultan and I sitting outside the deck salon, the others beyond ... The Sultan feels very uncomfortable at sea. He was constantly retiring below and can have seen very little, which was a pity, as it was a very fine sight.'

The queen invested the sultan with the Order of the Garter, though, as she wrote in her diary, 'she would have preferred the Star of India as more suitable for a non-Christian, but he had set his heart on having the Garter.' The sultan and his entourage were then entertained in a final round of parties and other entertainments. The event that Abdül Aziz most enjoyed, as he said himself, was the fireworks display at the Crystal Palace, which impressed him so much that he contributed a thousand pounds from his privy purse toward the restoration of the burned-out wing of the building.

The sultan and his party then returned to the Continent, being received in turn by King Leopold in Brussels, Kaiser Wilhelm in Koblenz, and the Emperor Franz Josef in Vienna. After a last party at Schönbrunn Palace Abdül Aziz and his entourage left Vienna on the imperial Ottoman yacht, the *Sultaniye*, and headed down the Danube, their ship and those of the accompanying Austrian flotilla garlanded with flowers from the emperor, who accompanied his guests as far as the frontier between the two empires.

When the *Sultaniye* arrived in Istanbul the harbour was filled with ships packed with spectators, their masts flying pennants to celebrate the sultan's return. The rest of the populace of the city lined the shores of the Bosphorus, everyone cheering Abdül Aziz and his entourage as their ship passed on its way to the landing-stage at Dolmabahçe Sarayı. Leyla Hanım describes the scene:

His Majesty was on the imperial yacht, the Sultaniye, *which was a gift of Said Pasha, the Viceroy of Egypt . . . An escort vessel preceded the imperial yacht, which was surrounded by boats carrying officials who had all come to meet the Sultan and was followed by other boats which carried the suite of His Majesty. Thousands of steamboats and vessels of all sizes literally covered the surface of the sea and they were all decked out with flags. Everybody stood up in the vessels and there was an immense crowd on both banks of the Bosphorus – hundreds of thousands of voices were raised together with the acclamation 'Padasahim çok yasa!', which is about the same as 'Vive l'Empéreur!' During all of this the military bands played the fanfare of Selam or salute. The enthusiasm of the people was such that some ladies were even crying with emotion.*

The sultan's tour had so impressed him with Western European progress that he ordered from Britain the newest locomotives, although there were as yet no rail lines in Turkey, and iron-clad warships, when there were no trained personnel in the Ottoman Navy to man and operate them. He also decorated and furnished his new palaces on the Bosphorus in the European style, purchasing a large number of British pianos, all in preparation for receiving the royal guests whom he had invited after his grand tour.

The first of these guests was the Empress Eugénie, who stayed in Beylerbey Sarayı for three days in October 1868, *en route* to the dedication of the Suez Canal the following year. After a banquet in her honour at Dolmabahçe Sarayı, Abdül Aziz took Eugénie to see his mother Pertevniyal. But the *valide* was outraged by the presence of a foreign woman in her harem, and she greeted the empress with a sharp slap across the face, almost provoking an international incident.

According to Karal, the sultan's extravagances reached a new level after his European tour, just as his sexual preferences changed to those for which some of his ancestors had been infamous:

His attitude towards women was extremely contradictory. As crown prince he was totally opposed to the presence of hordes of women in the palace, and on becoming sultan he dismissed the numerous palace household, declaring his intention of living a simple life with a single woman. This did not prevent him, however, from launching out, after his European tour, into extravagances that put those of his predecessors in the shade. Apart from the great stone buildings of Çırağan and Beylerbey, he also constructed summer palaces at Kâğıthane, Çekmece and Izmit, and then felt the need for fine furniture and beautiful women to adorn and enliven these palaces. The number of these women, eunuchs and female slaves soon rose to two thousand five hundred ... The abundant supply of women soon aroused a certain feeling of revulsion in the Sultan, who now

Abdül Aziz (1861–76);
photograph by Abdullah Frères, c. 1873

switched his preference to boys. This unnatural inclination was
nothing new for the Ottoman sultans, but during Abdül Mecit's
reign it had begun to disappear. Now it recurred, exactly like some
virulent disease . . .

The extravagances of Abdül Aziz surpassed those of his predecessor, emptying the treasury. There was little continuity in the
government to deal with this and other problems, for Abdül Aziz
changed grand vezirs at the rate of one a year. All political and
military appointments were up for sale, with the largest bribes going
to the sultan, who was degenerating rapidly in both mind and body.
Lady Brassey, who had met Abdül Aziz at the Paris Exhibition in
1867, saw the sultan in the early 1870s and said that he seemed to
have aged fifteen or twenty years in the interim. She remarked that

he had sunk into a state of melancholia and semi-derangement, and had become little more than a puppet in the hands of his ignorant but highly ambitious mother, the *valide sultan* Pertevniyal. He seemed tranquil only when he was with his new favourite, Nesrin, a beautiful sixteen-year-old Circassian girl he took into his harem early in 1876, after having heard her singing in the palace garden.

The political instability of the government, together with the deepening financial crisis, allowed the conservative elements in Turkey to begin undermining the Tanzimat programme, claiming that the reforms were responsible for the numerous problems of the empire. These also included revolts in both the Asian and European dominions of the empire, most notably in Bosnia and Bulgaria. But nothing was done, and the feeling grew that a democratic regime should be instituted under the Tanzimat movement. As the British ambassador Sir Henry Elliot later wrote:

From the pashas down to the porters in the street and the boatmen on the Bosphorus no one thinks any longer of concealing his opinions. The word 'constitution' is in every mouth and, should the sultan refuse to grant one, an attempt to depose him is almost inevitable.

Abdül Aziz tried to appease the demonstrators by shuffling his cabinet once again. But his new minister of war, Hüseyin Avni Pasha, soon came into conflict with the sultan, who was showing signs of severe mental instability. This led Hüseyin Avni to confer with Midhat Pasha and Süleyman Pasha, head of the military academy, and they decided to depose Abdül Aziz in favour of his nephew Murat, eldest of the four surviving sons of Abdül Mecit.

The conspirators made their move on the evening of 29 May 1876, when Midhat went to the Ministry of War, while Hüseyin Avni went to the barracks near Dolmabahçe, where he mustered a regiment of troops and surrounded the palace. Hüseyin then made his presence known at the main gate of Dolmabahçe Sarayı, where he informed the chief black eunuch that he had come to take Abdül Aziz to the Ministry of War as his prisoner. The *kızlar ağası*, a giant Nubian dressed in a white nightgown, went to wake the sultan, who had gone to bed in a good humour after watching a cock-fight in the throne room, taking along with him his new favourite Nesrin. Abdül Aziz had already been awakened by the commotion, and when Hüseyin Avni and Süleyman entered the throne room, they saw the sultan standing half-naked at the top of the great staircase, an unsheathed sword in his hand and his *haseki* Nesrin clinging to his arm in terror, trying to cover her face with her veil. Abdül Aziz's first inclination was to resist, but the *fetva* sanctioning his deposition was read to him and he acquiesced quietly, muttering that it was *kismet*, his ordained fate. At that moment Pertevniyal appeared at the top of the stairs, unveiled and with her hair in wild disorder, her face contorted with fury. She charged at Hüseyin Avni, gouging his face with her long nails, and then knocked him to the ground with a kick in the groin. The pasha's men soon subdued the *valide* and her servants took her back to her apartment, after which Abdül Aziz was allowed to dress before being taken from the palace.

Süleyman went to wake Prince Murat at his place of confinement, where he was deep in a drunken sleep. After the pasha quieted his fears, Murat was informed that he was going to succeed his uncle Abdül Aziz as sultan. A cannon was then fired to signal to Midhat at the Ministry of War that all was going according to plan.

After Murat dressed he was taken by caique to the old city and then by carriage to the Ministry of War. There Midhat and the grand vezir Mehmet Rüştü Pasha were waiting with the *şeyhülislam* Hayrullah Efendi, who administered the oath of allegiance to Murat as the prelude to his succession. The ministers were alarmed at Murat's appearance, for he was deathly pale, his lips covered with sores, and seemed barely able to walk. Murat was then brought back to Dolmabahçe Sarayı for his formal enthronement, as the warships on station in the Bosphorus and the batteries along the shore fired a cannonade to announce to the populace that a new sultan was on the throne. The plan had been to bring the golden Bayram Throne from Topkapı Sarayı for the ceremony, but the arrangements went awry, and instead a gilt armchair had to serve the purpose, and the new sultan was enthroned there as Murat V.

Meanwhile Abdül Aziz had been transported in another caique to a landing-stage of Topkapı Sarayı, from where he was taken to his place of confinement in the old harem. The chamber chosen for his imprisonment was the music room where the deposed Selim III had been assassinated in 1808. He remained there for three days with hardly any food, sleeping on the floor in his wet clothes, having been refused a nightshirt, all the while closely guarded and roughly handled as if he were a common criminal. On the third day he sent a message to Murat, congratulating him on his succession, and then on the following day the new sultan ordered that his uncle Abdül Aziz be transferred to Ferriye Sarayı, an annexe of Çırağan Sarayı. When he arrived there he rushed into the main salon looking for his mother Pertevniyal, but a soldier prodded him in the chest with his bayonet to hold him back, saying that she was coming. Looking around to see that he was surrounded by armed soldiers, Abdül Aziz cried out, 'Mother! Mother! They're going to kill me!', and then he broke down in tears as he was led away to the room in which he was to be imprisoned.

Abdül Aziz was kept under close guard at Ferriye Sarayı, where he grew increasingly morose over his ignominious confinement. He told his mother and others who attended him that he thought he was going to be murdered at any moment. One day he said to his chamberlain Fahri Bey, 'This world has no more interest for me,' which led his mother to fear for the worst. The end came on Sunday 4 June 1876, when Abdül Aziz was found bleeding to death in his room, having apparently cut his wrists with a pair of scissors. The first doctor to arrive on the scene was Avni Pasha, who said that he could do nothing, and soon afterwards he pronounced Abdül Aziz dead.

A group of nineteen doctors, including Dr Julius Millingen, who had been personal physician to every sultan since Mahmut II, subsequently wrote a report on the death of Abdül Aziz, whom they concluded had committed suicide by slashing his wrists with the scissors he had been given to trim his beard. Rumours that the deposed sultan had been murdered were heard, as Sir Henry Elliot

Ferriye Sarayı, an annexe of Çırağan Sarayı

notes, but after conferring with Dr Millingen he concluded that Abdül Aziz had in fact taken his own life. Dr Millingen told Elliot of his efforts to give some soothing medicine to Pertevniyal, who blamed herself for having allowed her son to have a pair of scissors, given his suicidal state of mind. 'It is I who am responsible for my son's death,' she said. 'You should send an executioner, not a doctor.'

The day after his death Abdül Aziz was buried in the *türbe* of his father Mahmut II. His mother Pertevniyal was duly replaced as *valide sultan* by Şevkefza, the mother of Murat V, who appointed her chief ally Damat Nuri Pasha as Lord Chamberlain. Şevkefza and Nuri then confiscated all of the gold coins and jewellery that Abdül Aziz and his mother Pertevniyal had hidden away in the harem of Dolmabahçe Sarayı, transferring the treasures into their own strongboxes.

Murat was nearly thirty-six when he became sultan, having spent the previous fifteen years in nominal confinement in the Cage. Abdül Aziz had allowed him considerable freedom as crown prince, most notably when he and his brother Abdül Hamit were taken along on the sultan's tour of Europe in 1867. Murat's fluency in French, his ability as a ballroom dancer and the ease with which he conversed with European ladies won Murat approval in the British court. Queen Victoria tried to arrange a match with Princess Marie of Mountbatten, and the proposal was made by the Prince of Wales to Fuat Pasha, the foreign minister, who transmitted it to Prince Murat. Murat mentioned the proposal to his brother Abdül Hamit, who immediately informed Abdül Aziz. The sultan was furious and rejected the proposal out of hand, severely criticizing Fuat Pasha for his role as intermediary.

Murat had been allowed to have his own harem in Dolmabahçe Sarayı throughout the reign of Abdül Aziz. The names of four of his concubines are known, and altogether his women bore him seven children while he was crown prince, two of them dying in infancy.

Murat was a voracious reader and had a deep interest in music and architecture. He was also very interested in contemporary politics, and while crown prince he met a number of the liberal Turks known as the Yeni Osmanlılar, the Young Ottomans. The prince's Greek doctor Capoleone initiated him into the society of Freemasons, where he befriended the poet and playwright Namık Kemal, one of the leading spirits of the Young Ottomans.

By the time that Murat came to the throne he was already a hopeless alcoholic, and his mental condition had so deteriorated that he was in no condition to rule. The traditional ceremony of the girding of the new sultan at Eyüp was postponed because of Murat's condition, and then a decision was made to abandon it altogether. Murat was unable to control himself sufficiently to receive visitors or foreign ambassadors. His subjects waited expectantly to see him in the *selamlık*, the procession for the Friday noon prayer. But usually he rode to the mosque in a closed carriage and was brought directly to the screened-off imperial *loge*, so that he remained invisible to the faithful.

*Murat V leaving Dolmabahçe Sarayı for the Friday noon
prayer at the Dolmabahçe Mosque*

The death of Abdül Aziz deeply troubled Murat, aggravating his
already severe mental illness. Then, during the next two weeks, he
was subjected to further traumatic experiences. A week after the
death of Abdül Aziz the departed sultan's *haseki* Nesrin died in
childbirth, and an enormous crowd of mourners followed her funeral
cortège to the cemetery of Karaca Ahmet in Üsküdar. The mourners
were led by Nesrin's brother Çerkez (the Circassian) Hasan, a young
officer who had been devoted to the late sultan. After the funeral
Hasan was posted to Baghdad by the minister of war Hüseyin Avni
Pasha, who wanted to get the hot-headed Circassian out of Istanbul

before he caused trouble. Hasan was outraged by this, and on 15 June he armed himself with four pistols and burst into a cabinet meeting at the Sublime Porte, where he immediately began shooting. With his first two shots he killed Hüseyin Avni Pasha and the foreign minister Raşit Pasha. When the attendants rushed in and tried to disarm Hasan he picked them off one by one, killing seven of them and wounding eight others before he was finally disarmed. He was then imprisoned, tried and convicted within two days, and on 18 June he was hanged.

All of this further unhinged Sultan Murat, whose behaviour became increasingly bizarre. Once he happened to see the famous clown Vehbi Molla in a crowd of people, and he burst out in uncontrollable laughter until his attendants led him away. On another occasion a group of Greek Orthodox clerics came to offer him their congratulations, but the sight of their black robes so terrified him that he jumped up from his throne and attempted to flee from the room. His mother, the *valide* Şevkefza, attempted to cure him with spells and charms, and when these proved ineffective she called in Dr Capoleone, who used old-fashioned methods such as blood-letting and the application of leeches and cupping-glasses as well as the prescription of tonics. Finally the imperial council called in Dr Leidesdorf, a renowned Viennese physician who specialized in mental disease. After an examination he informed the government that he could cure Murat if he could bring the sultan to his clinic in Vienna. His diagnosis was that the sultan was suffering from acute alcoholism, which, together with the emotional traumas he had suffered, had unbalanced him. A three-month course of treatment in the doctor's clinic in Vienna would cure the sultan, he said. But the ministers decided that they could not take the responsibility of allowing the sultan to go abroad in his condition, whereupon Dr Leidesdorf abandoned the case and departed abruptly for Vienna.

Meanwhile, Midhat Pasha pushed ahead with his programme to establish a constitutional monarchy. By that time Midhat Pasha had already consulted with Prince Abdül Hamit, who assured him that if he succeeded to the throne he would be willing to accept a constitution. Everyone concerned had now given up hope that Murat's condition would improve, and so Midhat Pasha gathered support for a move to have the sultan deposed on grounds of mental incapacity, to be replaced by Abdül Hamit. The grand vezir Mehmet Rüştü Pasha agreed, and at a meeting on 30 August the cabinet voted unanimously to depose Murat. The *şeyhülislam* issued a *fetva* declaring that Murat was unable to rule because of his insanity, and this was supported by a medical statement signed by several physicians stating that it was unlikely that the sultan would ever recover. The minister of war sent orders for Dolmabahçe Sarayı to be surrounded by troops, while the grand vezir went to inform Murat that he had been deposed. Murat received the news with resignation, his face expressionless except for a wry smile, and he allowed himself to be led away to his place of confinement.

Early the following morning the minister of war was sent to inform Abdül Hamit at the house of his foster-mother Perestu. He received the news calmly, and dressed, after which he was brought to Topkapı Sarayı, accompanied by the minister and an honour guard of 150 mounted soldiers. He arrived at the palace at eight o'clock in the morning and went directly to the Imperial Hall, where all of the ministers and other grandees of the empire acclaimed him as Sultan Abdül Hamit II. At ten o'clock a cannonade of one hundred guns signalled to the populace that the old sultan was deposed and a new one enthroned, after which Abdül Hamit embarked in the imperial caique at Saray Burnu and, accompanied by a flotilla carrying all of the dignitaries of the court, proceeded to Dolmabahçe Sarayı. There he was congratulated by the imperial household and received the obeisance of his ministers and subjects. He began his reign on 31 August 1876, the third sultan in three months to occupy the Ottoman throne. Thus for long afterwards the people of Istanbul referred to 1876 as 'the year of the three sultans'.

Chapter 17

IMPRISONED SULTANS

On the day that Abdül Hamit II became sultan he received the congratulations of the women of the imperial harem in the Blue Salon of Dolmabahçe Sarayı. After the women took their assigned places and individually offered their congratulations, there was a momentary silence and then Seniye Sultan, a granddaughter of Mahmut II, rushed up to Abdül Hamit and cried out, 'Your Majesty, I beg you, don't kill Sultan Murat.' Abdül Hamit was deeply shocked, and he replied in a hurt tone, 'How can you say such a thing! He is my brother. It's the work of fate. I never wanted the throne, they summoned me after three months.' Şerefnaz Hanım, one of the women in the harem, rebuked Seniye, shouting in a shrill voice, 'It's God's will! Sultan Hamit has ascended the throne. How can you say such a thing, Sultan Efendi!' The new sultan then left the salon in an embarrassed silence, an inauspicious beginning to his reign.

The ceremony of *kılıç kuşanması*, the girding of a new sultan with the sword of Osman Gazi, was delayed for a week after Abdül Hamit succeeded to the throne. It was finally performed on 7 September 1876, when Abdül Hamit was rowed from Dolmabahçe Sarayı to Eyüp in the imperial caique, with the populace of the city lining the shores of the Bosphorus and the Golden Horn to watch his progress. One of those who saw him pass was a young French naval officer named Julien Viaud, later to become famous as the novelist Pierre Loti. As Loti wrote of the new sultan in his *Aziyadé*:

'He was thin and pale and sadly preoccupied, with large black eyes surrounded by dark patches; he looked intelligent and distinguished.'

Abdül Hamit was nearly thirty-four when he became sultan, having been nominally confined to the Cage for the previous fifteen years. When he became sultan he confined his three surviving brothers, with Mehmet Reşat and Mehmet Vahidettin continuing to live in their apartments at Dolmabahçe Sarayı, while the deposed Murat V and his family were imprisoned in Çırağan Sarayı.

Since Abdül Hamit's mother was dead, his foster-mother Perestu assumed the role of *valide sultan*. She had cared for him since his boyhood, and his feeling for her was as deep as if she had been his real mother, whose loss had left him desolate. Perestu gave him the only parental love he knew during his lonely childhood and youth, for he was shunned and then later distrusted by his father Abdül Mecit.

Perestu encouraged Abdül Hamit to pursue his hobbies of wood-carving and cabinet-making, interests that he maintained throughout his life. She also taught him the good manners which so impressed even the foreign observers who otherwise had nothing good to say about him. He was particularly courteous and gentle in his dealings with women, an attitude that was credited to Perestu's influence. When Abdül Hamit set up his court Perestu received his guests with the attitude of an empress, dressed in old-fashioned costumes that had been worn when the harem was still in Topkapı Sarayı, bedecked in the most precious jewellery from the imperial treasury. Lady Layard, wife of Sir Austen Henry Layard, the British ambassador, describes Perestu as 'a small fair woman still bearing traces of great beauty'.

The only other one who showed him affection in his early years was Pertevniyal, mother of Abdül Aziz. When Abdül Aziz was confined in the Cage after Abdül Mecit came to the throne, the sultan permitted Pertevniyal to remain in the imperial harem. Abdül Hamit often came to sit with Pertevniyal as she puffed on her *çubuk*, the long Turkish pipe, and listened as she instructed him in the arcane lore of number-mysticism, astrology, necromancy and magic, interests that had led the black eunuchs in the harem to fear her as a witch. He also listened with rapt attention as she rambled on about the gossip of the court and the bazaars in the days when she was the *haseki* of Mahmut II. She knew far more about life in the city than any other woman in the palace, for she had been working as a bath attendant in Istanbul when she first came to the notice of Mahmut II, who saw her carrying a load of fresh linen to the hamam and was struck by her voluptuous beauty and charmed by her peasant wit. After the death of her son Abdül Aziz, Pertevniyal was forced to relinquish her title of *valide sultan*, whereupon she decided to retire to the old harem in Topkapı Sarayı, where she had first lived when she was the *haseki* of Mahmut II. There she spent the rest of her days, attended by only a few of her old maids, virtually forgotten by the sultan and his court.

Abdül Hamit's lonely childhood undoubtedly contributed to the paranoia which became increasingly evident as he grew older, as did his mania for spying on everyone around him. While his mother Tirimüjgan was still alive, though confined to her room by tuberculosis, she encouraged him to bring her news and gossip from the harem, and he was often seen eavesdropping on his brothers and sisters and those with whom they came in contact. He and his older brother Murat had been given a better education than most of their predecessors, and both of them could speak French. This allowed Abdül Hamit to learn more about what was going on in the outside world than was customary for Ottoman princes in times past, particularly those who had been strictly confined in the Cage. When Abdül Hamit was fifteen he met Armenius Vambéry, the Hungarian orientalist and traveller, who at the time was giving French lessons to Abdül Mecit's eldest daughter, Fatma Sultan. Vambéry wrote of how Abdül Hamit always attended his sister Fatma's lessons, remarking that the young prince was far more interested in his sister's affairs than in learning French. Vambéry describes Abdül Hamit as he appeared at these lessons:

... *sitting silent and immobile, only changing position when the eunuch in attendance brought him his usual cup of coffee, his*

*black eyes fixed on the teacher's face, as if anxious to snatch every
French word from his lips, and when his sister was called away on
some domestic affair, addressing him in a timid, slow voice, rarely
touching the subject of instruction, but asking questions about
Reshid [Reşid Pasha, Fatma's father-in-law], his sister and her
husband.*

A few years later Abdül Hamit and his brother Murat began
making excursions in the European world of Pera. While Murat
enjoyed the company of the liberal intellectuals of the Young Ottoman movement, whom he met in the political cafés of Pera, Abdül
Hamit preferred to spend his time with the financiers among the
Christian minorities, befriending the Greek banker Zarifi and the
Armenian broker Assani. Under Zarifi's guidance he invested his
money judiciously, and by the time he came to the throne he had
amassed a personal fortune worth about £70,000.

Abdül Hamit liked to wander around Istanbul on his own, usually
stopping in the fashionable shops and cafés along the Grand Rue
de Pera. The shop that he favoured most was that of a young Belgian
milliner named Flora Cordier, described by one of her admirers as
'the fair-haired girl with the laughing eyes'. Abdül Hamit fell in love
with Flora, and she went through a form of marriage with him,
though this was never officially acknowledged, and he lived secretly
with her in his seaside villa on the Bosphorus at Therapia. The first
mention of their union is in a letter from Benjamin Disraeli to Lord
Salisbury, written just after Abdül Hamit came to the throne, based
on information sent to the prime minister from the British Embassy
in Istanbul:

The new Sultan has only one wife, a modiste *from Pera, a Belgian.
He was in the habit of frequenting her shop, buying gloves, etc.,
and much admired her. One day he said 'Do you think you could
marry me' and she replied 'Pourquoi non', and it was done. It was
she who set him against Seraglio life and all that. In short a Roxelana.
Will he be a Suleyman the Great?*

Abdül Hamit's romance with Flora Cordier lasted little more than a year, for the opposition of Perestu and others made it impossible to bring a European woman into the imperial harem. There is no mention of her after 1876, when it was noted that her shop on the Grand Rue was closed, and there were rumours that she had been sent back to Belgium.

Abdül Hamit already had a harem before he became sultan. His first known concubine was Nazikeda, who in 1869 bore him a daughter named Ulviye. When Ulviye was seven she burned to death playing with matches, while Nazikeda, who tried to save her, also suffered severe burns. Leyla Hanım, in telling the story of this tragedy, writes that 'The Sultan and his consort were plunged into desolation, and for a long time they did not meet or even see one another.'

Abdül Hamit's first wife was Bedrifelek, whom he married on 15 December 1868. On 11 January 1870 Bedrifelek gave birth to his first son, Mehmet Selim, and on 12 January of the following year she bore him a daughter named Zekiye. Abdül Hamit had a total of twelve wives and concubines, who between them bore him eight sons and eight daughters, including a pair of twin boys, with four of his children dying in infancy or early childhood.

At the outset of his reign Abdül Hamit decided to move from Dolmabahçe to Yıldız Sarayı, the Palace of the Star, in the hills above Çırağan Sarayı. During the next two decades Abdül Hamit transformed Yıldız, rebuilding the existing structures and adding others so as to make it his principal residence, for he far preferred its secluded and wooded site to the exposed position of Dolmabahçe Sarayı. Yıldız was not a palace in the conventional sense, but a series of kiosks and pavilions embowered among the surrounding woods and gardens, with a lake fed by a stream spanned by little rustic bridges, and glass-enclosed cafés set here and there so that the sultan could stop for a coffee as he walked along the woodland paths. Mrs Max Müller, wife of the renowned orientalist, describes the gardens of Yıldız Sarayı, where she and her husband were invited to tea by the sultan one afternoon:

*A sultana of the imperial harem, second half of
the nineteenth century*

On our right rose the high bare Harem walls, higher than any prison
wall in England; a close and carefully guarded doorway admitted
us inside these walls. Leaving a beautiful kiosk to our left, and
passing through a narrow passage, we came suddenly on a scene of
marvelous beauty. Yildiz stands on the summit of the highest hill
of the capital, and before us lay a large lake or artificial river, covered
with kaiks and boats of all shapes, an electric launch among others.
The gardens sloped to the lake on all sides, the lawn as green, the

turf as well kept as in the best English gardens. Exquisite palms and shrubs were planted in every direction, while the flower borders were a blaze of colour. The air was almost heavy with the scent of orange blossoms and gardeners were busy at every turn sprinkling the turf, even the crisp gravel walks, with water. The Harem wall, now on our right, rose no longer bare, but covered to the very top with yellow and white Banksia roses, heliotrope, sweet verbana, passion flowers, etc. Thousands of white or silvery-grey pigeons – the Prophet's bird – flew in and out of a huge pigeon-house, built against the walls, half hidden by the creepers, and the whole scene was lighted up by the brilliant Eastern sunlight, in which every object stands out so clearly that one's sense of distance is almost lost. At the end of the lake is a duck decoy, where H. I. M. often amuses himself with shooting, and far beyond this we could catch glimpses of the park sloping away towards the Bosphorus.

Abdül Hamit built a furniture factory and a ceramic works within the palace grounds, both of them renowned for the high quality of their products, which were used in Yıldız Sarayı and the other imperial residences along the Bosphorus. Other structures included a theatre, a library, an observatory, a photography laboratory, an embroidery workshop, a museum of stuffed animals, another museum for the sultan's pictures and antiquities, a hospital and four clinics, a pharmacy, a carpentry workshop for the sultan's own use, a sawmill for the furniture factory, kennels and a hospital for the sultan's dogs, five stables for his horses, an aviary for his tropical birds, and a zoo for his pet animals, which included a lion.

Abdül Hamit also built a nursery and a schoolroom in Yıldız for his children, both of which are described in the memoirs of his daughter Ayşe, who was born to Müşfika Kadın on 1 November 1887. Ayşe's earliest memories are associated with the nanny who gave her such loving care in the nursery:

When I was small she would put me to bed and sit at the end of the bed and sing lullabies until I slept. She dressed and cared for me with infinite devotion, solicitude and love. I would kiss her and call

Two young sons of Abdül Hamit II and their servant,
a black eunuch; photograph by Basile Kargopoulo, c. 1870

her 'my dear nanny', and she would call me 'my one only, my angel princess'.

After Ayşe left the nursery she went every morning with her older brothers and sisters to the schoolroom. Members of Abdül Hamit's staff gave them lessons, which, from her account, provided them with a broader education than that of the royal children in earlier times:

Before we arrived, the servants would set out red velvet cushions and lecterns in the big hall. Our pen cases and quills were placed on the lecterns. Our teachers were Hasib Efendi, the private secretary, and Kamil Efendi, the cipher clerk. Hasib Efendi taught the Koran, Arabic and Persian, and Kamil Efendi taught Turkish and reading, Ottoman principles, arithmetic, history and geography. My mother had prepared my school bag. The bag was of very beautiful purple velvet embroidered with silver thread, and contained a precious gilded alphabet book, and gold pointers with diamond tips. Purple was my favourite colour, and so my bag was made in this colour.

A mosque known as Hamidiye Cami was erected at the upper entrance to the palace grounds, so that Abdül Hamit would not have to venture out into the streets of the city for his *selamlık*, the imperial procession for the Friday noon prayer.

The theatre at Yıldız had been built for Abdül Hamit by Sarkis Balian in 1888–9. Four years later the sultan hired a company of travelling Italian players headed by Arturo Stravolo, which included the maestro's father, brother, sister, wife and daughter. Abdül Hamit sometimes asked for the plots of plays and operas to be changed, for he hated unhappy endings, so that *La Traviata* became *Madame Camélia*, in which Violetta is restored to health at the final curtain.

The sultan was a voracious reader, particularly of detective stories and police thrillers, which were read to him by Ismet Bey, chief of the imperial wardrobe, who was seated out of sight behind a screen. His favourite was Sherlock Holmes, and as soon as a new work by Arthur Conan Doyle came out he had it translated into Turkish and often went through one in a single night. His translation department also prepared for him a selection from foreign-language newspapers, both from Istanbul and abroad. Otherwise he spent his nights reading his voluminous correspondence or going over the multitudinous *djournals*, or dossiers, compiled for him by his army of spies. His ministers and secretaries could expect to be summoned to see the sultan at any hour of the day or night, for he suffered from insomnia and seldom slept other than in short dozes.

By the time that Abdül Hamit came to the throne another crisis had arisen in the Balkans. The threat of war between the Turks and Russians led the Great Powers to convene in Istanbul on 4 November 1876. Their stated aim was to protect the territorial integrity of the Ottoman Empire, while calling on the sultan to consider reforms in governing Bulgaria and Bosnia.

Midhat Pasha advised Abdül Hamit to show up the Europeans by proclaiming a constitution, for the sultan had already agreed to establish a constitutional commission. The commission, headed by Midhat Pasha, drew up a constitution that was approved by the cabinet on 6 December of that year, with the sultan retaining the right to exile anyone whom he considered a threat to the state. Abdül Hamit appointed Midhat Pasha as grand vezir, and on 19 December the new Ottoman parliament was created.

The Istanbul conference was a complete failure, and on 20 January 1877 the delegates disbanded. This gave Abdül Hamit the opportunity to rid himself of Midhat Pasha, whom he stripped of his seals of office on 5 February 1877, sending him off into exile that same day on the royal yacht *Izzeddin*. That evening the sultan went to visit his foster-mother Perestu in the harem of Dolmabahçe Sarayı, where she played the piano to calm his nerves. Offenbach and Meyerbeer were his favourites, so she played some of their tunes while Abdül Hamit looked out the window and watched the *Izzeddin* leaving the quay with his arch-enemy aboard. He raised his hand to stop Perestu's playing, and she heard him murmuring to himself, 'It was foolish of Midhat to cross his Sultan.'

Abdül Hamit formally opened the first Ottoman parliament in a ceremony at Dolmabahçe Sarayı on 19 March 1877, after which the Chamber of Deputies convened in the Palace of Justice beside Haghia Sophia. The parliament had little autonomy, for Abdül Hamit had made sure that all real power remained in his own hands.

Czar Alexander II declared war on the Ottoman Empire on 24 April 1877, and within nine months the Russian army had advanced to the suburbs of Istanbul at San Stefano. The Great Powers intervened and peace terms were settled in the Treaty of Berlin, signed on 13 July 1878. The Ottoman Empire lost an enormous amount of territory in the Balkans and northeastern Anatolia, and the Porte was forced to pay a huge indemnity to the Czar. Meanwhile Abdül Hamit dissolved the Ottoman parliament, which would not meet again for more than thirty years.

Now that he had rid himself of parliament Abdül Hamit took

direct control of every aspect of government operations, both civil and military. Layard reported to London that 'His Majesty reigns supreme as hitherto, everybody and everything being more than ever under his absolute management and control.'

Abdül Hamit was afraid that there would be a plot to restore his brother Murat to the throne, and this aggravated his natural tendency toward paranoia. Early in his reign he created a network of spies who informed him about everything that was going on in his empire, particularly in the bazaars and coffee-houses of Istanbul. The sultan and his informers recorded their information and observations in *djournals*, an activity that became an obsession with Abdül Hamit. The sultan was never without his *djournal*, as Layard observed: 'The Sultan rarely forgets anything that is told to him, and is in the habit of noting in a *djournal*, which he carefully keeps, and which he usually has at hand, any observation or statement which he considers worthy of remembering, and which he frequently refers to in our interviews.'

On 20 May 1878 an Islamic fundamentalist named Ali Suavi attacked Çırağan Sarayı with a force of about a hundred Balkan refugees, his aim being to free the deposed Murat V and restore him to the throne. The attempt was foiled by the local gendarmerie, who killed Ali Suavi and about half of his men, capturing or dispersing the others. As soon as the situation was under control Abdül Hamit removed Murat and his family from Çırağan and kept them under close confinement in the Malta Köşk at Yıldız Sarayı, where he could keep an eye on them himself. Eventually they were allowed to return to Çırağan Sarayı, but under much tighter security than before, restricted to a wing of the palace known as the Mabeyn.

The abortive revolt heightened Abdül Hamit's fears for his personal safety, and he closed off the extensive grounds of Yıldız Sarayı to the public, so that the palace became a closely guarded fortress. Thenceforth he was seldom seen in public except for the Friday *selamlık*, when he usually went to the Hamidiye mosque at the upper entrance to Yıldız Sarayı, or on ceremonial occasions when he had to go to Topkapı Sarayı, always accompanied by a company

Ali Suavi's attempt to free the deposed Murat V

of heavily armed Albanian guards. His paranoia visibly increased and he underwent a mental crisis so serious that for two weeks he could not leave his room, with his foster-mother Perestu and his Greek physician Mavroyeni effectively acting as regents in his absence.

Layard was recalled from his post as ambassador to the Porte in April 1880. At Layard's last audience with Abdül Hamit the sultan presented to him Bellini's portrait of Mehmet the Conqueror, which now hangs in the National Gallery in London. Abdül Hamit had a deep affection for Layard and his wife, and he maintained his friendship with Lady Layard even after recriminations about the Treaty of Berlin brought her husband into disfavour with the sultan. She was the first woman ever to be invited to eat at the sultan's table, and he had permitted his children to go to tea with her at the British Embassy in Pera. She had often visited the harem and seen him playing with his children, watching him as he repaired a broken doll for one of his little daughters, listening while he recited Turkish folk-tales or played the music of Offenbach on his pianola, discussing with him his plans to open a girls' school where the daughters of good Turkish families could receive a Western education without running foul of Islamic opposition.

Layard gives an interesting description and character sketch of Abdül Hamit, mentioning the apocryphal rumour that the sultan was not really the son of Abdül Mecit, as well as another story that he had Armenian blood in his veins through his mother Tirimüjgan:

The Sultan was somewhat below middle height. His figure was slight and lithe. His beard and hair jet black. His features showed no trace of Tartar origin, nor did he appear to resemble any of his predecessors – except perhaps Sultan Mohamet, the Conqueror, whose portrait by Gentile Bellini, taken from life, is in my possession. The type was rather that of the Armenian or Jewish race; which seemed to give some countenance to the scandal current in the gossiping circles of Pera and Galata that he was not the son of Abdul Mejit, but had Armenian blood in his veins . . . He was very simple in his dress, wearing a frock-coat and nothing to distinguish him from a European except the red Turkish fez on his head . . .

He leant towards mysticism and was often subjected to excesses of fanaticism. But on the other hand his incontestably sharp mind brought him into collision with theories founded on supernatural matters, and in spite of his first decision to keep up his holy character as a successor of Mahomet, he would enter into the discussion of delicate religious matters by which he betrayed a good deal of scepticism . . . the Sultan was not at all an unshakable believer, but accommodated himself in public life to the duties of a pious moslem.

Abdül Hamit had felt compelled to recall Midhat Pasha from exile in 1878 and appoint him governor of Syria, where he remained for two years before being posted to Izmir. Then on 17 May 1881 Midhat was arrested and brought back to Istanbul, where he and nine others were put on trial on the charge of having murdered

Abdül Hamit II (1876–1909) in the middle years of his reign

Sultan Abdül Aziz. The trial, which Sir Henry Elliot called 'a disgraceful mockery', began and ended on 27 June, with the verdict being a death sentence for all ten defendants. The news produced an outcry in Western Europe, forcing Abdül Hamit to commute the death sentences to life imprisonment, and on 28 July Midhat Pasha and Hayrullah Efendi were sent off to a prison camp in Arabia. The end came for Midhat Pasha on 8 May 1884, when, according to the testimony of Hayrullah Efendi, he was strangled by his guards, after which he was buried in an unmarked grave.

Kaiser Wilhelm II paid a state visit to Istanbul in the early autumn of 1889, just a year after he came to the throne. Abdül Hamit gave him a warm welcome, housing the Kaiser and his entourage in the Merasim Köşk, a new pavilion that he had built at Yıldız Sarayı in anticipation of their visit. This was the first step in Germany's projected penetration of Asiatic Turkey, to be facilitated by the building of a Berlin to Baghdad railway. Abdül Hamit was delighted by the success of the Kaiser's visit, but he remained wary of the Germans, even after a second visit by Wilhelm nine years later. Count Ostrorog, a nobleman of Polish-French origin who spent many years in the service of Abdül Hamit, wrote, 'The Sultan was charmed but not intoxicated by the Kaiser. He was fascinated but not convinced.'

The welfare of the Armenians in the Ottoman Empire had been a point of contention with the Great Powers since the beginning of Abdül Hamit's reign. The rise of Armenian nationalism, encouraged by Russia, greatly exacerbated the problem. Two Armenian revolutionary groups, the Hunchaks and the Dashnaks, began terrorist activities in the Ottoman Empire that resulted in savage reprisals by Kurds of the Hamidiye cavalry, units of the Ottoman army named for Abdül Hamit.

On Wednesday 26 August 1896, a group of Hunchak terrorists seized the Ottoman Bank in Galata, killing two employees and holding one hundred and fifty staff and customers hostage as they threatened to blow up the building. Then on Friday a bomb was thrown at Abdül Hamit as he was going to attend the noon prayer in Haghia Sophia, and though he was unharmed a score of his guards were killed. This led to reprisals in which some ten thousand Armenians were killed in Istanbul. The surviving Hunchak terrorists in the Ottoman Bank had by then negotiated their safe conduct from the city, having alerted the world to the cause of Armenian independence.

The Armenian massacres caused an outcry in Western Europe, with Gladstone calling Abdül Hamit the 'Great Assassin' and Clemenceau castigating him as the 'Monster of Yildiz, the Red Sultan'. The Great Powers sent the sultan a cable warning him that 'the massacres must cease immediately and that if the situation continued it would imperil both his throne and dynasty.' Abdül Hamit heeded their warning, and on Friday 28 August an order was issued to stop the killing.

Abdül Hamit celebrated his Silver Jubilee as sultan and caliph in

1901. He marked the occasion by announcing his plans for the construction of a railway from Damascus to Mecca and Medina, which would make it easier for Muslims to make the Hejaz, or pilgrimage to the Holy Cities. Only Muslims were allowed to subscribe to the building of what came to be called the Hejaz Railway, with Abdül Hamit starting the drive by donating the equivalent of £50,000.

During the twenty-five years that Abdül Hamit had reigned thus far his deposed brother Murat V had been languishing in Çırağan Sarayı, imprisoned along with his family. Murat's mother Şevkefza, the former *valide sultan*, had died in 1889 and was buried beside her husband Abdül Mecit in his *türbe* at the mosque of Selim I. Murat had fathered three sons and two daughters before he became sultan, two of the boys dying in infancy, only Selahattin surviving. After he was deposed he fathered two girls, one of whom died in infancy, his daughter Fatma surviving. Murat's son Selahattin and his daughters Hadice, Fehime and Fatma were confined with him in Çırağan Sarayı along with their mothers. The harem in Çırağan Sarayı was headed by Murat's *birinci kadın*, Ebru, who held that position though she never bore him any children. This is mentioned by the Turkish historian Haluk Şehsuvaroğlu, whose account is based on conversations with three of Murat's favourites who shared his imprisonment in Çırağan Sarayı:

Ebru, Murat V's Baş (Head) Kadın, was a very good seamstress. She was a very well-informed, polite, well-bred woman. Although she had no children herself, when Murat acceded to the throne he refused to leave her as one of the ikbals *(female slaves) and created her Baş Kadın in direct contravention of Ottoman tradition . . .*

Şehsuvaroğlu goes on to write of some of the other women in the deposed sultan's harem, most notably Tarzi Nevin, an accomplished musician who was tormented by her unrequited love for Murat:

Tarzi Nevin was one of the court women who had been passionately in love with Sultan Murat ever since his years as prince. Abdül

*Circumcision party: three young sons of Abdül Hamit
flanked by two older boys; anonymous photograph, 1897*

*Hamit Efendi, who was fully aware of the affair, even advised his
brother to respond to her affection. 'For heaven's sake, brother,
she's in a sad way. Why don't you take her?'*

*Tarzi Nevin underwent a number of great crises of passion in
Çırağan Sarayı. She wouldn't wash, wouldn't comb her hair, would
even forget who she was. This state of affairs continued for some
time, but never, either when he was prince or later, did Murat ever
regard her as an object of love or passion.*

*Tarzi Nevin was the moving spirit of Çırağan. She set up a
remarkable group of actors and arranged theatrical performances.
Some of the girls would dress up in male costume and perform
before Murat V. She also established a remarkable band of musicians.
She both trained them and arranged a variety of concerts, while at
the same time teaching the young şehzades [princes] and sultanas*

Persian and Arabic. She composed a number of pieces, including waltzes and polkas. On concert evenings Tarzi Nevin would sit down at the piano, filled with intense excitement at being in the presence of Sultan Murat. When she was playing two girls would hold her by the shoulders. She appeared to be in a sort of trance, and played the most difficult pieces with great skill.

After the former Sultan was imprisoned in Çırağan, the education and upbringing of his children had been entrusted to these women. Some of them knew Arabic and Persian, while some others had a good command of French. But the inmates of Çırağan Sarayı were really distinguished by their skill on the piano and oriental instruments.

Murat V spent his days in Çırağan Sarayı in reading or listening to music. He was himself a very good pianist. He took a keen interest in his children's education and upbringing . . . The children also learned to play the piano very well. His younger daughter would sometimes take part in the theatrical performances, while another daughter would sit at the piano . . . At Çırağan everyone could read and write, and were familiar with music. At the same time, the necessity of managing their own affairs had made all the girls skilled in handicrafts . . .

Abdül Hamit kept a close watch on his imprisoned brother through the chief black eunuch Cevher Ağa, known as the Baş Musahib, who reported everything he learned to the sultan. Murat took advantage of this on one occasion to poke fun at his brother, as Şehsuvaroğlu reports:

The Baş Musahib would frequently come to inquire if there were any requests, but throughout all the years of confinement Murat V never asked his brother for anything. Once he declared, 'Let me ask my brother for anything that'll make him think I'm mad. He'd love that!', and asked to be sent a bird in a cage!

Murat's mental health greatly improved during his confinement, for he was free from the strain of being sultan and reduced his consumption of alcohol, though he continued to drink wine or beer with his meals instead of water. The primitive conditions in Çırağan made him more resourceful, increasing his self-respect, and he was proud of the fact that, lacking the services of a dentist, he had learned to pull his own teeth when they went bad. Also, his freedom from responsibilities enabled him to pursue his cultural interests, as Şehsuvaroğlu remarks:

He had a very rich library, and used to spend his time reading, writing, playing the piano and talking of old times with those who lived there with him. He was one member of the Ottoman dynasty with a good knowledge of Western music, and he composed a number of pieces during his years as prince and crown prince. The most famous of these was the Silistre March. He also wrote some new compositions in Çırağan, and in 1882 he composed a polka for his second granddaughter Celile Sultan.

Murat V would often talk of his father, his uncle, and his European trip. He would often give his children long descriptions of France and England and the freedom enjoyed there. 'One day we'll be free,' he would say, 'and I'll take you to all these countries in a boat.'

But Murat never regained his freedom, for he died of diabetes on 29 August 1904 in Çırağan Sarayı, where he had been imprisoned for two days short of twenty-eight years. By his last request the Kuran was read to him by his son Selahattin, who closed the book when his father passed away peacefully. The following day Murat was buried in the *türbe* of Yeni Cami, the sixth and last sultan to be laid to rest there.

Thus Murat was freed from his imprisonment by death, while his brother Abdül Hamit, reviled in the West as the Red Sultan, was beginning the last years of his oppressive reign in Yıldız Sarayı, a prison of his own making.

Chapter 18

THE FALL OF THE HOUSE
OF OSMAN

Another attempt was made to assassinate Abdül Hamit on 21 July 1905, when a carriage loaded with dynamite exploded in the square outside the Hamidiye mosque during the sultan's weekly *selamlık*, killing seventeen people. Abdül Hamit was inside the mosque when the explosion took place, and thus escaped injury.

The police chief blamed the explosion on Armenian terrorists, but arrests and confessions under torture provided no believable explanation as to who was behind the assassination attempt. The paranoiac sultan began to fear everyone, suspicious of the loyalty of his army and even of his own staff. His rule became even more despotic, with censorship of books, newspapers and plays, as well as the imprisonment and exile of anyone suspected of liberal thinking.

Opposition to Abdül's Hamit's dictatorship was led by the liberals known as the Young Turks, among whom a party called the Committee of Union and Progress (CUP) eventually came to the fore. The CUP convened two congresses in Paris, the first in February 1902 and the second in December 1907, with their final declaration in the latter meeting calling for the overthrow of Abdül Hamit and the creation of a democracy, using violence if necessary. On 23 July 1908 the leaders of the CUP sent a cable giving their ultimatum to Abdül Hamit, informing him that unless the constitution was restored within twenty-four hours the army in Macedonia would march on Istanbul. Abdül Hamit got the message, and on the following day he restored the constitution and declared that the parliament would be reconvened.

Elections for the new Ottoman parliament were held in the autumn of 1908, with the CUP winning all but one of the 288 seats in the Chamber of Deputies. The second parliament convened in the Palace of Justice at noon on 17 December 1908, with Abdül Hamit giving a speech from the throne, a dramatic occasion described by H. G. Dwight:

The Sultan stood with his hand on his sword of empire, looking down, a figure of dignity in his plain, dark military overcoat, visibly bowed by years and anxiety, yet not so grey as one might expect, keen-eyed, hawk-nosed, full-bearded, taking in one-by-one the faces that represented every race and region of his wide domains. The silence and the intentness of that regard grew dramatic as the seconds gathered into minutes. 'A wolf in a cage!' whispered some one behind me . . .

Muslim fundamentalists demonstrated against the new constitution, demanding a return to the sacred law of the *şeriat*. During the night of 12–13 April 1909 soldiers in the First Army joined the religious students of the *medreses* in storming the parliament building, killing two of the deputies and forcing the remainder to flee in terror. The CUP members who were still in Istanbul also fled, leaving Abdül Hamit in complete control of the government once again.

The opposition to Abdül Hamit was led by Mahmut Şevket Pasha, commander of the Third Army in Salonica, who brought his Macedonian troops by train to the town of Çatalca outside of Istanbul, effectively putting the capital under siege. On 22 April most of the dispersed deputies and cabinet ministers met secretly in San Stefano at the National Public Assembly under the chairmanship of the former grand vezir Sait Pasha. They voted to depose Abdül Hamit in favour of his younger brother Mehmet Reşat, though their decision was to be kept secret until the army took control of the capital.

Mahmut Şevket Pasha moved his troops into Istanbul on the

morning of 24 April, and before the day was over his forces had taken control of the city. The sultan's guards at Yıldız Sarayı at first advanced to meet the intruders, but on seeing the Macedonian infantry they quickly retreated to within the grounds of the palace. The guards began deserting and eventually Yıldız was left defence-less. Then, when electrical power was cut off, the sultan's enormous household panicked, particularly the women of the harem. The scene is described by Francis McCullagh:

The hundreds of hapless ladies believed that the Palace might at any moment be stormed by a licentious soldiery. Some of them fainted, some of them fell down in hysterics, and once during the night the rest began to scream until the place seemed like a Bedlam. Saturday night was as still as death and the screams were conse-quently heard by some of the Macedonians, 10,000 of whom, with a powerful artillery, now surrounded the Palace. They must also have been audible in the Imperial Kiosk, but no sign was made, and mystery continued to brood over that mysterious retreat.

Abdül Hamit sent word to Mahmut Şevket that the garrison at Yıldız would surrender, after which he retired to the pavilion known as the Little Mabeyn, along with his son Abdurrahim, who was then fifteen. On Monday morning a battalion of Macedonian troops quietly entered the precincts of Yıldız and took control of the palace, leaving the sultan undisturbed but evicting all of the male members of his staff except for two secretaries and four domestics. McCullagh again describes the scene:

All who were not women were immediately summoned to leave the Harem, and nearly all obeyed the summons immediately. The eunuchs hesitated, but were boldly cast forth by the more energetic of the young ladies inside . . . At noon next day I met in the European quarter of Pera a procession half a mile long, consisting solely of domestics, door-keepers, parasites, spies, cooks, eunuchs, slaves, and unarmed officers, surrounded by a thin line of keen-eyed Mace-donians with rifles in their hands.

On the following day, Tuesday 27 April 1909, the *şeyhülislam* issued a *fetva* deposing Abdül Hamit, declaring that he was unworthy to reign. A group of deputies headed by Essad Pasha was sent to inform Abdül Hamit of the *fetva*, while at the same time another deputation was instructed to tell Prince Mehmet Reşat of his accession to the throne.

When Essad Pasha and his associates reached Yıldız they were conducted to the pavilion known as the Çitli Köşk, where the sultan's secretary Cevat Bey received them and asked them the purpose of their visit. They replied that they wished to communicate a message to Abdül Hamit on behalf of the National Assembly, whereupon Cevat Bey warned them that the sultan was armed and might shoot them, adding that he was a good marksman and never missed. When the delegation insisted on seeing the sultan, Cevat Bey led them to the Little Mabeyn, where Abdül Hamit was waiting with Abdur-rahim. The sultan rose to meet them and asked them why they had come, to which Essad replied that a *fetva* had been pronounced deposing him. Essad reassured him that he was safe, whereupon Abdül Hamit requested that he be allowed to live in Çırağan Sarayı, where he had kept his brother, the deposed Murat V, confined for so many years. Essad said that he would pass his request on to the National Assembly, and that he hoped that it would be granted.

As Essad and the others left the palace they heard Prince Abdurrahim weeping, his father Abdül Hamit remaining silent in his desolation. He had reigned for more than thirty-two years, during all but the first few months of which he had been an absolute despot, and now he was reduced to the pathetic status of a completely powerless old man, begging to be allowed to live on in a dilapidated palace where he had previously imprisoned his deposed brother.

The assembly decided that Abdül Hamit should be exiled to Salonica. At nine that evening Hüsnü Pasha came to Yıldız Sarayı to inform Abdül Hamit of the assembly's decision. The pasha's report tells of Abdül Hamit's shocked reaction to the news:

I tried hard to make the sultan yield, but then he fainted. His women rushed towards him, brought him water, and wept bitterly over him. Finally he yielded, largely owing to the persuasions of his sons, his daughters, and the women of his harem, and the carriages were ordered to get ready.

Later that evening Abdül Hamit and his entourage left Yıldız Sarayı in a fleet of carriages and were taken to Sirkeci station. There they boarded the royal coach that the Oriental Railway Company had presented to Abdül Hamit twenty years before. The sultan's party included two of his sons, two daughters, three wives, four concubines, four eunuchs and fourteen servants, as well as his Angora cats and his giant Saint Bernard. After a journey of twenty hours they arrived in Salonica, where they were housed in the Villa Allatini, a large and comfortable seaside mansion. Abdül Hamit seemed pleased with his accommodations, and he settled in to begin a new life in exile.

Even before the removal of Abdül Hamit the new regime was cleaning out the old one, as the Macedonian army arrested over six thousand suspects, setting up courts-martial to try those charged with having been responsible for the overthrow of the previous government and other crimes against the people. Among those executed were the chief black eunuch Cevher Ağa, who was hanged from a lamp-post on the Galata Bridge. Cevher's possessions were then confiscated, including his villa on the Bosphorus, where the authorities discovered that he had been keeping a beautiful Egyptian slave girl, who was heartbroken when she learned of her master's death.

The authorities also evicted all of the members of Abdül Hamit's harem who had remained behind in Yıldız Sarayı when he was sent off into exile. McCullagh describes the scene:

One of the most mournful processions of the many mournful processions of fallen grandeur that passed through the streets during these days was composed of the ladies from the ex-Sultan's harem on their way from Yildiz to the Top-Kapou Palace. These unfortunate ladies were of all ages between fifteen and fifty and so numerous

that it took thirty-one carriages to convey them and their attendants.
Some of them were sent to the Old Seraglio in Stamboul, but this
old palace of the early sultans had fallen into such a state of disrepair
that it was found to be unsuitable for them and they were sent back
again to Yildiz.

The new government contacted the Circassian villages from which
most of the women in the imperial harem had come, notifying them
that they were at liberty to take home any of their family members
who had been living in the household of Abdül Hamit. Some of
the older women were left unclaimed, whereupon the government
announced that they would be maintained by the state 'until they
are asked for in marriage'.

Early in May the parliament sent a commission to Yıldız Sarayı
to take an inventory of Abdül Hamit's property. McCullagh writes of
a bizarre incident that occurred when the parliamentary commission
began its search of Yıldız Sarayı:

As the deputies were saying their prayers like good Mohammedans
on the first day of their search, they were astounded to hear hoarse
voices proceeding from an empty adjoining room, which they them-
selves had locked and sealed only a few moments before; and their
astonishment was turned into something like alarm when they
distinguished the words 'Padishahim tchok yasha!' *('Long live the*
Sultan!'). The cry came, however, not from reactionaries, but from
hundreds of hungry caged parrots who had been taught this phrase.

Meanwhile, the elder of Abdül Hamit's two surviving brothers
was officially raised to the throne as Mehmet V Reşat. The new
sultan was sixty-four, and had spent the previous forty-eight years
in the Cage, which in his case was the luxurious apartment of the
crown prince in Dolmabahçe Sarayı. After his accession to the throne
he moved into the sultan's apartment in Dolmabahçe, which once
again became the principal imperial residence.

On the day of his enthronement the new sultan went to the
Ministry of War and then on to the Sublime Porte, receiving the

Mehmet V Reşat (1909–18)

homage of his ministers and other grandees in both places, after which he made a pilgrimage to the Pavilion of the Holy Mantle in Topkapı Sarayı to kiss the hem of the Prophet Mohammed's mantle. Then on Friday of that week, 30 April, he performed his *selamlık* at the mosque of Haghia Sophia. Sir Andrew Ryan, then a young diplomat at the British Embassy in Pera, was present on both of those occasions, as he writes in his memoirs, describing the new sultan:

In this case there was no difficulty in arranging for the succession of the Heir Apparent, Mehmed Reshad, next brother to the deposed Sultan and a prince eminently suitable from the Young Turk point of view to occupy the Sultanate as a figurehead. He was an elderly man, who had long lived in a sort of gilded captivity, amiable but without political experience or any apparent desire to assert himself.

His mental calibre was so low that he frequently seemed almost gaga, although I was to discover on one subsequent occasion that he was not nearly such a fool as he looked.

The ceremony of girding the new sultan with the sword of Osman was deferred to Monday 10 May. Mehmet Reşat was extremely corpulent, and so when the *şeyhülislam* tried to stretch his arms around the sultan's capacious waist to gird him the sword nearly fell to the ground; luckily it was caught by Ali Haydar, the Sherif of Mecca, who thus prevented an accident that would have been a portent of disaster.

Mehmet Reşat had three known wives before he came to the throne: Kamures, Dürradem and Mihrengis. Kamures bore his son Mehmet Ziyaeddin on 25 August 1872; an unidentified concubine bore his son Mahmud Necmeddin on 23 June 1878; another unknown girl in his harem gave birth in 1887 to a daughter named Refia, who died in infancy; and on 2 March 1888 Mihrengis bore his third son, Ömer Hilmi, the last child that he would sire.

The sultan's mother, Gülcemal, had died in 1851, so there was no *valide sultan* during his reign. His younger brother, Mehmet Vahidettin, remained confined in his comfortable apartment in Dolmabahçe Sarayı, as were Yusuf Izzeddin and Abdül Mecit, the surviving sons of the late Sultan Abdül Aziz.

According to Çelik Gülersoy, 'Mehmet V was a pleasant, affable, good-natured but rather senile old man ... he was a spendthrift prodigal only too delighted when he could get his hands on a few jewels, meticulous in his prayers and almost equally devoted to brandy and liqueur.' Gülersoy writes of how the sultan would make excursions to the kiosk of Ihlamur in the hills above the Bosphorus, after which 'he would return to the palace in the evening with a couple of roses for his *kadin efendi* and remark to his first secretary,"We had a lovely time today, didn't we?"'

Three months after Reşat came to the throne, he reluctantly gave permission to have Çırağan Sarayı used to house the Ottoman parliament, for the Palace of Justice had proved to be too small.

Çırağan was then reconverted and the palace was formally inaugurated as the new home of parliament on 2 November 1909, the sultan presiding. But then on 6 January 1910 the building was totally gutted in a fire, and parliament was forced to move to the Fine Arts School in Fındıklı. Çırağan Sarayı, reduced to a fire-blackened shell, was abandoned and fell into ruins.

The new government severely limited the authority of the sultan, so Reşat was largely a ceremonial figure. The two power centres in the new regime were the CUP, which controlled parliament, and the military, headed by Mahmut Şevket. The sultan only had power to appoint the *şeyhülislam* and the grand vezir. The government drastically lowered the sultan's budget, so that Reşat had to make do with a much smaller staff than in times past, and there was little money for the upkeep and repair of the imperial palaces. Thus Çırağan Sarayı was never rebuilt, and Dolmabahçe and other imperial palaces soon began to look dilapidated.

Meanwhile, Abdül Hamit was whiling away his time in the Villa Allatini in Salonica. McCullagh describes the changed mood of the deposed sultan:

. . . people marvelled at how well he was bearing up, how completely he had rid himself of his habitual nervousness, at the interest he took in external things, at the eagerness with which he asked his head eunuch every evening for news, and at the affability wherewith he spoke to the officers who had charge of him . . . For the first time in many years he began to take an interest in the details of material life and to ask the names of flowers. He walked in the garden and smoked incessantly. He sat down on the stone steps and the stumps of trees like a prosperous farmer pottering in his shirt sleeves around his garden of a bright Sunday morning.

But then after a few months the ex-sultan's mood changed again and he became increasingly depressed, as McCullagh writes:

During the last few weeks the ex-Sultan has fallen into a condition bordering on melancholia . . . He has become morose and taciturn, and a prey to some terrible anxieties. Insomnia has now been added to his other troubles and he often sits all night in his room before an open window looking in the direction of Constantinople.

Political events had been developing rapidly, as the Ottoman Empire went to war with Italy in 1911, followed by the two Balkan wars of 1912–13. The Ottoman government was forced to bring Abdül Hamit back to Istanbul, where he was confined in Beylerbey Sarayı. By his own request he was given an apartment at the rear of the palace, sparing him the agony of looking across the Bosphorus to his beloved Yıldız Sarayı.

The CUP had by then taken control of the Ottoman government, under the triumvirate of Talat, Cemal and Enver, who in the autumn of 1914 brought Turkey into the First World War on the side of Germany. This proved fatal to the Ottoman Empire, which four years later went down in defeat with Germany and the other Central Powers.

Abdül Hamit had been pining away in Beylerbey Sarayı. By 1917 all but one of his *kadıns* had asked for and received permission to leave his harem, and they departed with his blessing, for he had nothing more to offer them. Müşfika Sultan was the only one of his women who stayed with him to the end, and he died in her arms on 10 February 1918. The following day he was laid to rest in the *türbe* of his grandfather Mahmut II. As Müşfika said of her departed husband: 'He was the kindest and most understanding of masters, but he never loved anyone, least of all himself.'

By then Sultan Mehmet V Reşat was approaching his end, too. 'There's nothing more for me to live for,' he kept repeating in the last weeks of his life, when he rarely left Dolmabahçe Sarayı other than for the weekly *selamlık*. The sultan's only comment on the effect that the Great War had upon his life as sultan was that 'The Palace excelled in two things, prayer and food; both have gone off.' The sultan's only other excursions from Dolmabahçe were to Topkapı Sarayı for the annual ritual of venerating the sacred relics of the Prophet Mohammed. On his last visit to Topkapı Sarayı he entered the Pavilion of the Holy Mantle alone to pray. He remained there so long that his anxious attendants went in and found him lying across the golden casket containing the sacred mantle of the Prophet, where he had fallen asleep in his exhaustion while praying. His attendants woke the sultan and brought him back to Dolmabahçe, where he remained until the early summer of 1918. He then moved up to Yıldız Sarayı, settling into the harem, as was his custom during the summer months. He died there of heart failure on 3 July 1918, aged seventy-three years and eight months. The following day he was buried in a *türbe* in Eyüp, the last of the imperial Osmanlı line to be interred in his own country.

He was succeeded by his younger brother, Mehmet VI Vahidettin, the last surviving son of Abdül Mecit. The ceremony of the *kılıç kuşanması* at Eyüp was delayed until 23 July. The girding with the sword of Osman was performed by both the *şeyhülislam* and the Senusi Şeyh Seyyid Ahmet, with the Sherif of Mecca Ali Haydar also present, the presence of the last two dignitaries being due to Vahidettin's desire to represent himself as Caliph of Islam as well as sultan.

Vahidettin was midway through his fifty-seventh year when he came to the throne, having been confined to the harem and then the Cage since his infancy. His mother Gülüştü died when he was three months old, and he was brought up first by one of the women in his father's harem, and then by his stepmother Sayeste, another wife of Abdül Mecit. He was confined to the Cage in the latter years of the reign of his uncle Abdül Aziz and throughout the reigns of his older brothers Murat V, Abdül Hamit II and Mehmet V Reşat. Counting the period of his infancy, when he was in the harem, his total period of confinement amounted to fifty-seven years, longer than that of any other sultan in the Osmanlı line, of whom he was fated to be the last.

Vahidettin had married four times before he came to the throne, his second and third marriages, which produced no children, ending in divorce. His first wife, Emine Nazikeda, whom he married in 1885, bore him three daughters. The first was Fenire, who was born

in 1888 and died in infancy; then came Fatma Ulviye in 1892, and
Rukiye Sabiha in 1894. His fourth wife Müveddet, whom he married
in 1911, bore his son Ertuğrul on 10 September 1912.

The British diplomat Andrew Ryan gave his impression of the new
sultan: 'The Sultan was as good a Turk as any of his predecessors, and
in many ways a better man than any of his three brothers who had
preceded him – less cunning than Abdul-Hamid, infinitely more
intelligent than Mehmed Reshad.'

By the time that Vahidettin came to the throne the Ottoman
Empire was close to collapse, and at his formal enthronement the
new sultan said in despair to the *şeyhülislam*, 'I am at a loss. Pray
for me.' But Vahidettin's concern does not seem to have been for
the empire, as noted in the memoirs of Ali Haydar Midhat, who
quotes the response of the sultan to a query by Seniha Sultan, the
mother of Prince Sabahattin, a grandson of Sultan Abdül Mecit I:
'Don't worry about that,' answered the sultan. 'I'm not concerned
with what's going to happen to the country. I'm more interested in
my own future and the future of our dynasty.'

The Ottoman forces had by then suffered a series of defeats in
both Iraq and Syria, and at the beginning of October 1918 they
retreated to make a last stand in Anatolia under Mustafa Kemal
Pasha. As they did so Kemal sent a cable to the sultan urging him
to form a new government and sue for peace.

Talat Pasha resigned as grand vezir on 8 October, and soon
afterwards he and Enver and Cemal fled from Turkey on a German
warship. On 14 October the sultan appointed Ahmet Izzet Pasha as
grand vezir, and he immediately began making overtures to the
British for peace.

An armistice was signed at Mudros to take effect on 31 October.
The armistice called for the unconditional surrender of the Ottoman
forces, with all strategic points in Turkey to be occupied by the
Allies. A large Allied fleet sailed through the straits and reached
Istanbul on 13 November, landing troops to begin the occupation
of the city. When a group of Turkish parliamentarians came to
visit Vahidettin, offering him their condolences, he spoke to them

despondently, indicating with a wave of his hand the long line of Allied warships anchored in the Bosphorus, 'I can't look out of the window. I hate to see them.'

Istanbul was formally placed under Allied occupation, with the British admiral Calthorpe appointed as high commissioner. Vahidettin felt that the only hope for Turkey was to cooperate with the Allies, especially the British, and so he and a succession of his grand vezirs worked with the high commissioner in administering what was left of the shattered empire. Vahidettin dissolved parliament on 21 December 1918, and at the beginning of March 1919 he appointed his brother-in-law Damat Ferit Pasha as grand vezir. When Vahidettin was criticized for choosing the unpopular Ferit, he replied he could appoint anyone he pleased, 'even the Greek or Armenian Patriarchs or the Chief Rabbi'.

At the Paris Peace Conference, which began in January 1919, the Allies considered various plans for dividing up what was left of the Ottoman Empire, with Greece claiming Izmir and its hinterland. The Greek prime minister Venizelos received backing from Lloyd George and Clemenceau to send an expeditionary force to Asia Minor, and on 14 May 1919 an Allied armada landed a Greek division at Izmir. The news of the Greek invasion devastated Vahidettin and reduced him to tears. Supporting himself on the arm of his cousin Abdül Mecit as he left a meeting of the imperial council, he said to him, 'Look, I am weeping like a woman.'

The Ottoman government continued to function under the aegis of the Allied high commissioner, who used the sultan and his cabinet merely as puppets. Meanwhile, a national resistance movement was developing in Anatolia under the leadership of Mustafa Kemal Pasha. On 19 March 1920 Kemal announced the establishment of a Turkish parliament in Ankara, the Grand National Assembly (GNA). The GNA met for the first time on 23 April of that year, choosing Kemal as president. The sultan responded by condemning Kemal and six other nationalist leaders to death.

The Allies agreed on the post-war boundaries of the Ottoman Empire in the Treaty of Sèvres, signed on 10 August 1920. The treaty greatly diminished the extent of the Ottoman Empire, leaving only central and northwestern Anatolia to the Turks. Istanbul would be left under Ottoman rule, but the straits would be placed under international control. The sultan had no choice but to accept the provisions of the treaty, but the GNA denounced it and declared that all the Turks who had signed the agreement were traitors.

During most of September 1921 no foreign ambassador or official could contact the sultan, who was completely incommunicado. Sherif Ali Haydar gives the explanation for the sultan's behaviour in his memoirs, writing that 'He [Vahidettin] had taken a new wife, who so demanded his attention that he refused to see any visitors.' It seems that Vahidettin, who was then past sixty, had fallen in love with a nineteen-year-old girl named Nevzad, the daughter of a palace gardener. Nevzad was engaged to a young sea-captain, and both she and her family completely opposed the sultan's proposal of marriage to her. But Vahidettin overrode their opposition, and on 1 September 1921 he married Nevzad and took her into his harem.

Meanwhile, the Turkish nationalist forces under Ismet Pasha and Mustafa Kemal Pasha had driven back the Greek army, which was evacuated from Izmir in early September 1922. The war then officially ended with an armistice signed at Mudanya on 11 October of that year.

On 1 November 1922 the GNA enacted legislation separating the sultanate and the caliphate, with the former being abolished and the latter reduced to a purely religious role. The Allied high commissioners were informed that Istanbul would be under the administration of the GNA, and that Vahidettin was no longer sultan, though he retained the title of caliph. Thus ended a sultanate that had lasted for more than six hundred years, a title that had passed on through thirty-six successive rulers of the Osmanlı dynasty. Vahidettin, the last sultan, now clung to a vestige of power through his title of caliph.

On 4 November the grand vezir Ahmet Tevfik Pasha resigned,

along with his cabinet, delivering up his seals of office to Vahidettin at Yıldız Sarayı. Vahidettin, alone and completely isolated, now felt that his life was in imminent danger, and he confided his fears to General Harington, the new British high commissioner. As he wrote to Harington on 16 November: 'Sir: Considering my life in danger in Istanbul, I take refuge with the British Government and request my transfer as soon as possible from Istanbul to another place.'

Harington made the necessary arrangements, and the following morning he sent two ambulances to Yıldız Sarayı to pick up Vahidettin and his party, which included his ten-year-old son Ertuğrul, his bandmaster, and six servants, headed by his head chamberlain, the chief black eunuch. By agreement with Harington, Vahidettin's wives would be sent to join him later under the care of his chamberlain. Vahidettin and his party were driven to Dolmabahçe Sarayı. There they boarded a motor launch that took them out to the British battleship HMS *Malaya*, which was waiting for them with a full head of steam, with orders to head for Malta.

A press photograph shows Vahidettin's departure, as he steps with his right foot on the launch, his left foot on the quay, a Turkish gentleman in a fez behind him holding a bouquet of flowers, a black eunuch following with baggage, a British officer saluting. Then the launch took Vahidettin out to HMS *Malaya*, which soon weighed anchor and steamed down the Bosphorus, bearing the last sultan of the Ottoman Empire into exile, never to return.

When Ali Haydar Midhat learned of Vahidettin's flight he wrote in his diary: 'May God preserve us from such a weak-kneed Sultan.' He later noted that 'The Turkish Imperial Family are largely to blame' for what he called the 'disintegration' of the Muslim world.

The day after Vahidettin's departure the GNA formally deposed him as caliph, citing a *fetva* that 'he had taken sides with the enemy against the Defenders of the Faith, had sowed fratricidal discord, and had finally placed himself under foreign protection and deserted the seat of the Caliphate to take refuge on board an English ship.'

The position of caliph was tentatively offered to Vahidettin's cousin, the crown prince Abdül Mecit Efendi, son of Sultan Abdül

Mehmet VI Vahidettin stepping aboard the launch
of HMS Malaya, the British warship that will take him
into exile, 17 November 1922

Aziz by his first wife, Hayranidil, and the eldest surviving male in the imperial Osmanlı line. Abdül Mecit indicated that he would accept the title, and on 19 November 1922 he received a cable from Mustafa Kemal Pasha informing him that he had been chosen as caliph. His installation took place the following Friday 24 November 1922, in a ceremony held in Topkapı Sarayı, which had been virtually abandoned since the first half of the nineteenth century. George Young, the only British observer, thought that the ceremony was a farce: 'a delegation of Angora [Ankara] deputies notifying an elderly dilettante that he had been elected by a majority vote like any Labour leader.'

The new caliph attended the Friday noon prayer at Fatih Camii, after which he paid a visit to the shrine of Eyüp. There he simply said a prayer and then departed for Dolmabahçe Sarayı, the customary *kılıç kuşanması* being omitted because the sword of Osman was the symbol of the temporal power of the sultan. Young remarked that 'The Caliph has been denied his Sword of Othman, but he has been given his Sword of Damocles.' Abdül Mecit eschewed the traditional costume worn by his predecessors in the Osmanlı line for appropriate civilian clothing, leading Young to describe him as 'a portly person in a fez, frock-coat and green ribbon'.

Abdül Mecit was fifty-four when he became caliph, having been for the past forty-six years confined in the Cage, which in his case was his luxurious apartment in Dolmabahçe Sarayı. By all accounts he was a cultured gentleman, an amateur painter and musician of some talent, content with his ceremonial role as the religious leader of Islam.

Abdül Mecit had married four times before he became caliph. He fathered only two children, a son Ömer Faruk born to his first wife Şehsuvar on 28 February 1898, and a daughter Dürrüşehvar, born on 12 March 1913 to his second wife Hayirnissa. His third and fourth wives, Mihisti and Behrus, bore him no children.

The final articles of the Treaty of Lausanne, signed on 24 July 1923, established the present boundaries of the Republic of Turkey, except for the province of the Hatay, acquired after a plebescite in 1939.

The Allied occupation of Istanbul came to an end on 2 October 1923, when the final detachment of British troops embarked from the quay at Dolmabahçe. Four days later a division of the Turkish Nationalist army marched into Istanbul. On 13 October the GNA passed a law making Ankara the capital of Turkey. Then on 29 October the assembly adopted a new constitution that created the Republic of Turkey, and on that same day Mustafa Kemal Pasha,

Caliph Abdül Mecit in procession for the Friday noon prayer, winter of 1923–4

later known as Atatürk, was elected president, choosing Ismet (Inönü) Pasha as prime minister.

On 3 March 1924 the GNA passed a law abolishing the caliphate, thus severing the last, tenuous bond that linked the new Republic of Turkey with the Ottoman Empire. This same law deposed Abdül Mecit as caliph, also stating that he and all of his descendants were forbidden to reside within the boundaries of the Turkish Republic.

At eleven o'clock that evening the Vali (governor) of Istanbul, Haidar Bey, came to Dolmabahçe Sarayı with four representatives of the GNA to inform Abdül Mecit of the assembly's decision. A special carriage had been prepared for the royal family on the Simplon Express, which was due to leave at midnight from Sirkeci station in Istanbul. The caliph and his immediate family, along with two servants and three officials, would be obliged to join the train outside the city at Çatalca, for the authorities were afraid of public demonstrations if they departed from Istanbul. They would leave the palace before dawn, while the others would have to be out an hour before midnight.

One of the painful scenes on the eve of departure is described in the memoirs of the Princess Musbah, daughter of Ali Haydar, Sherif of Mecca. She and her two sisters had come to say goodbye to their brother Mecit and his wife Rukiye, a granddaughter of Murat V, who were living in a kiosk near Dolmabahçe. Among those present were Rukiye's aunt Selma and her former wet-nurse Taya. As Musbah writes, referring to herself and her sisters as the Sherifas and to Rukiye as Yenga, or sister-in-law:

That evening they all gathered for the last time in Yenga's drawing room. A cold, biting wind howled outside. No one spoke very much.

Selma Hanoum asked Roukhia to play something. Yenga rose and went towards her Erard grand. Her fingers passed lingeringly, caressingly over the polished lid; the others could feel what was passing in her thoughts: this house, these rooms, the familiar objects around her which had become part of her life since that day when she had come as a bride to her new home.

She began to play the 'Moonlight Sonata' of Beethoven. The noble, wistful melody, with its rippling sombre accompaniment of the opening Adagio, moved the silent listeners to tears. Someone sobbed openly. Roukhia turned round, her face was covered with tears.

'I cannot play any more,' she said simply.

At eleven that night Medjid and Roukhia said goodbye to their friends and household, and accompanied by the Sherifas they got into their car.

Tears, tears on all the faces. And as the car moved off Musbah could hear Taya's wail of despair.

'Allah, protect the Light of My Eyes!'

It was a night of bitter cold and driving wind. When they reached Sirkeji, Musbah saw that the entrance to the station was guarded by troops and police. It seemed an unnecessary precaution in view of the apathetic attitude adopted by the police towards the banish-ment of the House of Osman from Turkey.

They passed through the double line of police onto the platform, where the Simplon Express stood waiting to carry the Imperial Family to exile. The platform was crowded with relatives, friends and retainers to bid their last farewell.

Here on the platform of Sirkeji station, a tragic end to the close of a chapter in Turkish history was being enacted.

A shrill whistle: the last embraces, the last words.

The Sherifas stood back. Behind them stood Akil Efendi, Medjid's faithful Greek steward, weeping bitterly. He had served his master since the latter was a boy.

The three sisters watched the train slowly move out and disappear into the darkness – a red light glimmered for a moment and then vanished. The royal exiles had departed.

How long ago was it that Musbah had been taken by her new imperial sister-in-law, Roukhia Sultan, to see the dolls that had been prepared for her?

Someone touched her on the shoulder. It was Akil Efendi.

'Come Highness! They have gone – it is all over.'

Meanwhile, Abdül Mecit and his family were still in Dolmabahçe Sarayı. Haidar Bey had informed them that they would have to pack up and depart within five hours, otherwise they would have to leave everything behind. The ensuing scene is described by the American journalist Constantine Brown:

Crying and shouting with despair, all the servants, well over two hundred men and women, began to bring out old-fashioned Turkish carpetbags and luxurious silver and gold dressing-cases and to fill them with the most unbelievable things, which might have done for a bric-a-brac shop but not for the journey of a large family. They were piling up all kinds of Persian and Arabic silks and velvets, antique coffee-cups in gilded holders, rosewood-framed hand-mirrors inlaid with mother-of-pearl, court dresses and gold-braided uniforms. No one thought of packing some practical every-day clothes or linen. At half past two in the morning nothing had been done. The commissioner of police, who, together with the other four representatives, was all the time in the palace, keeping a close watch over the crown jewels, decided to intervene, and in a business-like manner, assisted by a few other men, brought the Caliph's personal belongings, together with other things the family might need in exile, and packed everything in seventy-two trunks and bags.

At last everything was packed and loaded on to the convoy of motorcars and lorries that were going to take the royal exiles to Çatalca. At four o'clock in the morning the caliph and his family walked out of the palace and said goodbye to those who were remaining behind, some two hundred servants along with women who had been in the harem of departed sultans going back to Murat V, all of them weeping as they individually bade their farewells. The caliph turned to Haidar Bey and said: 'I hope the nation will not allow these people to starve; they are guiltless.' The Vali promised that they would all be provided for. A detachment of troops with fixed bayonets presented arms as the caliph passed them to board his motorcar. Abdül Mecit was deeply moved, and he turned to address the soldiers, saying, 'Goodbye, children, I shall always pray for you.'

As the motorcade made its way out of the palace driveway an old woman servant threw a basin of water into the roadway after the last car passed, the traditional Turkish custom at departure, meant to ensure that those who were leaving would some day return.

But Abdül Mecit would never return, and he must surely have known this as his car drove him along the Bosphorus road and then across the Golden Horn. There in the first light of false dawn he could see the pavilions of Topkapı Sarayı amid the spectral cypresses on the First Hill above the confluence of the Golden Horn and the Bosphorus, where his ancestors had lived for four centuries before they had abandoned the old palace in favour of Dolmabahçe and Yıldız. But now the Ottoman Empire was no more and the House of Osman had fallen, the last caliph following the last sultan into exile, as the ghosts began gathering in the abandoned House of Felicity.

Chapter 19

THE GATHERING PLACE OF
THE JINNS

HMS *Malaya* brought Vahidettin to Malta, where he stayed through the winter of 1922–3. Then in the spring of 1923 he accepted an invitation from King Hüseyin and made a pilgrimage to Mecca, the first of the Osmanlı line to do so. He was trying to gain recognition as caliph, but nothing came of this and he eventually abandoned the effort.

Vahidettin then sailed to Alexandria, hoping to settle in Egypt. But the British had no desire to have an ex-sultan living in a country that had once been part of his empire, and so he was forced to move on. King Victor Emmanuel III invited him to live in Italy, where he rented a villa in San Remo. He then sent his chamberlain to Istanbul to fetch his *haseki* Nevzad and the other two wives he had left behind. News of this reached the tabloid press in the US, prompting an American theatrical producer to send a cable to the British Embassy in Istanbul. It read: 'Hippodrome New York could use wives of ex-Sultan kindly put me in touch with party who could procure them.'

Vahidettin spent the remaining three years of his life in San Remo, where he died of heart failure on 15 May 1926, in his sixty-sixth year. His last years were plagued by debt, and his burial was delayed by the crowds of bill-collectors demanding payment from his penniless family. The Turkish authorities refused permission for Vahidettin to be buried in Turkey, but the French allowed his interment in Damascus at the mosque of Sultan Selim I.

After Vahidettin's death his wives returned to Istanbul, where Nevzad married the sea captain to whom she had been engaged before she was taken into the sultan's harem. The rest of his family scattered to various places of exile, his only son Ertuğrul moving to Egypt, where he died in 1944.

The families of earlier sultans were also sent off into exile. As Ayşe Osmanoğlu, a daughter of Abdül Hamit II, wrote in her memoirs: 'We are a group of human beings without fatherland, without a home, without shelter. The history of our family in exile was just a sequence of tragic deaths.' Her brother Mehmet Abdülkadır played in an orchestra in Sofia, and when he died in 1944 he was buried in a pauper's grave. Her sister Zekiye spent her last years dependent on charity at a hotel in southern France, where she died in 1950. Another brother, Abdurrahim Havri, committed suicide in Paris in 1952, leaving barely enough money to pay for his funeral.

Meanwhile Abdül Mecit, the last caliph, lived in Switzerland for a time before settling in Nice, where he remained until the Second World War. He then moved to Paris, where he died of heart failure on 23 August 1944, just as the Allies were liberating the city from the Germans. The excitement over the liberation of Paris overshadowed the death of Abdül Mecit, whose passing was not even noted by an obituary in *The Times* of London. The Allies gave permission for his burial in Medina, where he was revered as the last of the Ottoman caliphs, a moribund title that died with him.

After the death of Abdül Mecit the title of head of the Osmanlı line passed to Ahmet Nihat (1884–1954), a grandson of Murat V. When he died the title passed in turn to Osman Fuad (1895–1973), another grandson of Murat V; Mehmet Abdülaziz (1901–77), a grandson of Abdül Aziz; Ali Vasib (1903–84), a great-grandson of Murat V; Mehmet Orhan (1909–94), a grandson of Abdül Hamit II; and Osman Ertuğrul (1912–), another grandson of Abdül Hamit II, who now lives quietly in retirement in New York City.

Mehmet Orhan was the most colourful of the imperial exiles, and his life story reads like a picaresque novel. He left Nice at the age of seventeen and worked as a porter and tramway conductor in Buenos Aires, where he learned to fly and became a barnstorming acrobatic pilot. He was then appointed as chamberlain to King Zog of Albania, for whom he also served as personal pilot up until the beginning of the Second World War, when he returned to France. When the Allies landed on Normandy he enlisted in the US Army and served through the remainder of the war, after which the American government gave him a pension of $300 a month. He later supplemented his income by working as a guide at the American cemetery in Paris. He was married and divorced three times, fathering a son and a daughter. He was invited back to Turkey by President Turgut Ozal in 1992, by which time the law forbidding the return of the royal family had been rescinded. Mehmet Orhan had been fifteen when he left Istanbul with his family from Sirkeci station that cold and windy night in 1924, waving goodbye to the Princess Musbah and the others who had come to bid them farewell. And now he came back as an old man with just two years to live, treasuring the bitter-sweet memories of his return until his death in Nice in 1994. His nephew, Prince Bülent Osman, had some earth sent back from Turkey for the funeral, and he and the few other mourners each cast a handful of this soil into the grave of Mehmet Orhan when he was laid to rest.

When Prince Mehmet Orhan returned to Istanbul he was greeted royally by President Ozal in Çıragan Sarayı, which had been rebuilt as a five-star hotel. By that time all of the other surviving imperial Ottoman palaces had also been restored, most of them as museums. Dolmabahçe Sarayı at first served as a residence for the President of Turkey, and it was there that Atatürk died on 10 November 1938.

The old palace of Topkapı Sarayı was in a sorry state when the Ottoman Empire came to an end, for the sultans had not been in residence there since the first half of the nineteenth century. During the latter years of the empire the only residents there were a few old eunuchs and the discarded concubines and slaves of departed sultans, including those Circassian women who had gone unclaimed when Abdül Hamit's harem was disbanded in 1909. By then the

*The Rivan Kiosk and the Marble Pool in the Fourth Court
of Topkapı Sarayı*

palace was dilapidated and partly in ruins, its once beautiful gardens neglected and overgrown, the embowered pavilions in its lower terraces destroyed along with its seaside kiosks when the railway line for the Orient Express was built in the late 1880s. At that time an ancient grove of boxwood trees was uprooted from the lower gardens of Topkapı Sarayı, its loss bewailed by an old servant named Memiş Efendi, who had served in the palace since the days of Mahmut II. As he lamented: 'Alas, in that grove of boxwood trees every Wednesday night the king of the jinns holds council. Where will he go now?'

Topkapı Sarayı ceased to be royal domain in April 1923, when a decree of the GNA declared that the palace was the property of the Turkish Republic, attached to the administration of the museums of Istanbul. Years of restoration followed before the various parts of the palace could be opened to the public as the Topkapı Sarayı

Museum, whose collections include many of the treasures belonging to the sultans, as well as the objects which they and their household used in their daily life.

The last part of the palace to be opened was the harem, though there are still parts of that ancient labyrinth that have not yet been completely restored and made accessible to visitors. Among these are the Hall of the Favourites and the Cage, though the site of the infamous Kafes is still not absolutely certain, probably because it was located in various places at different times. The most likely location for the Kafes is an unrestored congeries of rooms off the long passageway that leads into the open courtyard below the Hall of the Favourites. Old maps of the harem note that this passageway

The Goths' Column and the outer gardens of
the harem of Topkapı Sarayı

The tower of the harem of Topkapı Sarayı

is called the Gathering Place of the Jinns, a name whose origin is unknown to those who are not aware of the lament of Memiş Efendi.

The present author made his way surreptitiously into this lost labyrinth in the autumn of 1960, before the harem had yet been opened to the public, and not having obtained permission to be there he very quietly made his way through the dark rooms of the Kafes and on into the even more shadowy chambers of the Hall of the Favourites. Midway between the two he explored a small chamber at the top of a creaking wooden staircase, identifying it from his reading as the room where Ibrahim the Mad was imprisoned after his deposition, when for nine days and nights his ceaseless weeping was heard by his women in the Hall of the Favourites, until Black Ali came to strangle him.

These rooms have still not been opened to the public, and perhaps they never should be, for shuttered and abandoned as they were at the time of the author's unauthorized visit they evoked the presence of those who lived there in the past, the imprisoned princes who lived in their gilded cage and the sequestered favourites whose beauty could not be seen beyond the palace walls. The windows were shuttered and the rooms in almost total darkness; an old brass bedstead under a tottering canopy was shrouded in cobwebs, its rotting mattress giving off an odour of sepulchral decay. Through the gathering shadows the mirror of a baroque dressing-table reflected the dark image of a deserted room. And when night fell the presence of ghosts could be felt, returning along the Gathering Place of the Jinns to this haunted palace, once the House of Felicity.

Glossary

The following are some Turkish words and technical terms that are used frequently in the text. Turkish words enclosed in parentheses are the form that they take when they are modified by a noun; e.g. Yeni Cami = the New Mosque, whereas Sultan Ahmet Camii = the Mosque of Sultan Ahmet.

acemoğlan: a Janissary recruit, or apprentice of the Outer Service of Topkapı Sarayı
ağa (ağası): title given to commandants of army corps, especially those of the Janissaries, and to high officials in the imperial palace, particularly the chief black and white eunuchs
bailo: Venetian ambassador
bakşis: gratuity
baş: head, chief of a corps
bayram: Muslim festival
bedesten: covered market
beylerbey: governor of a province
birinci: first
birinci kadın: first wife, or first woman (in the harem), by tradition mother of the sultan's eldest living son
bostancı: gardener; palace (foot)guard
bostancıbaşı: head gardener; head of the palace guards
büyük: big; elder
caique: fishing boat or rowing barge
caravanserai: inn for travellers
cariye: female slave

cihad: holy war

çırak: apprentice

cirit: game played on horseback with darts

damat: son-in-law

daye hatun: wet-nurse

defterdar: accountant, treasurer

devşirme: levy of Christian youths for Janissaries

divan: imperial council; room where assemblage is held; also a collection of poems

dragoman: interpreter, go-between

efendi: gentleman, master

eski: old

Fatih: Conqueror

fetva: *mufti's* opinion on a matter of religious law

firman: imperial edict

gazel: classical Turkish poem

Gazi: Warrior for the Islamic faith

gedikiler: chosen women in the imperial harem

genç: young

hane: house or room

hanım: lady

harem: women's quarters in a house or palace

has: royal

haseki: sultan's favourite woman

hatti şerif: imperial edict

hatun: woman, lady

haznedar: treasurer

hoca: teacher

hospodar: princely governors of Moldavia and Wallachia

ikbal: royal concubine

imam: prayer leader in a mosque

iskele (iskelesi): landing stage

Janissaries: élite corps of Ottoman army

kadıasker: head judge

kadın: woman, wife

kafes: cage

kalfa: qualified worker

kanun: law

kanunname: a collection of laws or rules

kapı (kapısı): door, gate

kapı ağası: chief white eunuch
kapıcı: doorman, gatekeeper
kapıcıbaşı: head gatekeeper
kara: black
karagöz: Turkish shadow puppets
kasır (kasrı): summer palace
kaya kadın: chief woman servant in the harem
kaymakam: provincial governor
kazan: cauldron
khan: title applied to the Ottoman sultans and other rulers
kılıç: sword
kılıç kuşanması: girding of a sultan with the sword of Osman
kira: woman agent used by the women in the harem
kismet: fate, destiny
kız: girl
kızlar ağası: chief black eunuch
köşk (köşkü): kiosk
küçük: little
külliye: building complex, usually surrounding a mosque
lala: tutor
lale: tulip
mabeyn: room, hall or suite separating the men's and women's
   quarters in a home or palace
medrese (medresesi): Islamic school of higher studies
meşkhane: music room
meydan (meydanı): public square
mihrab: niche in wall indicating direction of Mecca
millet: nation, or the members of a recognized religious creed
mimber: pulpit in a mosque
minaret: tower from which the *müezzin* gives the call to prayer
molla: a high-ranking teacher of theology
müezzin: one who calls to prayer
mufti: official learned in Islamic law who is in charge of Islamic law
   for a province or district
musahib: sultan's favourite page
namazgah: outdoor place of Islamic prayer
ney: Turkish flute
Nizamı Cedit: New Order of Selim III, particularly his reformed army
oda (odası): room
padişah: sultan

pasha: highest-ranking Ottoman official or officer

pazar (pazarı): market

pazar caique: royal barge

pilaf: cooked rice

sancak şerif: sacred standard of the Prophet Mohammed

saray (sarayı): palace

Segbanı Cedit: regiments of reformed army of Mahmut II

şehzade: prince

selamlık: men's quarters of a home or palace, also the sultan's
   procession to the mosque for the Friday noon prayer

serasker: commander-in-chief or minister of war

şeriat: Islamic law

şeyh: sheikh

şeyhülislam: the chief religious official in the Ottoman Empire

Sipahi: feudal cavalryman

süt anne: milk-mother

tanzimat: reform

tekke: dervish lodge

top: cannon

tuğra: imperial monogram

türbe: Islamic mausoleum

ulema: ruling body of Muslim jurists

usta: journeyman; superintendent

valide sultan: mother of a reigning sultan

veliaht: crown prince

vezir: member of imperial council

yalı: waterfront mansion

yamak: Janissary auxiliary

yeni: new

Ottoman Sultans (The House of Osman)

1. Osman Gazi, c. 1282–1326
2. Orhan Gazi, 1326–62
3. Murat I, 1362–89
4. Beyazit I, 1389–1402
   (Interregnum)
5. Mehmet I, 1413–21
6. Murat II, 1421–44, 1446–51
7. Mehmet II, 1444–6, 1451–81
8. Beyazit II, 1481–1512
9. Selim I, 1512–20
10. Süleyman I, 1520–66
11. Selim II, 1566–74
12. Murat III, 1574–95
13. Mehmet III, 1595–1603
14. Ahmet I, 1603–17
15. Mustafa I, 1617–18, 1622–3
16. Osman II, 1618–22
17. Murat IV, 1623–40
18. Ibrahim, 1640–48
19. Mehmet IV, 1648–87
20. Süleyman II, 1687–91
21. Ahmet II, 1691–5
22. Mustafa II, 1695–1703
23. Ahmet III, 1703–30
24. Mahmut I, 1730–54
25. Osman III, 1754–7

26. Mustafa III, 1757–74
27. Abdül Hamit I, 1774–89
28. Selim III, 1789–1807
29. Mustafa IV, 1807–8
30. Mahmut II, 1808–39
31. Abdül Mecit I, 1839–61
32. Abdül Aziz, 1861–76
33. Murat V, 1876
34. Abdül Hamit II, 1876–1909
35. Mehmet V Reşat, 1909–18
36. Mehmet VI Vahidettin,
    1918–22
37. Abdül Mecit (II) (Caliph
    only), 1922–4

Genealogy of the Sultans

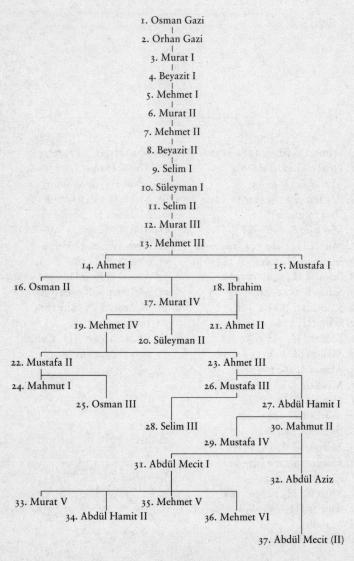

1. Osman Gazi
2. Orhan Gazi
3. Murat I
4. Beyazit I
5. Mehmet I
6. Murat II
7. Mehmet II
8. Beyazit II
9. Selim I
10. Süleyman I
11. Selim II
12. Murat III
13. Mehmet III

14. Ahmet I
15. Mustafa I

16. Osman II
18. Ibrahim
17. Murat IV

19. Mehmet IV
21. Ahmet II
20. Süleyman II

22. Mustafa II
23. Ahmet III
24. Mahmut I
26. Mustafa III
25. Osman III
27. Abdül Hamit I
28. Selim III
30. Mahmut II
29. Mustafa IV

31. Abdül Mecit I
32. Abdül Aziz

33. Murat V
35. Mehmet V
34. Abdül Hamit II
36. Mehmet VI

37. Abdül Mecit (II)

Mothers of the Sultans

Sultan	Mother (Italics denotes a *valide sultan*)	Sultan	Mother (Italics denotes a *valide sultan*)
1. Osman Gazi	?	22. Mustafa II	*Rabia Gülnüş*
2. Orhan Gazi	Mal Hatun		
3. Murat I	Nilüfer	23. Ahmet III	*Rabia Gülnüş*
4. Beyazit I	Gülçiçek		
5. Mehmet I	*Devletşah*	24. Mahmut I	*Saliha*
6. Murat II	Emine	25. Osman III	*Şehsuvar*
7. Mehmet II	Hüma	26. Mustafa III	Mihrişah
8. Beyazit II	*Gülbahar*	27. Abdül Hamit I	Rabia Şermi
9. Selim I	Ayşe	28. Selim III	*Mihrişah*
10. Süleyman I	*Hafsa*	29. Mustafa IV	*Ayşe Seniyeperver*
11. Selim II	Hürrem (Roxelana)	30. Mahmut II	*Nakşidil*
12. Murat III	*Nurbanu*	31. Abdül Mecit I	*Bezmialem*
13. Mehmet III	*Safiye*	32. Abdül Aziz	*Pertevniyal*
14. Ahmet I	*Handan*	33. Murat V	*Şevkefza*
15. Mustafa I	?	34. Abdül Hamit II	Tirimüjgan
16. Osman II	Mahfiruz (Hadice)	35. Mehmet V Reşat	Gülcemal
17. Murat IV	*Kösem*	36. Mehmet VI Vahidettin	Gülüştü
18. Ibrahim	*Kösem*	37. Abdül Mecit (II)	Hayranidil
19. Mehmet IV	*Hadice Turhan*		
20. Süleyman II	*Saliha Dilaşub*		
21. Ahmet II	Hadice Muazzez		

Bibliography

Ahmed Vasif Efendi, *Tarih-i Vasif*. Cairo, 1830

Alberi, Eugenio (ed.), *Relazione degli ambasciatori Veneti al Senato durante il XVI secolo*. Series 3, vols. 1–3. Florence, 1842–55

Alderson, A. D., *The Structure of the Ottoman Dynasty*. Oxford, 1956

Ali Seydi Bey, quoted in Pars Tuğlaci, *The Ottoman Palace Women*. Istanbul, 1985

Ambros, F. G., *Candid Penstrokes: the lyrics of Meali, an Ottoman poet of the 16th century*. Berlin, 1982

Andrews, Walter, 'The Sexual Intertext of Ottoman Literature: the story of Meali, magistrate of Mihaliç'. Ediyabat 3 (1989): 31–56

Angiolello, Giovanni Maria, *Historia Turchesa (1300–1514)*, ed. I. Ursu. Bucharest, 1909

Arifi (Fethullah Arif Çelebi), *Süleymanname*. Istanbul, Topkapı Sarayı Library, H. 1517

Aşıkpaşazade, Dervish Ahmed, *Die altosmanische Chronik des Aşıkpaşazade*, ed. Friedrich Giese. Leipzig, 1929

Atıl, Esin, *The Age of Süleyman the Magnificent*. Washington, DC, and New York, 1987

——, *Süleymanname: The Illustrated History of Süleyman the Magnificent*. Washington, DC, and New York, 1986

Babinger, Franz, *Mehmed the Conqueror and His Time*, trans. Ralph Manheim, ed. William Hickman. Princeton, 1978

Badoara, Andrea, cited in Alberi, *Relazione*, vol. 1, p. 362

Barozzi, Nicolo and Giglielmo Berchet (eds.), *Le Relazioni degli stati Europei*. Series 5: Turkey. 2 vols. Venice, 1871–2

Bassano da Zara, Luigi, *I Costumi et i modi particolari della vita de'*
   Turchi, ed. Franz Babinger, with a facsimile of the Rome 1545
   edition. Munich, 1963

Beauvau, Henry de, *Relation journalière du Voyage du Levant*. Lyons,
   1609

Bernardo, Lorenzo, cited in Alberi, *Relazione*, vol. 2, pp. 321–426

Bobovi, Albert, *Mémoires sur les Turcs* ×. Harvard University,
   Houghton Library. Count Paul Riant Collection, French 103

Bodnar, E. W., *Cyriacus of Ancona and Athens*. Brussels, 1960

Bon, Ottaviano, *The Sultan's Seraglio: an intimate portrait of life in*
   the Ottoman court, introduced and annotated by Godfrey
   Goodwin. London, 1996

Bordier, Julien, *Relation d'un voyage en Orient (1604–1619)* ×. Paris,
   Bibliothèque Nationale, Fr. 18076

Bragadin, Pietro, cited in Alberi, *Relazione*, vol. 3, p. 102

Brassey, Lady, *Sunshine and Storm in the East, or Cruises to Cyprus*
   and Constantinople. London, 1880

Brown, Constantine, article in *Asia*, June 1924, cited in Gülersoy,
   Dolmabahçe Palace and its Environs

Busbecq, Ogier Ghiselin de, *Turkish Letters*, trans. Edward Seymour
   Forster. Oxford, 1927

Cantemir, Demetrius, *The History of the Growth and Decay of the*
   Othman Empire, trans. N. Tindal. London, 1734–5

Capello, Girolamo, Calendar of State Papers, Venice, vol. 9, item 563

Cassels, Lavender, *The Struggle for the Ottoman Empire, 1717–1740*.
   London, 1966

Cevdet Pasha, cited in Gülersoy, *Dolmabahçe Palace and its Environs*

Clarke, Edward Daniel, *Travels in Various Countries of Europe, Asia,*
   and Africa. Vol. 2 of 11 vols. London, 1816–24

Clot, André, *Suleiman the Magnificent: the man, his life, his epoch*,
   trans. Matthew J. Reisz. Paris, 1989

Commynes, Philippe de, *The Memoirs of Philippe de Commynes*
   (1445–1509), ed. Samuel Kinser, trans. Isabelle Cazeaux. 2 vols.
   Columbia, South Carolina, 1969, 1973

Contarini, Alvise, quoted in Barozzi and Berchet, *Le Relazione*, 1:374

Contarini, Bartolomeo, '*Summario della relazione* [1519]', in Alberi,
   vol. 3, pp. 56–68

Contarini, Iacomo, 'Relazione [1507]', in Sanuto, vol. 7, pp. 7ff.

Contarini, Paolo, cited in Alberi, *Relazione*, vol. 3, pp. 209–50

Contarini, Simon, report in Barozzi and Berchet, *Le Relazioni*, 1:132–4

Courmenin, Louis Deshayes de, *Voiage de Levant fait par le Commandement du Roy en l'année 1621*. Paris, 1632

Covel, Dr J., 'The Diaries of Dr J. Covel, 1670–79', in J. T. Bent (ed.), *Early Voyages and Travels in the Levant*. London, 1893

Croix, François Petis de la, *État général de l'empire ottoman*. Paris, 1695

Dallam, Thomas, 'The Diary of Master Thomas Dallam, 1559–1600', in J. T. Bent (ed.), *Early Voyages and Travels in the Levant*. London, 1893

Dallaway, James, *Constantinople Ancient and Modern, with Excursions to the Shores and Islands of the Archipelago and to the Troad*. London, 1797

Davis, Fanny, *The Palace of Topkapı in Istanbul*. New York, 1970

Davis, James C. (ed. and trans.), *Pursuit of Power: Venetian ambassadors' reports on Spain, Turkey and France in the age of Philip II, 1560–1600*. New York, Evanston, and London, 1970

Dolfin, Daniele, *Dispacci, 1726–30*. Venetian State Archives, Filza 181

Donini, Marcantonio, cited in Alberi, *Relazione*, vol. 3, pp. 173–209

Doukas, *Decline and Fall of Byzantium to the Ottoman Turks by Doukas: an annotated translation of 'Historia-Byzantina'*, by Harry J. Magoulias. Detroit, 1975

Dwight, H. G., *Constantinople, Old and New*. New York, 1915

Edip (Adıvar), Halide, *Memoirs*. New York, 1926

Elliot, Sir Henry G., *Some Revolutions and other Diplomatic Experiences*. London, 1927

Emo, Giovanni, *Dispacci, 1720–26*. Venetian State Archives, Filza 183–5

Eremya Çelebi Kömürcüyan, *Istanbul Tarihi XVII asırda Istanbul*, trans. (Armenian to Turkish) H. O. Andreasyan. Istanbul, 1952

Evliya Çelebi, *Narrative of Travels in Europe, Asia and Africa [the Seyahatname]*, trans. Joseph von Hammer. London, 1834–6

Feridun Ahmet Bey, *Nüzhet el-esrar der sefer-i Zigetvar* ×. Topkapı Sarayı Archives, H1339

Fermanel, Gilles, *Le voyage d'Italie et du Levant, 1630*. Rouen, 1664

Flachat, Jean-Claude, *Observations sur le commerce et sur les arts d'une partie de l'Asie, de l'Afrique, et même des Indes Orientales 1740–1758*. 2 vols. Lyons, 1766, 1777

Freely, John, *Istanbul, The Imperial City*. London, 1996

Fresne-Canaye, Philippe du, *Le Voyage du Levant de Phillipe du Fresne-Canaye (1573)*, ed. M. H. Hauser. Paris, 1897

Garzoni, Costantino, 'Relazione del impero ottoman [1573]', in
  Alberi, vol. 1, pp. 369–436
Gibb, E. J. W., *A History of Ottoman Poetry*. 6 vols. London, 1900–09
Giovio, Paolo, *A Shorte Treatise upon the Turkes Chronicles*, trans.
  Peter Ashton. London, 1546, Folio C
Goodwin, Godfrey, *A History of Ottoman Architecture*. London, 1971
——, *The Janissaries*. London, 1994
——, *The Private World of Ottoman Women*. London, 1997
Grelot, Guillaume-Joseph, *Relation nouvelle d'un voyage de
  Constantinople*. Paris, 1680
Gritti, Andrea, 'Relazione fatta in Pregadi per sier Andrea Gritti
  ritornato orator del Signor turcho', in Sanuto, vol. 5, pp. 449–68
Gritti, Francesco, *Dispacci, 1723–27*. Venetian State Archives
Gritti, Ludovico, quoted in Anton von Gévay (ed.), *Urkunden und
  Actenstücke zur Geschichte der Verhältnisse zwischen Österreich,
  Ungern, und der Pforte in XVI. und XVII. Jahrhunderte*, vol. II,
  part 1, pp. 21, 31
Gülersoy, Çelik, *Dolmabahçe Palace and its Environs*. Istanbul, 1990
——, *The Çırağan Palaces*. Istanbul, 1992
Haidar, HRH Princess Musbah, *Arabesque*. London, 1944
Halman, Talat S., *Süleyman the Magnificent Poet*. Istanbul, 1987
Hamlin, Cyrus, *Among the Turks*. New York, 1878
Hammer-Purgstall, Joseph von, *Geschichte des osmanischen Reiches*.
  10 vols. Pest, 1827–35
Harington, General Sir Charles, *Tim Harington Looks Back*. London,
  1940
Hasan Kafi el-Akhisarı, cited in Ipsirli.
Haslip, Joan, *The Sultan: the life of Abdul Hamit II*. London, 1958
Hierosolimitano, Domenico, *Relatione della Gran Citta di
  Costantinopoli* ×. London, British Museum, Harley 3408, fols.
  83–141
Hobhouse, John Cam, *A Journey through Albania and Other
  Provinces of Turkey during the years 1809 and 1810*. London, 1813
Hornby, Lady, *Constantinople during the Crimean War*. London,
  1863
Ipsirli, Mehmet, 'Hasan Kafi el-Akhisarı ve Devlet Düzenine ait
  Usülü'l-hikem fi Nizami'l-Alem'. Tarih Enstitüsü Dergisi 10–11
  (1979–80): 239–78
Itzkowitz, Norman, *Mehmed Raghib Pasha: the making of an
  Ottoman grand vezir* (Ph.D. thesis). Princeton University, 1959

Jenkinson, Anthony, quoted in Lewis

Karal, Enver Ziya, *Osmanlı Tarihi*. Türk Tarih Kurumu publication, vol. 8, p. 258 (undated)

Kâtip Çelebi, *Fezleke*. 2 vols. Istanbul, 1869–70

Kemalpaşazade, *Tevarih-i al-i osman*, ed. Şerafettin Turan. 2 vols. Ankara, 1954–7

Knolles, Richard, *The Lives of the Othoman Kings and Emperors*. 2 vols. London, 1610

Kritovoulos of Imbros, *History of Mehmed the Conqueror*, trans. Charles T. Riggs. Princeton, New Jersey, 1954

Lane-Pool, Stanley, *The Life of Sir Stratford Canning, Viscount Stratford de Redcliffe*. 2 vols. London, 1888

Languschi, Giacomo, 'Excidio e presa di Costantinopoli nell'anno 1453 (dalla Cronica di Zorzi Dolfin)', in Agostino Pertusi, *Testi inediti e poco noti sulla caduta di Costantinopoli*, ed. Antonio Carile. Bologna, 1983, pp. 167–80

Layard, Sir Austen Henry, *Autobiography and Letters*. 2 vols. London, 1903

Lello, Henry, *The Report of Lello/Lello'nun Muhtirasi*, ed. O. Burian. Ankara, 1952

Lewis, Bernard, *Istanbul and the Civilization of the Ottoman Empire*. Norman, Oklahoma, 1963

Leyla Hanım, *The Imperial Harem of the Sultans*, trans. Landon Thomas. Istanbul, 1994

Lokman bin Seyyid Hüseyin, *Hünername* ×. 2 vols. Topkapı Sarayı Museum, H 1523–4

Loti, Pierre, *Aziyadé*. Paris, 1892

Ludovisi, Daniello de', cited in Alberi, *Relazione*, vol. 1, pp. 1–32

MacFarlane, Charles, *Constantinople in 1828*. 2 vols. London, 1829

——, *Turkey and its Destiny*. 2 vols. London, 1850

Magni, Cornelio, *Quanto di piu curioso e vago ha potuto raccaopgliere nel primo biennio da esso consumato viaggi e dimore per la Turchia*. 2 vols. Parma, 1673–4

Mansel, Philip, *Constantinople, City of the World's Desire, 1453–1924*. London, 1995

Mayes, Stanley, *An Organ for the Sultan*. London, 1956

McCullagh, Francis, *The Fall of Abdul-Hamid*. London, 1910

Melek Hanım, *Thirty Years in the Harem*. Istanbul, 1872

Menavino, Giovantonio, *I cinque libri della legge, religione, et vita de'*

Turchi et della corte, & alcune guerre del Gran Turco. Florence, 1548

Merriman, Roger Bigelow, *Suleiman the Magnificent, 1520–66*. Cambridge, Massachusetts, 1944

Midhat, Ali Haydar, *Hatıralarım, 1872–1946*. Istanbul, 1946

Miller, Barnette, *Beyond the Sublime Porte: the grand seraglio of Istanbul*. New Haven, Connecticut, 1931

——, *The Palace School of Muhammed the Conqueror*. Cambridge, 1941

Moltke, Helmuth von, *Briefe aus dem Turkei*. Berlin, 1873

Montagu, Lady Mary Wortley, *The Complete Letters of Lady Mary Wortley Montagu*, ed. Robert Halsband. Vol. 1: 1708–1720. Oxford, 1965

Morgenthau, Henry, *Secrets of the Bosphorus: Constantinople, 1913–1916*. London, 1918

Moro, Giovanni, cited in Alberi, 'Relazione [1590]', vol. 3, pp. 323–80

Morosini, Gianfrancesco, 'Relazione [1585]', in Alberi, vol. 3, pp. 251–322

Moryson, Fynes, *An Itinerary Containing his ten yeeres Travell*. Vol. 2. Glasgow, 1907

Müller, Mrs Max, *Letters from Constantinople*. London, 1897

Mustafa Ali, cited in Babinger, p. 428

Naima, Mustafa, *Annals of the Turkish Empire from 1591 to 1659*, trans. Charles Fraser. London, 1831

Nani, Agostino, Calendar of State Papers, Venice, vol. 9, item 950

Navagero, Bernardo, cited in Alberi, *Relazione* [1553], vol. 1, pp. 33–110

Necipoğlu, Gülrü, *Architecture, Ceremonial and Power: the Topkapı Palace in the fifteenth and sixteenth centuries*. Cambridge, Massachusetts, 1991

Osman II, Sultan, Letter to James I of England, quoted in Ross

Osmanoğlu, Ayşe, *Babam Abdülhamid*. Istanbul, 1960

Ostrorog, Count Leon, *The Turkish Problem*, trans. Winifred Stevens. London, 1915

Palmer, Alan, *The Decline and Fall of the Ottoman Empire*. London, 1992

Palmer, J. A. B., 'Fr. Georgius de Hungaria, O. P., and the *Tractatus de Moribus Condicionibus et Nequicia Turcorum*', Bulletin of the John Rylands Library 34 (1951), 44–68

Papadakis, A., 'Gennadius II and Mehmet the Conqueror', Byzantion 42 (1972)

Pardoe, Julia, *The Beauties of the Bosphorus*. London, 1839

Pears, Sir Edwin, *Forty Years in Constantinople*. London, 1916

——, *Life of Abdul Hamid*. London, 1917

Peçevi, Ibrahim, *Tarih*. 2 vols. Istanbul, 1864–7

Peirce, Leslie P., *The Imperial Harem: woman and sovereignty in the Ottoman Empire*. New York and Oxford, 1993

Penzer, N. M., *The Harem*. London, 1936

Pingaud, Léonce, Choiseul-Gouffier: *La France en Orient sous Louis XVI*. Paris, 1887

Porter, Sir James, *Observations on the Religion, Government and Manners of the Turks*. 2 vols. London, 1761

Postel, Guillaume, *De la République des Turcs*. Poitiers, 1560

Ragazzoni, Jacopo, cited in Alberi, *Relazione*, vol. 2, p. 97

Roe, Sir Thomas, *The Negotiations of Sir Thomas Roe in His Embassy to the Sublime Porte, 1621–1628*. London, 1740

Rosedale, H. E., *Queen Elizabeth and the Levant Company*. London, 1904

Ross, E. Denison, 'A Letter from James I to the Sultan Ahmad'. From the Bulletin of the School of Oriental Studies, London, vol. vii, part 2, 1934

Roth, Cecil, *The House of Nasi: the Duke of Naxos*. Philadelphia, Pennsylvania, 1949

Ryan, Sir Andrew, *The Last of the Dragomans*. London, 1951

Rycaut, Paul, *The Present State of the Ottoman Empire*. London, 1680

Sadeddin, Hoca, *Tacü't-tevarih*. 2 vols. Istanbul, 1862–3

Safi, Mustafa bin Ibrahim, *Zübdetü't-tevarih*. 2 vols. Istanbul, 1862–3

Sagredo, Giovanni, quoted in Babinger, p. 408

Sagundino, Alvise, '*Relazione* [1496]', in Sanuto, vol. 1, p. 323; '*Relazione* [1499]', in Sanuto, vol. 2, p. 600

Salomone, Rabbi, quoted in Rosedale, p. 23

Sanderson, John, *The Travels of John Sanderson in the Levant, 1584–1602*, ed. Sir William Foster. London, 1931

Sanuto, Marino, *I Diarii di Marino Sanuto (1496–1533)*, 58 vols. Venice, 1879–1903

Şehsuvaroğlu, Haluk, *Sultan Aziz hayati hal'ım ölümü*. Istanbul, 1949

——, *Çırağan Sarayına dair bazı hatırılar*. Aksam newspaper, 26 November 1947

Selaniki, Mustafa, *Mustafa Selaniki's History of the Ottomans* (Ph.D. thesis), ed. Mehmet Ipsirli. University of Edinburgh, 1976

Seymour, Sir Hamilton, Collected papers. British Library.

Shaw, Ezel Kural and C. J. Heywood, *English and Continental Views of the Ottoman Empire, 1500–1800*. Los Angeles, 1972

Shaw, Stanford, *Between Old and New: the Ottoman Empire under Sultan Selim III, 1789–1807*. Cambridge, Massachusetts, 1971

Shaw, Stanford, *History of the Ottoman Empire and Modern Turkey*, Volume I: *Empire of the Gazis: the rise and decline of the Ottoman Empire*. Cambridge, Massachusetts, 1976

Shaw, Stanford and Ezel Kural Shaw, *History of the Ottoman Empire and Modern Turkey*, Volume II: *Reform, Revolution, and Republic, 1808–1975*. Cambridge, Massachusetts, 1977

Shay, Mary Lucille, *The Ottoman Empire from 1720 to 1734, As Revealed in Despatches of the Venetian Baili*. Urbana, Illinois, 1944

Sherley, Sir Thomas, *Discourse of the Turkes*, ed. E. Denison Ross. London, 1936

Sitwell, Edith, *Victoria of England*. London, 1936

Skilliter, S. A., *William Harbone and the Trade with Turkey, 1578–1582*. London, 1977

Soranzo, Jacopo, cited in E. Spagni, 'Una Sultana veneziana'. Nuovo Archivio Veneto 19 (1900), pp. 241–348

Spandugino, Teodoro, 'De la Origini delli imperatori ottomani, ordini de la corte, forma del guerreggiare loro, religione, rito et costumi de la natione', in C. Sathas (ed.), *Documents inédits relatif à l'histoire de la Grèce*. 9 vols. Paris, 1880–90, pp. 138–261

Süleyman the Magnificent, *Tagebuch* [diary of the Vienna campaign], ed. and trans. W. F. A. Behrnauer. Vienna, 1858

Sumner-Boyd, Hilary and John Freely, *Strolling through Istanbul*. Istanbul, 1972

Swallow, Charles, *The Sick Man of Europe: Ottoman Empire to Turkish Republic, 1789–1923*. London, 1973

Tavernier, Jean-Baptiste, *The Six Voyages . . . through Turkey into Persia, and the East Indies, finished in the Year 1670 . . . Together with a New Relation of the present Grand Seignor's Seraglio*, trans. J. Philips. London, 1678

Tott, François Baron de, *Mémoires du Baron de Tott sur les Turcs et les Tartares*. 2 vols. Paris, 1785

Tournefort, Joseph Pitton de, *A Voyage into the Levant* . . . London, 1741

Tuğlacı, Pars, *The Ottoman Palace Women*. Istanbul, 1985

Tursun Beg [Bey], *The History of Mehmed the Conqueror by Tursun Beg*. Facsimile with commentary by Halil Inalcık and Rhoads Murphey. Minneapolis and Chicago, 1978

Uluçay, M. Çagatay, *Osmanlı Sultanlarına Ask Mektuplarını (Love Letters of the Ottoman Sultans)*. Istanbul, 1950

——, *Harem'den Mektuplar (Letters from the Harem)*. Istanbul, 1956

Valier, Cristoforo, report in Barozzi and Berchet, *Le Relazioni*, 1: 302–3

Vambéry, Armenius, *His Life and Adventures, told by himself*. London, 1896

Vandal, Albert, *Une ambassade française en Orient sous Louix XV: la mission du Marquis de Villeneuve, 1728–1741*. Paris, 1887

Venier, Maffeo, *Description dell'Imperio Turchesco* (1582). Biblioteca Patriarchalis, Sala Monico Cod. 34, and Biblioteca Marciana Classe VI, Cod. DCCCLXXXII (8505)

Venier, Marco, quoted in Rosedale, pp. 36–40

Walsh, Robert, *A Residence at Constantinople*. 3 vols. London, 1836

Wheatcroft, Andrew, *The Ottomans*. London, 1993

White, Charles, *Three Years in Constantinople*. 3 vols. London, 1844

Yalman, Ahmed Emin, *Turkey in My Time*. Norman, Oklahoma, 1956

Young, George, *Constantinople*. London, 1926

Zographos, Dr Xenophon, *Les derniers Jours de S. M. le Abdulmedjid*. Paris, 1892

Index